THE EVOLUTION OF RELIGION

How Religions Originate, Change, and Die

AND WHY IT AFFECTS US ALL

Alex Shelby

THE EVOLUTION OF RELIGION:
How Religions Originate, Change, and Die – And Why It Affects Us All

Copyright © 2014 by Alex Shelby

All rights reserved
Published in the United States of America

Cover design elements acquired from:

http://old.richarddawkins.net/articles/3534
http://www.technologyreview.com/view/416910/a-microbial-encyclopedia/
http://bpier2012.homestead.com/pier-index.html

All images contained herein were either created by Alex Shelby explicitly for THE EVOLUTION OF RELIGION or obtained from the following sources:

http://www.age-of-the-sage.org/psychology/social/asch_conformity.html
http://www.myfellowamerican.tv/blog/?p=15
http://fivethirtyeight.blogs.nytimes.com/2013/03/26/how-opinion-on-same-sex-marriage-is-changing-and-what-it-means/?_r=0

Includes bibliographical references
ISBN-13: 978-1494974787

CONTENTS

FOREWORD: *Is Religion the Answer?*   3

1
INTRODUCTON: *You Can't Compare Religion to Evolution!*   9

2
RELIGION'S STORY: *In the Beginning...*   24

3
COGNITIVE ANALYSIS: *It's All In Your Mind*   38

4
RELIGIOUS BRANCHING: *Part 1 – Why So Many?*   54

5
RELIGIOUS BRANCHING: *Part 2 – What's the Difference?*   68

6
WAR: *What is it Good For?*   87

7
ECONOMICS: *Expensive Bibles Sell Better*   100

8
COMPARISON: *The Stats*   109

     Far East Religions   112

     Indo Iranian Religions   120

    Near East Religions   130

    Indo European Religions   168

    Indigenous Religions   174

9 CONCLUSIONS: *Where Are We Headed?*   182

EPILOGUE: *The Burden of Proof*   203

REFERENCES   213

FOREWORD

Is Religion the Answer?

A few months before I published this book, a small dream of mine was auspiciously realized. Part of my inspiration for writing this book stemmed from my recent addiction to Oxford-Style theological debates on the existence of God, supplied copiously by YouTube. For me it seemed nearly impossible to possess both the knowledge and poise to successfully debate such a vast topic as religion: spanning multiple millennia of human history, continents of culture, thousands upon thousands of biblical verses, as well as biological and cosmological data as both support and opposition. My enjoyment of watching these debates was analogous to a varsity football player watching the NFL playoffs. I was intimidated and moved as I watched these champions of philosophy match wits. And then, around the time I entered the proof-reading phase of this book, I was invited to step on the field.

It was a typical afternoon at my local shopping mall when I was suddenly approached by a young man. Maybe that quiet section of the outdoor walkway was an ideal place for a conversation, or maybe I just looked bored; whatever the reason, I landed on his radar. He had an enthusiastic 'salesman-esque' vibe about him, and opened with a line about conducting a 'survey on morality' as a part of his college research. I can't remember the name of his college, but I do remember it was a 'Christian' institution. I knew where this was headed, and if this had happened five years ago I would have immediately tensed up; my modus operandi when I'm being 'preached' to. This time, however, things were different. Thanks to the research I had done for this book I was armed with heaps of data on this precise topic, and I was dying to unload it on someone. But I would never have envisioned it happening under these circumstances. Nevertheless, I accepted his invitation.

His opening question, although simple in its presentation, was actually quite complex: where do we get our morality? This is among the top three topics volleyed at atheists during religious debates, the other two being the origin of the universe, and "what's our purpose?" Two things immediately popped into my head. One was my response to his question. The other was whether or not this young believer was prepared for a spirited debate, because this conversation would inevitably sprout legs, and I had at least a half-hour to kill.

My response was about as succinct as I could make it, basically linking our morality back to our primate ancestors, and social mammals before them. I wasn't sure how scientific he was prepared to get until he asked, "And where did our morality come from before that?" That was the first real sign that this was less a survey and more an excuse for a religious lecture. I was, however, pleased that he maintained the etiquette of an actual dialogue. In other words, he allowed for my rebuttals, which he would soon discover were around every corner.

Believe it or not, this is the first time anything like this had ever happened to me. I, like most people in America, have been approached numerous times by religious proselytizers, but I had never once challenged them. I used to sit back and wait for an opportune moment to receive their pamphlet and excuse myself as quickly as possible. Most of them don't approach you at a mall, and they usually come right out and ask if you've been saved. On this particular occasion, instead of wishing I could snap my fingers and disappear, my adrenaline was pumping, and in a good way. But our encounter had merely begun, and I'm the furthest thing from a seasoned debater. Underestimating this youngster's body of knowledge could do a real number on my confidence, which was the last thing I needed before pulling the trigger on a self-published book.

My response to his opening question led to whether or not I believed morality was *objective* or *subjective*, as well as if I considered the Bible to have actual historical value. His view on the Big Bang made its way into the discussion, as did my view on the afterlife. I was genuinely excited to discover this young man was quite knowledgeable when it came to countering my responses, which probably means I'm not the first atheist he's debated. However, I think I caught him off-guard when I told him that, according to Christian beliefs, I was destined to go to Hell, and I seemed at peace with this. He assured me this didn't have to be the case (subtext: you can still be saved). I suppose the fact that I maintained a smile gave him the impression that I was unaware of, and interested in, Christian theology. Ironically, I probably knew as much about Christianity as he did. That's when the conversation steered towards, and settled on, the Bible.

The Bible was this young man's suit of armor, so when I pointed out several divinely instructed biblical events that I perceived to be highly immoral, like genocide and slavery, he spent very little time defending these and, quite understandably, diverting the conversation back towards more agreeable passages.

I lost track of the time, but we must have conversed for a half-hour, and ultimately ended on very civil terms. Was anything actually accomplished? I highly doubt I put a dent in his armor. And he presented the typical points I've heard many times over from the apologist community. But after musing over our discussion, it became obvious to me that the 'great debate' over the existence of God was utterly futile. Not because there weren't valid arguments at hand, but because we were essentially speaking different languages.

Two brothers purchase the same stock from their father's company. After a year the first brother tells the other they should sell. The second brother asks why. Somewhat astounded, the first brother says the stock has lost over half its value and shows no signs of recovering. Somewhat confused, the second brother responds, "I don't care about that. Owning stock in our father's company makes me happy."

It's easy to find the good in something if you ignore the bad, especially when the 'bad' is grounded in cultural evolution (e.g. what was acceptable to a war-torn society thousands of years ago may be considered depraved to others in modern times). But why invest emotion in something like religion, science, or history? Because the young believer and I – as well as most of the planet – want the same thing: *justice*. This was actually the note our conversation ended on; a fitting testament to the issue that lies at the heart of almost any religious discussion.

All around us, day in and day out, we witness bad deeds going unpunished, be it road rage on our commute, or biological warfare on the news. We are essentially helpless to do anything about it, and many of us refuse to accept this. On one hand, the *atheist* is bound by their conscience alone to take an active part in 'correcting' these injustices. Some make political stands while others post their annoyances on Facebook. On the other hand, the *theist* is bound by their spiritual beliefs to make sure others know what will happen to them if they sin without repentance. Several problems arise from the mindset of the latter. The first being the definition of 'sin', which is often subject to one's perspective (e.g. one man's sin is another man's excuse to search for weapons of mass destruction). The second problem is if the knowledge of eternal punishment in Hell actually affects our decision making? The third, and perhaps most important, is the very existence an afterlife, a heaven, a hell, or God. From the atheist standpoint, the theist is approaching the very real problem of global injustice by essentially warning everyone that the Boogeyman is watching them. Boogeyman or not, if this threat works, why not go with it? Superstitious as the human race is, beliefs like this haven't always existed in religion.

Gods and goddesses entered religious belief around 75,000 years ago, but the concepts for Heaven and Hell arose only a few thousand years ago, and it completely evades many religions altogether, including Judaism – the forefather of Christianity and Islam. Based on the amount of calories Christian preachers burn warning us about the torments of Hell, you'd expect to find entire gospels devoted to it. In fact 'Hell' is mentioned only 23 times in the New Testament, and there isn't a single detailed description. To help put this in perspective, the evils of 'usury' are addressed 14 times and in stark detail, yet you never see Christians boycotting the banks or credit card companies. The graphic depictions of eternal torture and demons we so often hear about were 'borrowed' from non-Biblical sources, like Plato's *Myth of Er* and Dante's *Divine Comedy*.

So why would social injustice, an issue so critical to us today, not be addressed in more primitive religious beliefs? Because what happens to a 'criminal' is not nearly as important as your family's survival. Before the industrial revolution, if you factor in the astoundingly high rate of infant mortality, we died in our 30's. It wasn't until after vaccinations and electricity that we were afforded the luxury of worrying about what happens to those around us. History demonstrates that religion evolves with the needs of society. This doesn't necessarily negate religion's effectiveness, but, to the atheist, it does seem oddly convenient. In other words, God appears to align his needs with ours. But it doesn't stop at our approach to injustice. The beliefs and rituals surrounding religion have always mirrored the desires of society, from which Gods we worshipped to the sacrificial methods we employed.

Like all aspects of culture, the characteristics of something that is supposed to be divine – religion – more closely resembles the characteristics of something manmade. What this says to me is that historical perspective plays almost no role in our emotional desires. In other words, the dogma of religion can appear to hold water if we ignore the history and opposition that surround it. One of the reasons I wrote this book is to demonstrate how the evolution of religion reveals strong ties to the evolution of government, culture, economics, technology, warfare, and social oppression – just to name a few – all of which are manmade concepts. That said, can we honestly profess that religion is the answer? As much as we'd like to believe that ghost stories will keep people in line, when 'actual' imprisonment and capital punishment provide only a semi-adequate deterrent, we should look beyond our own needs and consider what's happening around us, as well as what's happened before us.

There's no denying that religion has endured for some very viable reasons. But even as we enter an era of technology where information is exceedingly plentiful and social media allows us to speak our minds to the masses, on a more personal level we are no further along than we were centuries ago. The closer I got to publishing this book the more I had to prepare myself for the impending fallout I would receive from friends and family. And it makes sense – why would a chemo-patient entertain the second opinion of a doctor who tells them their cancer is no longer in remission? I have willingly accepted a role as a messenger of bad news to over half the people on this planet (i.e. the approximate amount of people who believe in heaven). So why write this book?

Do I expect to change minds, or make an impact of any kind? I'd be lying if I said "no". The more data I uncovered the more obvious it became that we are basically no different than any other social animal. Almost every passion we exhibit is geared toward advancing the survival of our species, but when it relates to an animal we call it an 'instinct'. Yet, as far as we know, animals don't have religion. But they also lack a method by which to communicate complex fears and questions to one another, as well as the capacity for detailed problem solving. We are forward thinking creatures, which means, we worry. We don't just survive for today; we worry whether or not we'll survive to see tomorrow. Religion alleviates much of this burden. Unfortunately it also provides a barrier for foreign relations, self reliance, and moral progression. I believe we can create a stronger society if we hone our capacity to differentiate reliable evidence from ambiguous evidence, as well as base our decisions in general on evidence rather than emotion.

Notice I used the word 'emotion' instead of *religion* or the *Bible*. If there was only *one* religion, and *one* holy book, then emotion would play a smaller role. But religions and holy books number in the thousands and they're all relatively similar, which leads us to trust the beliefs of our family, friends, and countrymen. It's a lot easier to believe the doctor who tells you your cancer is in remission, but unfortunately that doesn't make it so. Living your life based on bad information guided by emotion can have greater consequences than one may realize.

In and of itself, religion is not necessarily the problem, but it sets a dangerous precedent. Most modern faiths reinforce the most mindless aspect of the conservative agenda: *change is bad*. They base their decision making on the notion that it's acceptable to treat many forms of ancient politics as 'perfect', and therefore eternally enduring. The fact is that societies change in accordance with technology, and morality changes in accordance with survival salience and cultural pressures. If government policy is stifled by obsolete conventions, our social advancement could be the least of our worries.

A great example of what can happen when politics and religion collide has been demonstrated in recent Congress hearings where 'global warming' was addressed. In 2009, during a House Subcommittee on Energy and Environment, Illinois Representative John Shimkus opened with the following claim, after quoting Genesis 8:21-22 (God's covenant after the Great Flood) and Matthew 24:31 (God's sign for the Rapture):

"The earth will end only when God declares it's time to be over. Man will not destroy this earth. This earth will not be destroyed by a flood... I do believe God's word is infallible, unchanging, perfect."

In summary, global warming is not something we can manage. Also, in 2013, when asked about the Keystone XL pipeline's possible contribution to climate change, Texas Representative Joe Barton had this to say:

"I think you can have an honest difference of opinion on what's causing that [climate] change without automatically being either all-in that it's all because of mankind or it's all just natural. I think there is a divergence of evidence. I would point out that if you're a believer in the Bible, one would have to say the Great Flood is an example of climate change, and that certainly wasn't because mankind overdeveloped hydro-carbon energy."

In summary, global warming is not something we can manage.

I don't think these two men gained an ounce of support because people believe the Bible made a good point. I think they receive support, if any, because people tend to trust other people who share their values, and if you believe the Bible is infallible, you'll likely side with either of these politicians. And if voters are convinced to ignore scientific data because a politician quotes their favorite book, we'll be setting up future generations for severe failure.

If we want real solutions to real problems – like global warming, healthcare, and foreign policy, to name but a few – we need to realize that our world will always be 'a work in progress'. This paradigm can make us feel rather small and helpless, but that brief feeling of powerlessness can inspire people to make important changes. You don't have to be an elected official to sway the public these days. We should never take for granted that we live in an age where we can share our viewpoint with literally the entire world. And if our instincts guide us properly, we can find a way to rise above the benign chatter and grab people's attention.

CHAPTER 1

INTRODUCTION:

You Can't Compare Religion to Evolution !

"If it were proven that there is no God there would be no religion. But also if it were proven that there is a God, there would be no religion."

-Ursula K. Le Guin

Personal Evolution
Christian Apologists
Religion versus Evolution
The Evolution of Culture
Defining the Argument

I was an eight-year-old boy who opened his eyes during prayer in church wondering if I was somehow negating its affects. I secretly searched the auditorium for fellow dissenters, and it appeared I was the only one brave enough, or stupid enough, to attempt this. "Talking to someone we can't see is serious stuff," I deduced. Dad was at home watching television while mom stood by my side the one day a week I wore my only pair of slacks and collared shirt. We never prayed, much less mentioned Jesus, outside church. We had a dusty Bible or two in our house. Needless to say, Christianity never stood much of a chance with me. But this wasn't always the case. Some of my earliest beliefs about death were influenced by religion. I remember clearly thinking that the actors who died in the movies were brave volunteers who actually gave up their life. Death was merely an inconvenience.

I spoke to God often at that age, never quite sure if I was doing it properly. Speaking to God was the one time I could truly be myself, which slowly felt like the wrong thing to do. Nothing really seemed to change when I prayed. Life wasn't going any smoother, which was a confusing outcome. The possibility of God being 'too busy' to deal with me was not an option, so I was told. I was years away from realizing there were other religions in the world, much less actually questioning my own. I gradually entered a state of religious limbo where I didn't really believe, but I certainly didn't deny His existence. I knew God could hear my thoughts, so I tried to put it out of my mind entirely. And then something significant happened that would alter my entire outlook. After graduating high school and embarking on a journey to discover who I was, death somehow lost its power with me. I was secretly my parents' worst nightmare: a fearless teenager.

I developed a mysterious obsession with religion, one I didn't fully understand. I discovered that every possible permutation for God, the afterlife, creation, and the soul had already been thought of and debated for centuries. At this point I still wasn't entirely sure what an 'atheist' was. Did they hate God? Did they worship Satan? The convenience of the internet was years away, and I wasn't very outspoken or much of a reader, so many of my questions remained unanswered.

And then I saw something that changed my outlook forever. Comedian George Carlin put into words what I assumed was unthinkable. He came right out in front of a cable audience and said, "There is no God". His rant focused mostly on prayer, breaking down its logic, or lack thereof, and essentially stripping it naked for everyone to laugh at[1]. I was watching it with my best friend who happened to be Catholic and, quite understandably, failed to appreciate its humor. We had a mutual respect for each other's views, but it occurred to me that religion wasn't something an insightful comedian could talk someone out of. My friend didn't view it the way I did at the time: he didn't see religion as a choice.

I never saw the point in persuading someone to change their view, especially on something as personal as religion. I had entered the 'free thinker' phase. I was proud that I could finally give myself permission to believe or not believe as I saw fit. The one person I could have a candid religious conversation with was my father. I never really cared or knew why he stayed at home all those Sundays until now. And through no deliberate influence on his part we saw eye to eye on matters of spirituality, or lack thereof. Our discussions satisfied my appetite for religious understanding until around the time the internet began to flourish.

I didn't use the internet till it was effectively forced upon me. And I wasn't motivated to do research till social media outlets like *YouTube* turned into a battleground for religious debate. I was scared to watch videos boasting such titles as, "Undeniable Proof There is a God". This was a Pandora's Box I was not mentally prepared to open. If God was real he watched me wander about for the last twenty years questioning his

---

[1] This bit was featured in George Carlin's HBO stand-up comedy special "You Are All Diseased" (1999).

existence while tracking sin after un-confessed sin. But I had to do it; I owed it to myself to have all the information, not just the parts that felt comfortable. I watched video after video of rainbows, flowers, sunsets, waterfalls, and of course, images of the Bible. This was the proof? Granted, rainbows and sunsets are aesthetically pleasing occurrences in nature, but I thought less pleasing phenomenon like tornados, leprosy, and cockroaches came from the same source.

2007: the end of Catholicism as we know it hit the media. The San Diego diocese filed for bankruptcy to avoid paying lawsuit settlements for 144 claims of sexual abuse. It was undisputable – Catholic priests, guided by the divine will of God, appointed child molesters into their clergy. How could a God that allows this to happen possibly be justified? The illusion of perfection had been exposed. One of two things was sure to happen: the Pope was going to drum up the mother of all rationalizations to diffuse the situation, or a worldwide de-conversion of Catholics would snowball into reality. What seemed to be a death blow for religion was merely a slap on the wrist. The church doors reopened and life went on. I was beginning to understand the power of faith.

Christian Apologists

I craved theological information more than ever. What was it about religion that glided past me only to sink its claws into my neighbor? Plausible deniability was understandable for the bulk of society, but what out the intellectuals? Thanks to the internet, atheists now posed a viable threat to theism, so the Christians, Muslims, and Jews put aside their differences to do battle with the non-believers. I found academic debates between Christian apologists like Dinesh D'Souza and Frank Turek versus atheists like Christopher Hitchens and Sam Harris. I was in awe of the knowledge these men wielded, not only about religion, but about history, anthropology, and astronomy. I struggled to sort out what was undisputable and what was unfalsifiable. I found myself in a cold sweat after one of my atheist heroes fumbled over his rebuttal. I suddenly waffled: maybe there is a God. I'd watch another video and witness a counter-point scored for atheism. The unfortunate truth eventually became clear: all the logic and faith in the world wouldn't sway either side in the slightest. This was not a battle of facts, or even logic; this was a battle of egos.

Mark Smith is an atheist who created *Contra Craig* (www.jcnot4me.com), a website named after the king of Christian apologist debaters Dr. William Lane Craig. In August of 1998 Mark Smith asked Craig the following question:

"For the sake of argument let's pretend that a time machine gets built. You and I hop in it, and travel back to the day before Easter, 33 AD. We park it outside the tomb of Jesus. We wait. Easter morning rolls around, and nothing happens. We continue to wait. After several weeks of waiting, still nothing happens. There is no resurrection – Jesus is quietly rotting away in the tomb."

Craig told him he would still believe in the resurrection of Jesus, due to the "self-authenticating witness of the Holy Spirit." This was Craig's way of saying that God has blessed every human being with the innate instinct to worship Him, and it was up to each of us to embrace or reject this instinct. Craig is not alone when it comes to unwavering belief, just to list a few:

"How did [the Holocaust] happen? Because God allowed it to happen... because God said, 'My top priority for the Jewish people is to get them to come back to the land of Israel.'"
—Rev. John Hagee

"To those who say Ted Bundy should burn forever in eternity I would only say, so should I, so should all of us... "
—James Dobson (Focus on the Family)

"AIDS is the wrath of a just God against homosexuals. To oppose it would be like an Israelite jumping in the Red Sea to save one of Pharaoh's charioteers ... AIDS is not just God's punishment for homosexuals; it is God's punishment for the society that tolerates homosexuals."
—Rev. Jerry Falwell

"I want you to just let a wave of intolerance wash over you. I want you to let a wave of hatred wash over you. Yes, hate is good... Our goal is a Christian nation. We have a biblical duty, we are called on by God to conquer this country. We don't want equal time. We don't want pluralism."
—Randall Terry (The News Sentinel)

"Nobody has the right to worship on this planet any other God than Jehovah. And therefore the state does not have the responsibility to defend anybody's pseudo-right to worship an idol."
—Rev. Joseph Morecraft

"I don't know that atheists should be considered citizens, nor should they be considered patriots. This is one nation under God."
—George W. Bush

My interest shifted from researching the religion, to researching the people who follow religion. What was it that caused someone to believe or not believe? Was this genetic or environmental? Why are we so polarized in matters of faith and religious conviction? I happen to partially agree with Craig; we do possess an instinct to intimately understand (not worship) the entity or concept responsible for the origin of what's currently unknown (e.g. the origin of the universe). But to say that instinct originated "from God" is circular logic (i.e. the 'thing we can't prove' created the desire to worship the 'thing we can't prove').

Origin in nature can be a slippery slope, but it's a slope worth scaling. Are we hard-wired to worship a god, or gods, the same way we are hard-wired to hunt, gather, and socialize? And if so, when did these instincts first develop? As fascinating and mysterious as origins can be the final straw didn't come till the ultimate irony of religious beliefs eventually came to light: 'the truth' changes.

Religion versus Evolution

Evolution has been on religion's hit-list ever since Darwin published *The Origin of the Species* in 1859. Change over time – these three words raised questions about the divine nature of holy scripture. Even after the Catholic Church's quasi acceptance of the theory[2], some 50% of Americans still trust the 'good book' over the science book.

People won't necessarily accept what you say because you have a degree and wear a white lab coat – we generally need to understand what we're being told, and many intelligent people have difficulty following the principles of mutation, genetic drift, adaptation, speciation, etc. An all-powerful creator is a conceivable paradigm even a child can grasp, yet this theory comes from someone who sometimes wears a white gown and has studied a book few people understand as well. The problem is, unlike outer space through a telescope or weather patterns on radar, the layperson is unable to observe evolution taking place[3]. It consequently gets dumped into the category of 'not provable', and therefore supernatural.

Change over time is not only a fact of biology it is also a fact of religion. 99% of the religious beliefs that have graced human history evolved from a previous religion. Religious beliefs, just like biological creatures, develop, evolve, and go extinct. The evolution in biology comes from random genetic mutations, or, in other words, an imperfect copy. Evolution in religion however is not necessarily the result of the imperfect transfer of information. Religious evolution (i.e. the branching of religions into new beliefs, denominations, and sects) is often a conscious decision. German

---

[2] In July 2007 Pope Benedict made the following statement: "Currently, I see in Germany, but also in the United States, a somewhat fierce debate raging between so-called 'creationism' and evolutionism, presented as though they were mutually exclusive alternatives: those who believe in the Creator would not be able to conceive of evolution, and those who instead support evolution would have to exclude God. This antithesis is absurd because, on the one hand, there are so many scientific proofs in favor of evolution which appears to be a reality we see and which enriches our knowledge of life and being as such. But on the other, the doctrine of evolution does not answer every query, especially the great philosophical question: where does everything come from? And how did everything start which ultimately led to man? I believe this is of the utmost importance?"

[3] Biological evolution is observable in organisms with short life spans, like bacteria or fruit flies. On a slightly longer scale, the Atlantic tomcod evolved a resistance to poisonous PCBs that were dumped into the Hudson River from 1947 to 1976.

biblical scholar Julius Wellhausen applied this theory to religion in 1883 when he scrutinized the origins of the Torah, which led to his premise known as the 'documentary hypothesis' (*discussed further in chapter 5*). Wellhausen discovered that the divine scripture of Hebrews not only had multiple authors, but it was revised and rearranged over centuries to accommodate their evolving society.

In biology, genetic change may or may not give a life form a survival advantage in its natural environment. For example, peppered moths originally had a light, blotchy coloring which served as an effective camouflage. Before the industrial revolution a uniformly dark variant of the peppered moth made up 2% of the species. After the industrial revolution, 95% of peppered moths showed this dark coloration. Over time the light colored moths lost their advantage of camouflage as light surfaces were darkened by pollution, and were consequently eaten more frequently by birds.

In religion, variations in dogma and belief may or may not give a religion a survival advantage in a human society. Around 950 B.C.E. some followers of the Canaanite religion introduced the war god Yahweh to their pantheon. Over time they denounced the other hundred gods and goddesses they formally worshipped, creating one of the first monotheistic belief systems in history. Known today as Judaism, this opened the door for monotheism, and would eventually dominate 60% of religions around the globe. Yet Judaism today occupies a mere 0.5% of the world's population. Was Judaism the preverbal 'first land animal' whose offspring (e.g. Christianity and Islam) developed a superior and more desirable belief system, hence their dominant numbers?

The biological model of evolution provides a superbly similar template as a means to understanding theological evolution. As predators, climate, geography, and random mutation tend to dictate the path of biological evolution, these too apply to theology in analogous ways. Predators can take on the form of warmongers, which can wipe out entire cultures along with their religion, and can also come in the form of government corruption. Climate and geography can dictate the economic structure of a society, which can shape a community's survival needs, and can also guide the expansion routes of warfare. And random mutations simply account for the unpredictable 'human factor' responsible for manipulating religious values, sometimes gradually, and sometimes rapidly.

When examined on a more scientific level, theological evolution closely mirrors the specific characteristics of biology.

Mutation: Changes in the DNA sequence of a cell's genome (e.g. the deletion, change, or duplication of a gene).

Example in religion: The deletion or change of theological beliefs or rituals (duplication can come in the form of biblical redundancy – the same story expressed by two or more authors).

Gene flow: The exchange of genes between populations and between species (e.g. the movement of mice – of the same species – between inland and coastal populations to create a hybrid sub-species).

Example in religion: The West Africans (Yoruba religion) came in contact with Haitians (Catholics) to create a hybrid faith among the slaves called Vodou.

Natural selection: The process by which genetic mutations that enhance reproduction become and remain more common in successive generations of a population (e.g. the length of a giraffe's neck became a survival advantage, and therefore evolved in the direction of growing longer rather than remaining shorter).

Example in religion: Monotheism became a survival advantage amongst a polytheistic world as it reduced confusion amongst its followers for determining which God would reign supreme, and therefore, once adopted, rarely regressed to polytheism.

Biased mutation: When there are different probabilities at the molecular level for different mutations to occur (e.g. the loss of *sporulation* – asexual reproduction by the production and release of spores – in a bacterium during laboratory evolution, rather than natural selection against the cost of maintaining sporulation ability.

Example in religion: In the west, salvation through Heaven provided a reward system for followers, whereas in the east, reincarnation – arguably a lesser reward – has a higher probability of sustaining within the culture.

Adaptation: The process that makes organisms better suited to their habitat (e.g. the adaptation of horses' teeth for the grinding of grass).

Example in religion: Mazu (goddess of sailors) was one god amongst many in the Chinese Folk pantheon, and nowhere near as notable as Shangdi (the supreme sky deity), yet 1,500 temples dedicated to the sole worship of Mazu (i.e. Mazuism) are located almost exclusively in Asian coastal regions with prospering sea trade.

Co-evolution: When the interaction is between pairs of species – such as a predator and its prey – these species can develop matched sets of adaptations (e.g. the garter snake evolved a resistance to *tetrodotoxin*: a toxin that causes paralysis of voluntary muscles and irregular heart rate – which was an evolutionary defense of its amphibian prey).

Example in religion: Territorial battles between the Roman and Persian Empires became an ongoing struggle, which gathered momentum around 200 B.C.E. while both societies were polytheistic. Once monotheism (i.e. Christianity) was adopted by the Romans, the Arabs evolved a 'rival' monotheistic belief system (i.e. Islam) 300 years later.

Allopatric speciation: Speciation that occurs when biological populations of the same species become isolated from each other to an extent that prevents or interferes with genetic interchange (e.g. when finches became isolated throughout the Galapagos islands, a dozen new species evolved in accordance with their new environment).

Example in religion: Buddhism didn't flourish in its homeland of India, yet after it migrated to Asia (where it was no longer in competition with its predecessor: Hinduism) it flourished and branched into nearly 100 sects.

Extinction: The disappearance of an entire species (e.g. nearly 99% of all species of animals and plants that have lived on earth are now extinct – the most notable being dinosaurs).

Example in religion: Religious evidence relies highly on written documentation. Most religions that went extinct before 500 B.C.E. were likely oral (although art represented in artifacts may portray religious themes), and others since may not have matured to the point of developing texts. There are easily as many extinct religions as there are thriving religions, as well as the difficult to account for 'evolution within a belief system' that sheds and creates traditions without branching – the main difference being that as long as modern humans have knowledge of an extinct religion, it could theoretically be revived.

The Evolution of Culture

A question which should be asked is whether or not religion is man-made or truly an inspiration of divine sources. Philosophical arguments aside, there are correlations with cultural features that may offer insight. The evolution of culture, for example, is of particular interest when we take into account the catalytic factors involved.

Anthropologist Gerald Weiss defined 'culture' as our generic term for all human non-genetic, or meta-biological, phenomena. A more traditional definition would be our learned behavior, as opposed to instinctual behavior. There is survival based culture, like those associated with food (e.g. hunting techniques, cooking techniques, flavoring), shelter, and clothing. There is aesthetic based culture, like art, music, and dancing. And then there is territorial based cultural, whose purpose is to establish social identity, like language and religion. Language is tied into culture as a vehicle for unity and identity, and religion not only serves a similar purpose, it demonstrates an analogous chronological correlation.

Origin dates of language and religion

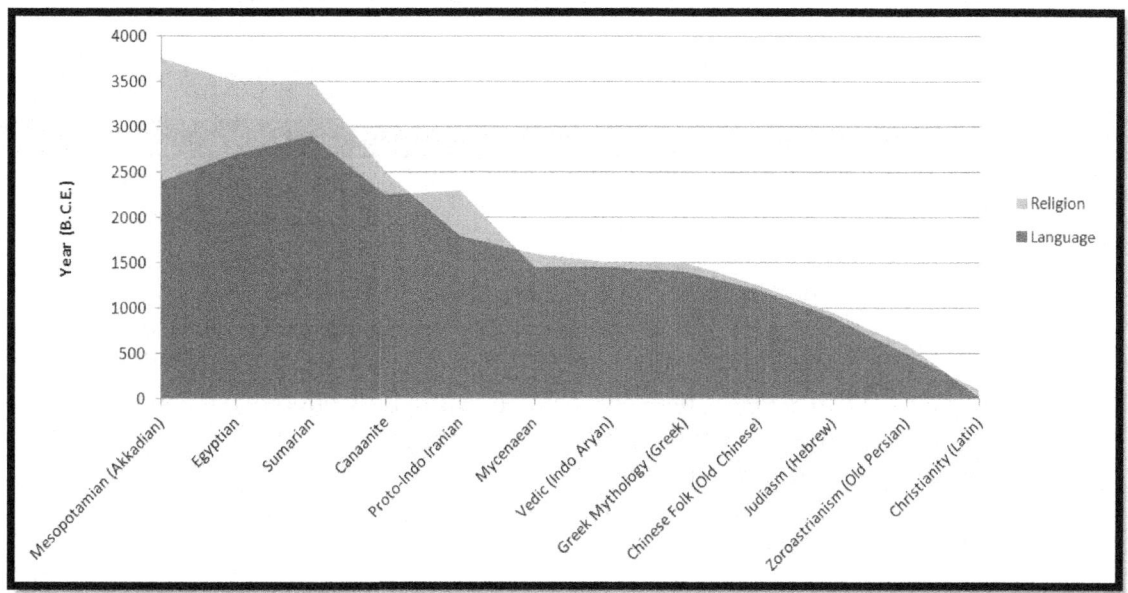

The focus now shifts to a culture's organic qualities. If the origins of culture are man-made, what does that suggest about religion? Is culture even specific to humans?

Variants in chimpanzee behavior show observable cultural differences. Gimbe chimps alter thin twigs to go termite fishing, whereas in West Africa they use large sticks to break holes in termite mounds and scoop them out with their hands. These food gathering techniques are largely environmental in nature and probably due to differences in rainfall and the hardness of termite mounds. Dr Klaus Zuberbühler from the University of St Andrews in Scotland presented chimps from different regions with a similar dilemma. A wooden log filled with honey with a narrow access hole was introduced to two chimp groups. Kibale Forest chimps used a stick to get the honey, while used Budongo Forest chimp used leaf sponges. These solutions were developed with surprising speed, enough to suggest engrained cultural influences at work.

But how does culture actually evolve? Survival based culture is primarily driven by advancements in technology, as with fire making and hunting techniques, which also influenced religious practices (*discussed further in chapter 2*). This evolutionary process became evident shortly after the hunter-gather society developed (130,000 years ago), followed by the Neolithic period (11,000 years ago), and lastly the Bronze Age (5,000 years ago), which saw the advent of large scale warfare.

The primary influence for aesthetic cultural evolution is linked to societal changes, like war and economics. These changes were slow, perhaps slower than technological advances. And certain aesthetics changed little or not at all, like traditional dances and music. Science (theory of evolution, big bang, etc) has only recently begun to influence religious belief, but its overall deterrent has been minimal. Religious evolution did however appear to shadow aesthetic evolution, or perhaps vice-versa.

*Comparison of **European** culture & religion*

Year	Culture	Religion
3,500 B.C.E. – 500 C.E.	*Classical*: elegant, realistic	*Polytheism*: Minoan, Mycenaean, Greek, Hellenistic
500 – 1,300 C.E.	*Medieval*: abstract, vivid, religious	*Polytheism*: Germanic, Slavic, Celtic – *and Monotheism*: Catholic
1,300 – 1,600 C.E.	*Renaissance*: back to realism, varied themes, contrasts in lighting, enhanced perspective	*Monotheism*: Catholic, Orthodox
1,600 – 1,800 C.E.	*Mannerism, Baroque, Rococo*: emotional, emphasized detail	*Monotheism*: Catholic, Protestant

*Comparison of **Mesopotamian** culture & religion*

Year	Culture	Religion
3,000 – 1,500 B.C.E.	*Pre-Assyrian*: simple, generally non-religious	*Polytheism*: Mesopotamian, Sumerian, Canaanite
1,500 – 600 B.C.E.	*Assyrian*: grandiose themes, high detail	*Polytheism*: Mesopotamian, Edomite
600 – 300 B.C.E.	*Neo-Babylonian*: cosmopolitan, expression of heritage	*Polytheism*: Mesopotamian – *and Monotheism*: Judaism

*Comparison of **Chinese** culture & religion*

Year	Culture	Religion
2,000 – 200 B.C.E.	*Neolithic*: jade, bronze casting	*Polytheism*: Chinese Folk
200 B.C.E. – 200 C.E.	*Imperial*: Terracotta Army, porcelain	*Atheism*: Confucianism
200 – 600 C.E.	*Period of division*: calligraphy, tomb painting	*Agnosticism*: Taoism – *and Atheism*: Confucianism
600 – 1,000 C.E.	*Sui, Tang*: landscape paintings, Buddhist sculptures	*Agnosticism*: Buddhism, Taoism

Aesthetic transformations tend to reflect the tone of society, and are essentially an expression of that attitude. The irony of religious transformation is that it contradicts its divine nature. In other words, culture changes but Gods are fixed – something had to give.

Defining the Argument

Clear theological definitions are needed to advance religious arguments. The definitions of *religion* and *theism* are technically similar: the belief in and worship of a superhuman controlling power. But for the purposes of the information presented in this book, *theism* represents the broad belief or mindset, while *religion* refers to the specific dogma as it pertains to a specific faith. *Atheism* and *agnosticism* both address the supernatural, but atheism addresses belief (i.e. I do not 'believe' in God(s)), whereas agnosticism addresses what is knowable (i.e. determining the truth about a God's existence is ultimately 'unknowable'). Atheism can also be defined as strong or weak atheism, *strong* being the assertion that there is no God, while *weak* arises as a counterpoint to theism (i.e. there is not enough evidence to justify belief in God(s)). This book applies the position of weak atheism to the evolution of religion, but more importantly quantifies the practical perspective of religion's purpose, which is, intentional or not, an alternative form of government.

To determine religion's effectiveness as a form of government, existence of God aside, it is important to consider religion's claim of divine influence. Arguments for and against the existence of God have become a popular method by which theological debates can address complex themes. A popular theistic argument that has persevered general critique is the *Kalam cosmological* (or first cause) argument, which states:
1. Everything that begins to exist has a cause.
2. The universe has a beginning.
3. Therefore, the universe has a cause (i.e. that cause is God).

In 1978 the *Chicago statement on biblical inerrancy* was formulated by more than 200 evangelical leaders as a defense against liberal interpretations, which, in general, states that the Christian Bible *"...is without error or fault in all its teaching, no less in what it states about God's acts in creation, about the events of world history, and about its own literary origins under God..."* Also, *"No falsehood can approach [the Qur'an] from before it or behind it",* has been a mantra of the Islamic faith. Claims of inerrancy tend to be partial to the Abrahamic faiths (i.e. Judaism, Christianity, Islam), but this is an accepted mindset for all religions whose purpose is to represent divine authority.

The goal of this book is to examine, demonstrate, and understand evolution within theology. To approach religion from a standpoint of 'inerrancy' would be to simply accept it as fact. Unfortunately, the issues surrounding religious rivalries stem from an innate contradiction in our moral development. Higher brain functions allow humans (and many primates) the ability to attach 'levels of degree' to values and punishment. This is how all modern justice systems are structured, and for good reason, otherwise petty crimes, like littering, would incur the same penalties as murder (i.e. someone guilty of littering would have nothing to lose if they murdered potential witnesses). The only 'degrees' applied to religion lie in the potential for 'second chances' via reincarnation, purgatory, or a reformative hell. This 'side note' to salvation has done little to prevent the true consequence of this moral paradox, thus resulting in religious evolution (e.g. the addition, deletion, and modification of scriptures), which has spawned the vast array of religious beliefs we have today. Based on this I'd like to pose an argument against the existence of God – or at the very least, against the validity of scripture – which can be referred to as the *argument from change*:

1. Entities that change or evolve cannot be considered 'free of error'.
2. Religious beliefs undergo change.
3. Therefore, religious beliefs are not free of error (i.e. they did not originate from God).

Even if agreement could be reached on religion's inerrancy, the fact is that religions continue to evolve in two primary ways: the beliefs of existing religions are modified thereby creating new denominations and sects, or undesirable beliefs of existing religions are no longer enforced or acknowledged by religious leaders. The latter negates the divine aspects of dogma, demoting it to a manmade construct. The former begs the question: which version of a religion is correct? Nevertheless, the primary argument of this book is to demonstrate that religion serves as an inferior influence for government due to its inherent characteristics. Governments evolve with the desires of its leaders and citizens, and, for better or worse, can be addressed via administrative policy, or, in some cases, public protest. Religious evolution indirectly mirrors the desires of the public but resides in an ambiguous context devoid of formal policy or procedure. The initial appeal of such an institution seems unlikely, yet it continues to flourish. This lends insight to the notion that perhaps 'lack of choice' is acceptable as long as the reward is substantial. Unfortunately, the reward offered by religion is an emotional placebo: a winning lottery ticket you can never scratch.

The evolution of both government and religion might benefit from some historical perspective. Laws we would consider archaic maintain relative consistency with modern morality. However, the degree and methods of punishment are antiquated by contemporary standards. Below is a listing of the more notably decrees in some of the most advanced societies of their time period.

2,050 B.C.E. – Sumerian: if a man is accused of sorcery he must undergo ordeal by water (drowning), if he is found innocent, the accuser must pay 3 shekels (3 silver coins).

1,790 B.C.E. – Babylonian: divorce was the husband's option; adultery was punishable by drowning.

1,500 B.C.E. – Hittite (Turkey): If a man rapes a woman in the mountain, it is his wrong, but if he rapes a woman in a house, it is her wrong (punishable by death for either).

1,075 B.C.E. – Assyrian: a man is allowed to strike his wife, pull her hair or ear.

500 B.C.E. – Crete: rape was punishable only by fines.

Some notable laws of modern democracy deal less with traditional crime and more with civil rights.

- *1865:* slavery abolished in America
- *1890:* polygamy officially outlawed in Utah
- *1920:* women's suffrage

Where religion and government collide are in their incompatibility. Be it government or religion, the rules they enforce tend to fall into the categories of 'do' and 'do not'. This listing is current, valid, and relatively tame when we consider the rituals of extinct belief systems involving cannibalism and human sacrifice.

- If you're a baptized Sikh, *do* carry a kirpan (dagger) at all times.
- If you're Rastafarian, *do* smoke marijuana as a worshipping ritual (illegal in most countries).
- If you're Jewish, *do* slaughter animals via shechita (often considered inhumane).
- If you're a Muslim female, *do* keep your face veiled in public even if it violates security identification measures.
- If you're a follower of the Christian Science religion, *do* pray for divine healing rather than provide professional medical care for your children.
- If you're a Catholic doctor or nurse, *do not* participate in abortions.
- If you're a follower of an Abrahamic religion, *do not* marry a member of the same sex or you will be denied legal marital status and privileges in many countries.

Government *do not's* primarily focus on protecting the freedom of its citizens. Religious *do not's* intended to protect individual freedom (e.g. murder, adultery, stealing) were influenced by previously established government policy – religion was just an alternative means of enforcement[4]. In general the rules of religion that do not mirror those of government are there to 'protect the faith' (e.g. do not worship other Gods – *Exodus 34:14*, kill non-believers – *Deuteronomy 17:1-5*, stone fortune tellers – *Leviticus*

---

[4] In the context of Abrahamic belief systems, the documentation of the story of the Ten Commandments (6th century B.C.E.) trailed local government policy by as much as a thousand years.

20:27). These tenets are not broadly enforced, as most 'faith protecting' dogma is aimed at strengthening one's conviction. So what's the harm?

Unlike most governments who have a judicial system set up for interpreting laws, religion's 'court of law' exists as a supernatural concept – in the physical world biblical interpretation is left in the hands of religious leaders and followers. These individuals, whose primary objective is to serve God before man[5], occupy seats in government, law enforcement, education, and science. When their faith is contradicted by law, curriculum, or the scientific method, truth and justice are often sacrificed. Worse yet, when a government is strongly influenced by religion, the primary focus of these institutions is to protect itself rather than its citizens (e.g. no freedom of speech or press).

Comprehending religious evolution is the first step to understanding where these rules originated, and whether or not their validity is justified. Aside from the political impact, there are many questions we must ask and answer if we want to understand contemporary religion, religion in the future, and whether or not religion actually works.

- Why did certain religions flourish while others faded away?
- Can we predict which modern religions will excel or decline?
- What factors that once affected religious evolution are no longer valid today?
- Can we predict how modern society will affect religion in the future?
- Will religion ever go away?

Is this knowledge relevant to anyone other than theologians and philosophers? I believe we are entering a pivotal moment in history, an era where ideas can accomplish more than warfare ever could due to the convenience and the power of social networking. The emotional pull of religion is in a heated tug-of-war with our propensity for logic, and the advantage will go to the side with popular support. Religion has always had the edge in this battle, but the tide is beginning to shift as vital knowledge which criticizes the authenticity of theological beliefs, once suppressed, or at least ignored, is now able to flourish. Perhaps we will be afforded the opportunity to discover our true requirements for survival: the logical mindset to conquer challenges (science), or the emotional tools to cope with our limitations (religion).

---

[5] Although there are biblical passages that empower government leaders with the authority of God (1 Peter 2:13), there are several passages in Romans and Acts that explicitly state to obey the word of God over man.

Demographics of global religious belief

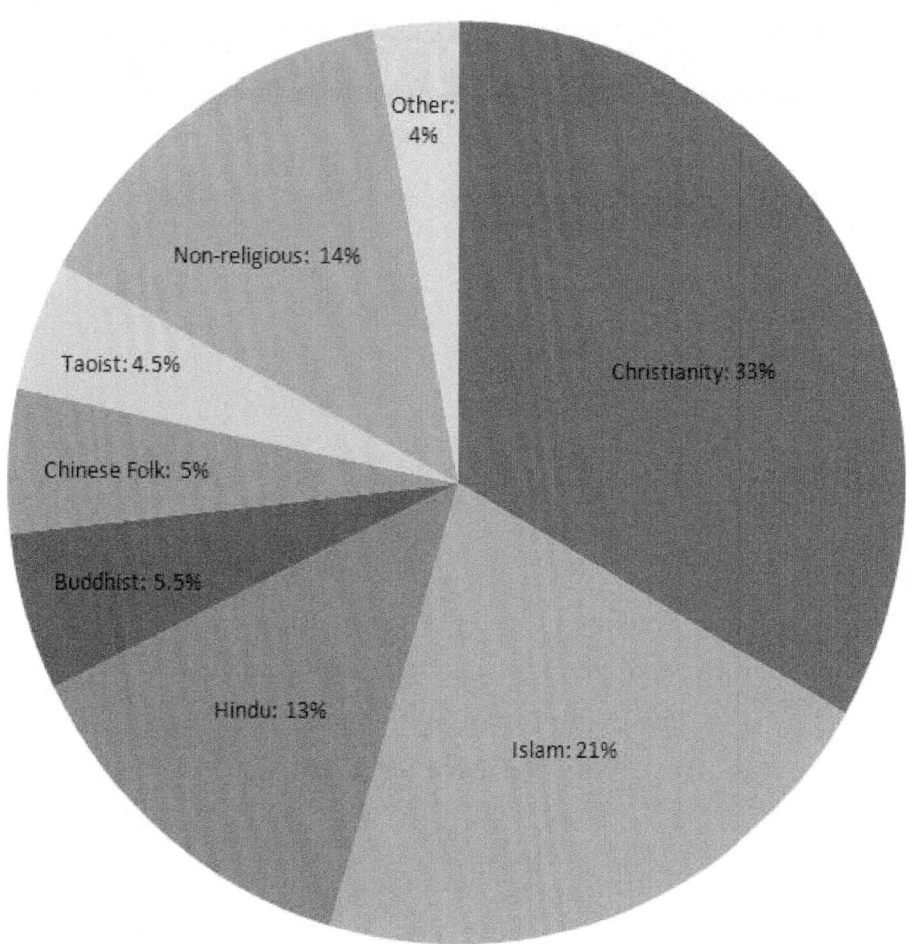

CHAPTER 2

RELIGION'S STORY:

In the Beginning...

"If triangles had a God, he'd have three sides."
-Old Yiddish Proverb

Timeline of Religious Development
From Many to One: The Rise of Monotheism
The Evolution of Myth and Ritual
Why We Have Religion

Are emotions just the 'human' version of instincts? If instincts are an involuntary compass for survival, almost anything that provokes an emotional reaction most likely has a survival benefit, especially if you imagine yourself back several thousand years. Take something as 'recreational' as music. You're a Paleolithic hominid and you're alone in the jungle. You have no weapons and you're starving. Your senses are all you have to keep you alive. You look for movement, be it predator or prey. You listen for the sounds of animals or running water. There is a sound, but it's like nothing you've ever heard. It's an exciting tone and rhythm impossible for nature to create on its own. This must mean you're within earshot of a band of prospering humans, which likely means food, shelter, and compassion.

Is there a survival benefit for religion as well? We can determine this by examining the similarities of religions in their fledging state. The first similarity, and a very telling clue, is that all religions began as polytheistic: belief in multiple gods. Today, 77% of religions that do believe in a god are monotheistic: belief in a single god. When did this shift occur, and more importantly, why?

Several benchmarks were achieved that shaped religion into its more modern structure. It began with a belief in the supernatural. This encompassed entities like the soul, afterlife, and a general notion of spirits affecting the physical world. The next phase was the gods themselves, each representing some aspect of nature and human limitation. After that came cosmology, creation myths, and the various stories surrounding the gods, their world, and how they interacted with mankind. Next came ritualistic practices, which were extensions of a society's culture and link to their cosmological origins. Lastly were rules and initiations, which was essentially the method by which societies personalized and attached identity to their beliefs (i.e. how to distinguish between 'us' and 'them'), as well as motivating an implied obedience (i.e. a primitive justice system).

The trigger for each of these milestones was not necessarily rooted in cognitive advancement but rather social advancement, which coincided with archeological evidence. Once the foundation for a religion was firmly established the details became the primary focus, and they would undergo evolutionary changes at an accelerated pace.

100 million years ago:

Mammals are flourishing, and so are primitive forms of communal empathy, including the ability to learn and follow the rules of a social group. For example, vampire bats who eat a surplus will regurgitate their meal for bats that did not eat to save them from starvation[6]. The 'golden rule' of morality at this stage went something like "do unto others in a manner that benefits the group".

60 million years ago:

The first primates arrive, specifically the, now extinct, tree inhabiting *Smilodectes,* similar to a lemur. Reciprocity evolves, or the cognizance to remember who did you a favor, as well as peacemaking. Those who don't abide are ostracized. This was one step beyond 'what's good for society is good for the individual', and slowly heads in a more intimate direction.

30 million years ago:

Monkeys evolve (e.g. gibbons, macaques, capuchins) as well as the brain capacity to add empathy to our morality timeline. This comes in the form of mutual grooming, sharing, and individual equality. Dutch primatologist Frans de Waal conducted a study with capuchin monkeys involving food rewards in the form of cucumber slices or grapes. If a monkey receiving only cucumber slices saw another monkey consistently receiving delicious grapes, he protested by throwing the cucumber

---

[6] Vampire Bats did not actually evolve until around 50 million years ago, but their communal instincts were evident in many of the more primitive mammalian species.

and jumping into the cage walls. Not always, but sometimes, the monkey who received the grapes would refuse it until the other also received a grape.

15 - 5 million years ago:

Anthropological: The monkeys lose their tails and leave the trees; apes have arrived. Orangutans, gorillas, and chimps develop specific awareness for another's well being, for example they will console the loser of a brutal fight with hugs and kisses, assist the elderly, and mourn death. Primitive humans have also evolved.
Religious: After a chimpanzee dies the others won't eat for a day, and go about their day in silence[7].

2 million years ago:

Anthropological and cultural: Homo erectus evolves, accenting the 'great split' between chimpanzees and future humans (both descended approximately 8 million years ago from one of three hominin species: *Ardipithecus, Sahelanthropus,* or *Orrorin* – a.k.a. CHLCA: chimpanzee-human last common ancestor). A recent theory links a decrease in a protein called MYH16, which is a chief component in developing powerful jaw muscles, like those in chimpanzees and gorillas. Weaker jaw muscles made it harder to chew raw meat, but also created less of a strain on the skull, allowing the brain to expand within a more flexible cranium casing. Unlike the more primitive species of Neanderthal, Homo erectus and Homo habilis established the first know forms of 'culture', which allowed for the transfer of knowledge from generation to generation.

Religious: The increased intelligence of Homo erectus adds a few more levels of morality to the mix: enforcing their society's moral codes more rigorously with rewards, punishment and reputation building, as well as incorporating 'degrees' of punishment.

500,000 years ago:

Cultural: The advantage of the expanded cranial capacity of Homo heidelbergensis becomes evident. Around this time the hominid brain, specifically the neo-cortex, tripled in size. Some of the archaic homo sapiens migrate from the caves and the first shelters were constructed. The first weapons are crafted in the form of spears.
Religious: There is little concrete evidence to speak of from this era, but it was around this time that the first burial and mourning 'rituals' developed. This was a result of what can be referred to as the 'projection of the mind', which established the empathetic framework for a belief in the afterlife.

---

[7] Donna Fernandes, president of the Buffalo Zoo, witnessed a wake for a female gorilla, Babs, who had died of cancer. Donna says the gorilla's longtime mate howled and banged his chest, picked up a piece of celery (Babs' favorite food), put it in her hand, and tried to get her to wake up.

200,000 years ago:

Anthropological: Homo sapiens evolve in East Africa. Disputed evidence is found for ritual burial with archaic forms of limestone grave marking. There was evidence of stone knives, most likely used for carving meat and creating other tools. Methods of controlling fire were highly unsuccessful. One's ability to survive came down to man versus nature, a daunting mission to wrangle methods and knowledge about this seemingly unpredictable living environment.

Religious: Animism is born: the belief that natural objects, natural phenomena, and the universe itself possess 'souls'. Primitive Homo sapiens analyzed their world through simple deductions: if it moves it possess life (e.g. plants *grow*, clouds *drift*, rivers *flow*, the sun *rises*). Sympathy for the dead was apparent in an infant burial located near modern day Syria. The joints, having been disarticulated, were methodically positioned with anatomical correctness in the grave site prior to burial. Belief in the soul and/or afterlife seems to coincide with a more highly evolved acceptance of death, yet this was apparent far in advance of deity worship or presumption of divine origin.

130,000 years ago:

Cultural: The first bands of hunter-gatherers start to form with numbers as low as ten to as high as a hundred. Social hierarchy was loose at this point with no clear tribal leaders. Some cultures find greater success in controlling fire, which leads to better methods for sharpening stone. Primitive art arises in the form of decorative beads.

Religious: Undisputed evidence of burial and ritual repetition arises. Bones uncovered in gravesites in Africa were found stained with red ochre, possibly symbolizing our efforts to offer a form of mystical protection in the afterlife.

75,000 years ago:

Cultural: The arrowhead is developed, a controlled use of fire, plant-based bedding, some cannibalism persisted, but most importantly a more sophisticated verbal language evolves. Changes in climate increased our short-comings due to our lack of technology and understanding. Genetic evidence shows a dramatic decrease in the human population around this time due to long periods of severe drought in eastern Africa. Entire bands and blood lines were dying off. There was always a need for more food and better hunting techniques, along with mysteries surrounding the weather, disease, and infertility. The exodus from Africa begins. Over the next several thousand years humans cultivated the Middle-East, India, and Australia.

Religious: Personalities are applied to our existing belief in animism – Gods are born. Innovations in language allows for a method to share supernatural theories to explain the unknown. The forces of nature, biology, astronomy, and pathology (i.e. weather, stars, disease, fertility, war) were explained through divine control. Ritualistic worship of gods was scattered, unorganized, and often a last resort. There was evidence of animal worship, a humble appreciation for the creatures whose flesh was keeping humans well fed.

50,000 years ago:

Cultural: Human migration extends to Europe. The sewing needle is invented, along with some simple musical instruments, a primitive bow and arrow, and poisoned tipped hunting arrows.

Religious: Idolatry and religious symbols emerge, as well as burial sites containing graven goods or personal items. This suggests more ritualized afterlife beliefs, as food and nourishment was often included in the burial chamber. Supernatural representation appears in cave art. As language improved so did the stories to explain the world of the gods, and the theories behind cosmology and creation. The stories that survived established archetypes and struck a chord in its listeners. They were more memorable and easier to pass on to future generations. This stage of god worship was known as *Hetaerism*, an egalitarian existence of god and goddesses, consistent with the communal hunter-gatherer lifestyle. For each and every mysterious aspect of nature there was a god who controlled it, and could provide aid if worshipped properly. Sacrificial rituals were fine-tuned based upon success, or lack thereof, which could be easily misconstrued (e.g. if a thunder storm broke the day after a sacrificial ritual, the gods were evidently offended).

40,000 years ago:

Cultural: Cloth is invented, along with iron smelting, better weapons, refined cave paintings, and the flute. As the migrations continued, cultures mixed. The values of one society did not always mesh with the values of another, leading to both conflict and compromise.

Religious: The first evidence of cremation is discovered. This was an indication that certain members of a band held a position of importance – the establishment of a social hierarchy is on the horizon. Community decisions are slowly moving into the hands of the alpha male. Religion was slowly evolving as a source of cultural human rights, adding importance to certain rituals that could not otherwise be justified (e.g. animal sacrifices would be counterproductive for survival were it not for religious purposes).

25,000 years ago:

Cultural: Migration extends to Japan and North America. Some of the more advanced cultures were experiencing population growth, which led to individual property. Primitive techniques for domesticating animals were also developed.

Religious: Figurines of Venus, the fertility goddess, emerge in Europe signifying some of the earliest forms of representational art. Even as individual property was attainable 'private' worship was still thousands of years away.

20,000 years ago:

Cultural: Pottery was soon to be invented in China. Environmental changes, in the form of a depleting ice age, give rise to new tropical forests. Plants suitable for domestication were available and primitive agriculture was invented, allowing prospering bands to end their nomadic migration and set up permanent villages. Trade was established with other camps, along with primitive governments. Bands would sometimes form alliances, or if extenuating circumstances occurred, engage in conflict.

Religious: When neighboring bands merged, often through small scale conflict, so did their gods. A 'polytheistic sympathy' existed between cultures as entire pantheons were attached to civilizations and regions. Society didn't question the existence of foreign gods, rather their importance or dominance. Foreign cultures were as much a learning tool as were their religions. In other words, another band may have been weak at war but successful with medicine, so not only were their medical techniques adopted, so was their 'god of healing'. This often led to redundancy in worship as obsolete gods never completely went away. Stories emerged of deities battling each other for supremacy in the heavens, and this was often mirrored on earth with the bands who worshipped them. To balance out our expanding blend of religious practices, and to underwrite obedience, inductive rituals were established. 'Rites of passage' proved to be an effective form of tribal unity to counter our growing distrust of 'outsiders'. For example, the severing of the foreskin of a newborn's penis served as a test of a parent's commitment to the tribe, as well as a 'brand' to identify cultural roots.

11,000 B.C.E.:

Cultural: Migration extends to, and settles in, Canada and South America. Agricultural techniques reach a pivotal zenith. The hunter-gatherer lifestyle comes to an end and a population explosion occurs on a semi-global level. Bands grew into tribes, now numbering from the hundreds up into the thousands. There was a dire need for justice and order.

Religious: Society has a new focus: agriculture. The fertility of the earth becomes the key to survival. The environment gradually takes on a female persona. Pantheons show signs of an evolution as goddesses begin to outnumber and outrank the gods, otherwise known as the *Agrarian* (or Neolithic) phase of worship. As survival becomes less mysterious and taxing, 'terror management' becomes less focused on environmental threats and more focused on mentally coping with death, amplifying religious camaraderie. As fellowships grow, taxes are collected to build churches and enforce laws. Society members bond through large-scale community projects.

5,000 B.C.E.:

Cultural: Populations double again. Tribes grow into chiefdoms with numbers ranging from the low thousands to the tens of thousands. Wheeled vehicles are invented. The barter system evolves into currency exchange. Government is more organized, and armies grow. Up until now territorial wars were rare. But now that mortality rates have decreased, leaders soon have something they've never had in their population: expendability.

Religious: Cultures all over the globe now have their own set of gods and goddesses (some numbering in the thousands), and their own modes of worship, many of which include human sacrifices. As our capability to survive increases, our anxiety towards foreign religions increases.

3,500 – 2,500 B.C.E.:

Cultural: The Bronze Age begins. Written language develops. Chiefdoms grow into States with populations numbering as high as 100,000, allowing armies to grow further.

Religious: Increased populations increase the devastation of war, which channels religion towards a new realm. The key to survival is a strong military. This stage of god worship is known as *Dionysian* and a more patriarchal representation arises. The male dominated mindset of war influences society and government. Gods (sometimes a single god) rather than goddesses claim supremacy in the pantheon. The Egyptians lead the movement to develop the first religious texts. Beliefs and principles are more easily spread and documented. Religious dogma is polished and solidified. The mystery surrounding religion began to dissipate and private worship is finally condoned.

From Many to One: The Rise of Monotheism

It's the year 2,500 B.C.E. and the shift from polytheism to monotheism is around the corner. Warfare became a viable tool once populations reached a relative abundance.

The spoils of war and its affect on the economy took its toll on many empires, and an increased dependence on proper worship evolved; not so much the rituals, but which god to worship. Many cultures had a long list of war gods, supreme gods, creator gods, protector gods, and destructor gods to worship just to ensure victory in battle. This ambiguity created rifts in morale and leadership.

Military failures led to discrepancies descending from a perceived disconnect with the will of the Gods, which was often in flux due to 'divine disagreements' in the heavens (i.e. the competing forces of nature in the material world were symbolic of competing deities). To retain social unity leaders had to assure their citizens that the will of the Gods was clear and understood. One way of accomplishing this was to consolidate leadership under one supreme god. As rulers were replaced decisions were made to promote their 'god of choice' as the primary deity of worship. Monotheism was still over a millennium away, but our social hierarchy was clearly being mirrored in the heavens, and almost every pantheon would soon have a king.

The first practices of monotheism occurred in, what was at the time, the most scientifically advanced region in the world: Mesopotamia[8]. They slowly became aware that certain minor deities were 'unnecessary' for their survival. Over generations the early musings of monotheism grew from determining a supreme god, to eliminating lesser gods, to choosing and believing in only one. When this was first put into practice it was not intended to revolutionize theology. In the case of the first two monotheistic faiths, Zoroastrianism and Judaism, it served a very common goal of religion: cultural identity. The ancient monotheistic Persians and Jews were simultaneously solidifying their own culture as well as segregating themselves from foreigners. Once proselytizing faiths like Christianity and Islam got a hold of monotheism, the theological respect offered by 'polytheistic sympathy' was removed. The worship of a single god would shift the mode of religious evolution from 'fusion' to 'destruction'. In fact, the concept of monotheism promoted the first notable forms of religious persecution, but it was 'against' the monotheists rather than in favor of it. In other words, the polytheists were trying to destroy what they didn't understand. Monotheism represented a major shift in cultural values, from the naturally inspired pantheons that represented our environment, to embracing technology that labeled all but one of these gods as 'superfluous'.

There are surprisingly few historical instances of a conclusive polytheistic conversion to monotheism. Only a few impactful evolutions were required to essentially shift global deity worship from 100% polytheism to the modern demographic of around 20%. Only a few doors needed to be opened to invite a seemingly endless permutation of monotheistic possibilities.

---

[8] Around 3,500 B.C.E. the Mesopotamians were the first to invent writing, the wheel, mathematics, the calendar (based on an astrological understanding of moon and planet cycles), and engineering in the form of the Archimedes Screw, glasswork, and advanced architecture (e.g. 50 mile long walls, towers over 100 feet tall).

1,500 – 1,000 B.C.E. – Zoroastrian (a monotheistic version of dualism; worship of Ahura Mazda) evolves from the polytheistic Proto-Indo Iranian and Vedic religion.

950 – 450 B.C.E. – Judaism (sole belief in Yahweh) evolves from the polytheistic Canaanite religion.

1,469 C.E. – Sikhism (sole belief in Waheguru) evolves from polytheistic Hinduism.

1,838 C.E. – Tenrikyo (sole belief in Tenri-O-no-Mikoto) evolves from the non-theistic following of Buddhism.

Creationists often argue against the possibility for the diversity of life through biological evolution (i.e. animal species are too abundant and too diverse to have originated from so few). If polytheism represented aquatic life, and monotheism represented land-based life, the process by which theological evolution occurred is not only evident but fast, given that biology took 500 million years (proto-amphibian origin) and theology took 3,500 years (monotheistic origin).

There is some dispute over the first true form of monotheism. The linguistic nature of the first Zoroastrian scriptures suggest that they were written between 1,500 and 1,000 B.C.E. (though documentation of the prophet Zoroaster doesn't appear till around 600 B.C.E.), and describe a consolidation of worship from the polytheistic Proto-Indo Iranian beliefs solely to Ahura Mazda. This principle, with its views on light and darkness, heaven and hell, and one supreme God is argued to have been the true inspiration behind Judaism, and ultimately Christianity.

In 1,344 B.C.E. pharaoh Akhenaten (Amenhotep IV) abolished the worship of all Egyptian Gods accept for the sun-disk Aten. This was the first documented practice of monotheism in history. Perhaps too progressive for its time, Akhenaten's successor restored traditional polytheism ten years later. The political advantages of monotheism were not vastly apparent. In fact, it was less about what monotheism could offer and more about economic timing (*discussed further in chapter 7*). It would be another four hundred years before monotheistic worship was attempted, but not necessarily accepted, at least not by the Egyptians.

In Asia, around the turn of the first millennium B.C.E., the Chinese were ahead of the curve in some respects. They shifted their primary worship to the god Shangdi. But the Babylonians thought along the same path some 500 years before the Chinese with their crowning of Marduk as their supreme deity. This was technically henotheism as both the Chinese and the Babylonians continued to recognize the existence of their pantheon.

Pure and sustainable monotheism came in the form of Judaism beginning around 950 B.C.E. The story behind it revolved around the war god Yahweh who supposedly led the Jews to freedom from Egyptian slavery. The Jews gradually (approx 500 years later) consolidated their worship to Yahweh and denounced all other Canaanite gods. This started a monotheistic chain reaction over the next few centuries in the Middle East with other Canaan based belief systems: Milkom became the sole deity in Amman, Chemosh in Moab, and Qaus in Edom. But polytheism wasn't going down without a fight.

It would be nearly a millennium before new branches of polytheism would cease to sprout. Interestingly enough, the road to monotheism (with the exception of Manichaeism) proved to be a one-way street – these superfluous gods were not as immortal as once believed. The Thelema faith aside (who revived Nuit, Hadit and Ra-Hoor-Khuit from the Egyptian archives), once the gods of the polytheistic world were officially dismissed, they stayed that way. Contrary in some ways to biological evolution, in which life forms tend to become more complex, religion streamlined itself with respect to deities. It did, however, grow more complex with respect to sacraments.

The Evolution of Myth and Ritual

Religions generally encompass specific deities, divine law, ethics, and lifestyle. These are not arbitrarily assigned but based on historical origins, which come in the form of divine myths and from those myths rituals are derived. One of the key objectives of religion is to establish an emotional connection with the origins on which a faith is based. For example, fasting rituals like Lent, Yom Kippur, and Ramadan are modern ways for contemporary worshippers to emulate historical religious events. Romanian historian and philosopher Mircea Eliade argues that this emotional connection derives from our desire for *nostalgia*: a time of presumed purity free from corruption. We desire to know something's origin in order to understand its nature, thereby gaining power over it through comprehension.

There are fictional myths (creative musings that are representational) which involve supernatural events and protagonists, and there are historical myths, which are stories that are intended to be true but have become exaggerated over time. The general consensus among believers range from a 'completely literal' interpretation of a fictional myth as true, to the notion that the details may vary but the essence of the story – the supernatural aspect – is historically factual. These myths originated before we had any formal scientific understanding, thus religion essentially served as science – a primitive way of explaining our physical world. The various creation myths associated with religion have ranged from the Abrahamic version (God willed the elements of cosmology into existence out of nothingness), to the Greek version (out of chaos was born the Earth, who gave birth to the sky, and then bred the Titans, one of whom bred Zeus), to the shaping of the earth by spiritual animals (Yoruba: rooster; Cherokee: beaver and buzzard; Japanese: wagtail bird).

American Mythologist Joseph Campbell argues that the power of metaphor was quickly realized as stories were passed down (e.g. "Jesus *is* the Son of God", rather than "the relationship of man to God is *like* that of a son to his father"), and these metaphorical myths were presented as fact. Take something as mundane as a thunderstorm. We might not fully understand the physics of static electricity, but modern minded adults understand that potentially dangerous weather is not a form of spiritual punishment. But describing a thunderstorm becomes difficult without a modern frame of reference. Today we might compare the sound of thunder to fireworks or a gun shot. With a sparse language base and only other elements of nature as a background, hyperbole and even supernatural imagery become the most effective way of encapsulating this mysterious phenomenon.

One problem with storytelling accuracy in Neolithic times was a lack of record keeping and limited communication options – there were only experiences, memory, and words. Today we can fact check, recreate conditions through scientific testing, and exchange information easier and faster to corroborate sightings. As meaningful accounts were little more than the retelling of events, it was apparent that history could be re-invented as the story-teller saw fit (i.e. editing outcomes to mean something more significant). If you weren't a political or military leader, having your version of history retold to future generations was the easiest way to achieve immortality.

Psychologist Richard H. Gramzow of the University of Southampton conducted studies which demonstrate distinct differences in our stress levels when lying as compared to exaggerating. Guilty consciences (e.g. calculated deception, withholding vital information) show greater signs of distress, whereas those who 'stretched the truth' for personal gain – whether it related to themselves or others – were considerably more relaxed. Our deterrents for exaggerating what we either saw or have been told, when compared to simply making something up, are almost non-existent.

Our motivation to study history is driven by a desire to find meaning in the past that will explain our present, or guide us into the future. Documented history tends to focus on negative events and man's flaws in judgment or corruption, whereas myths are often heroic, or, if they didn't start that way, a heroic angle was incorporated. Myths tend to have clear themes and morals, whereas the intrinsic value in historical events is often ambiguous. When a myth is retold often enough, and carries positive traits of its society, it becomes a piece of culture. Its authenticity becomes secondary if its message carries value for future generations. These myths were often coveted and sacred and incorporated into tribal initiations[9].

Rituals evolved as the myths they are based on evolved, and this was influenced by technology. The first era of mythology originated with the invention of spoken language during the *hunter-gatherer* period approximately 75,000 years ago. The primary purpose of myths was to justify the paradox between killing animals for survival and the divinity of the animals themselves, as they were often worshipped or sacred. For example, through myths humans interacted with animals and established a spiritual pact whereby the hunted were portrayed as willing victims, and that we would return their

---

[9] In primitive American cultures sacred myths were sometimes withheld from women, and not told to male children until they reached the age of maturity.

spirit to Mother Earth to be born anew through sacrificial rituals. The more established myths were publically reenacted as both a form of religion and entertainment.

The next phase was *agrarian* around 15,000 years ago. The fertility of the earth was the focus. There was a need to understand weather cycles, moon cycles, and seasonal changes for harvest. Myths revolved around ritualistic sacrifices for prosperous growth, which was essentially the early science of meteorology and botany. Snakes (also serpents and dragons) could symbolize the umbilical cord joining humans to Mother Earth. They also represented sexual desire, which related to fertility, as well as guardianship, vengefulness, and medicine (i.e. poison). Rain dances incorporated slithering maneuvers and would often involve live snakes.

The *celestial* phase came around 5,000 B.C.E. shifting curiosity from the earth to the sky. Myths incorporated stars, planets, the sun (e.g. Kings were often represented by the sun and a glowing crown), and adjustments were made to integrate a new understanding of mathematics. There was a better understanding of cosmology, and seasonal cycles and time. However the Europeans of the north-west would mingle – often forcibly – with the Arabs of the south-east, and war Gods would slowly overtake fertility gods. Thunder gods, like Zeus and Indra, featured a blend of Motherly weather, and Fatherly warfare. This era witnessed the decline of agricultural sacrifices (feminine) and saw the rise of military protection in the form of human sacrifices (masculine). Myths based on the constellations developed (Ursa Major: Bear; Orion: the Warrior; Pleiades: fishing or sailing; Milky Way: a River to Heaven), and involved much more diverse rituals.

As survival shed much of its mystery, the *Medieval* phase (500 – 1,500 C.E.) saw a major thematic shift. Our purpose for living shifted from 'survival of the fittest' to 'follow your bliss'. Courting for marriage was permitted allowing for a luxury that was considered quite rare: love. Romantic themes and love stories were now accessible and captured our passions. Stories like *Tristan and Isolde*, *Laxdaela saga*, and *Sir Gawain and the Green Knight* were enduring literally works of the period that would influence the classical fiction of Christopher Marlowe and William Shakespeare.

By this point the window of opportunity for hyperbolized mythology was closing. Religious rituals based on myths were essentially limited to variations on existing practices. Even as new creation stories would arise, like that of Mormonism or Scientology, unlike their predecessors these myths, once created, were quickly documented and were therefore resistant to modification. The death of tall tales and fables would pave the way for a genre of works unmistakably bound to the world of fiction.

Why We Have Religion

It can be argued that there were an abundance of agnostic civilizations prior to 5,000 B.C.E., but they were at a disadvantage. The tribes with religion operated as a cohesive unit. There was an inherent trust built into a community who engaged in group rituals. They took pride in their own, and developed an estranged empathy for those outside the group. Civilizations who worked as a unit were more prone to share ideas and exchange favors. Their technology advanced faster and they had a superior military.

If there were civilizations of atheists they were destined to fail. Extinction for religion, or a lack thereof, operated on the leadership level. The citizens of a non-religious tribe weren't eliminated – their government was. Their territory was occupied, their leadership replaced, and they were forced to worship as their conquerors did. Whether you were sincere or not about your beliefs mattered little. Your former leader's ability to spread atheism was effectively eliminated. Society's leaders controlled information, and essentially controlled religion. A system was established to contain beliefs and resist change. It seemed unfathomable that new religions were able to form, flourish, and ultimately surpass. But they did, and did so abundantly.

However, certain aspects of religion are contrary to our innate survival instincts. Prayer, for example, violates much of what evolutionary survival has taught us. If a tiger was chasing you, it would take an enormous amount of faith to resist the urge to run and instead focus on praying for divine intervention. But when our adrenaline is not pumping, prayer can be beneficial (*discussed further in chapter 3*). Individual prayer and worship was not practiced in early forms of religion. Instead, group prayers brought members of society together, and may have promoted collective problem solving afterwards.

Before the Neolithic period (c. 12,000 B.C.E.) bands were a fairly cohesive unit of around 50 people, most of which were family members. You were assigned a role and you did your job – life was relatively simple. Social bonding required little encouragement. After the population explosion, as many as twenty bands would untie to form a tribe of some 1,000 members. Social unity now required incentive if they wanted to take advantage of their collective knowledge and skills. Tribal chieftains tended to be a solitary unit of authority, along with the extended 'royal family' to serve as aids, and a few civilian deputies to serve as 'keepers of the peace'. There were no formal laws, there were no town meetings, and families tended to dwell within a communal home. Religion was the first 'member's only' social organization, and there were essentially no other options, nor was there a need for any. That is until cultures started mixing.

What does religion have to do with war? The political answer might involve a degree of xenophobia (fear of foreigners): how can we trust the morality of a tribe who sacrifices humans to their gods? The economic answer might involve the fact that this foreign tribe borders on a river that would be beneficial for trade. Which version do you think a chieftain would share with his tribe to establish military camaraderie? Simply living and working together accomplished little in the way of solidarity. Emotional bonds were much easier to form if society members believe that they 'thought alike' (i.e. shared a common cultural view), and were therefore collectively worth defending. This mindset illustrates the importance we place on morality.

Our ability to determine the moral compass in other humans is a flawed instinct. Not necessarily because we are unable to predict actions based on body language, but because intelligent beings are capable of manipulation. A Harvard anthropology study conducted in 2005 helped evaluate the tendency for deception in chimpanzees. When a human engaged in competition for food, chimpanzees would alter their behavior by hiding from the human until the 'coast was clear' before approaching an available meal. When humans engage in manipulation they don't always have to hide. We are perfectly capable of adjusting our speech patterns and body language to conceal deceptive motives. Until we evolve the sensitivities of a polygraph machine, we have little more that our instincts to guide us. Religion seeks to correct this need by applying an aspect of predictability. Whether or not it works doesn't negate the notion that we subconsciously lower our guard when amongst others who share our beliefs. The irony lies in the underlying deception often used by authorities to bond societies in this manner.

A non-violent way to put religious bonding into practice was for a chieftain to organize an architectural endeavor, like the construction of a church. Tasks rendered in the name of a deity were good for the tribe and the individual – provided their belief system involved accomplishing sacraments to receive salvation in the afterlife. The underlying theme is that 'exclusivity' works. People behave differently when they are part of a group, but the direction they lean is often in the hands of a charismatic individual.

CHAPTER 3

COGNITIVE ANALYSIS:

It's All In Your Mind

"Believe those who are seeking the truth. Doubt those who find it."
-Andre Gide

Seekers and Finders

Empathy and Survival

The Evolution of Prayer

The Meaning Behind Meaning

Religious Motivation

Does Religion Work?

Who Are the Religious?

Are humans hard-wired to be religious? In 2005 geneticist Gene Hamer proposed the highly criticized existence of the 'god gene'[10]. According to University of Michigan's associate research scientist Margaret Evans, children are indeed religiously hard-wired. When children under the age of ten were taught evolution by their parents and teachers they preferred and related to creationist explanations. Experimental evidence, including cross-cultural studies, suggests that three-year-olds attribute god-like qualities to a variety of different beings, suggesting that belief in a supernatural creator is our default mindset.

It can be argued that there are two types of information gatherers: seekers (generally liberal) and finders (generally conservative). Either is capable of theism or

---

[10] Gene VMAT2 plays a key role in regulating the levels of the brain chemicals serotonin, dopamine and norepinephrine, which consequently regulate the neurological activities associated with mystic beliefs.

atheism – the determining factor is in the upbringing. Early exposure aside, there are cognitive reasons why religion is compatible with the way our mind processes information. Some of it is specific to certain mindsets, some of it is universal.

When a 'seeker' is raised in a religious household, they can be very emphatic about their beliefs. The seeking portion of their subconscious is able to focus on other things like school, work, or hobbies – anything other than *how did we get here* and *what is my pur*pose. The problem is that religious explanations don't always hold up. There are contradictions with science, contradictions with human nature, and contradictions within their own dogma. Most of these are innocent enough to overlook. But depending on the tenacity of the seeker, they may reach a crossroads where they are forced to reevaluate their beliefs. The seeker can't live in a world of denial for very long, or they wouldn't be seekers. Scenarios like these often lead to family rifts, denunciation, and feelings of betrayal.

Whether a 'finder' is raised in a religious or non-religious household they tend to remain loyal to the belief system they were initially exposed to. The goal of the finder is to establish peace within themselves, and if denial carves the most efficient path to accomplishing this, compelling evidence will take a backseat to emotional satisfaction. But if a finder does happen to change their belief, it will likely be a quick and confident conversion.

What influences someone to be a seeker or a finder? This tends to go hand in hand with one's viewpoint on 'change'. The more conservative amongst us tend to resist change, and usually become finders. The more liberal are generally open to change, and often become seekers (e.g. the correlation between larger liberal populations in big cities ties into the fast-paced, fluid lifestyle associated with fluctuating media, diverse cultures, accelerated business, etc). A finder may value comfort over practicality, like Harry Harlow's rhesus monkeys who chose a cloth mother over a wiry bottle[11]. But these are broad categorizations with various overlaps. There are universal cognitive traits that are much more difficult to suppress.

Empathy and Survival

Our ability to empathize is bred into us ever since the first social mammals came into existence 100 million years ago. Without it there would be no subconscious motivation to bond with other humans, not unlike the anti-social lifestyle of koala bears, black bears, leopards, and panthers. But empathy doesn't stop there. We bond with other living things, like pets, sometimes more intensely than with other humans. Where empathy gets murky is when it drifts into the world of the non-living.

---

[11] In the 1950s American Psychologist Harry Harlow conducted various psychological experiments, one of which involved separating baby rhesus monkeys from their mother. When presented with a choice of surrogate mothers (one with a food bottle encased in a wire frame, the other made of soft cloth with no food) the monkeys overwhelmingly selected the cloth surrogate.

Children are notorious for forming bonds with inanimate objects (e.g. toys, blankets, bottles). Their creativity tends to elude our more mature social confines and essentially run amok. This is natural and healthy, and doesn't ever completely go away. As adults we tend to apply this same behavior when we find it emotionally appropriate. But a certain amount of skepticism is often – or at least should be – employed when someone offers you the intangible, like 'positive vibes', or more significantly, life after death. But when it comes to matters of emotional comfort, or even survival, Pascal's Wager tends to win over the majority[12].

We gain a survival benefit by being able to predict another's behavior. We recognize our own external triggers for certain mannerisms and apply them to the outside world. This comes from an analysis of behavior, facial expressions, and on a deeper level, pheromones. You can recognize another's anger, even if they profess otherwise. You wouldn't necessarily know if you've upset your economy-car after hauling a trunk load of cinder blocks, yet there is a tendency to humanize inanimate objects. And things get further complicated when we humanize the dead.

It's an easy biological step to take for granted when we allow for the mind to operate without a host brain. Thoughts are a fuzzy thing. Science offers a loose explanation based on electronic impulses, but this tends to be an emotionally unsatisfying definition when our understanding of electricity can also be something created by a revolving turbine. There's something about the 'life force' that spins our biological turbine that we assume continues on after our blood stops flowing. The secret, however, may lie in the receptors that interpret these electronic impulses.

Neuroscientist Michael Persinger has conducted experiments to study the effects of electromagnetic impulses on our brain's temporal lobes. The warping of our ability to process information and correctly interpret impulses can recreate some of the phenomenon associated with near-death experiences, including 'out of body' experiences. The employment of an artificial 'brain scrambler' inhibited receptors simulating the effects of opiates. Patients of the study were blindfolded and wore headphones, so impulses created by sensory receivers (eyes and ears) were not involved. Their experiences were created solely within the mind.

The validity of paranormal near-death experiences is not solely what's on trial. There are seemingly unavoidable side-effects when our empathy with the dead plays out to fruition. Once we project our empathy onto the deceased, the world of the supernatural and paranormal was suddenly realized. There's a kind of 'magical thinking' that can extend, without bounds, the limitations of what's actually possible in the spirit world. There's a vicarious projection of our own desires to live in a realm where our minds can function normally while violating the laws of physics. Projecting this ability onto the dead creates two scenarios that were properly absent: emotion and purpose.

---

[12] 17th century French philosopher Blaise Pascal proposed the only two possibilities for the existence of God: he is, or he is not. Based on loss versus gain, the benefits far outweigh the harm if we choose to worship God only to discover he never existed, as opposed to not worshipping and realizing he does.

Emotion attributed to the dead now allows for a deceased person to be psychologically affected by your thoughts and actions. Without physics to hinder their travels, they potentially know everything about you. It's subjective territory whether or not the spirits can 'affect' the physical world, which leads us to purpose. When things happen around you, good or bad, they now potentially have purpose. If the dead care what you do, and can influence the physical world you live in, you may find yourself adjusting your thoughts and actions accordingly. For many of us this is a positive thing. If you knew your dead mother was watching your every move, you might conduct yourself in a more proper manner beyond changing your underwear daily. But this can also lead to unnecessary guilt, or a belief that you deserve the bad things that happen to you. Needless to say, the leap from believing in a spirit world (animism) to believing in, and worshipping, Gods was a relatively small one.

The Evolution of Prayer

Prayer is a natural progression from believing in the supernatural, to linguistically communicating with them. Worshippers engage in prayer for different reasons: requests (e.g. knowledge, humility, health, financial assistance), experiential (e.g. to attain a divine experience), or purely conversational. The accepted methods of prayer have evolved as well, but before 2,500 B.C.E. prayer and sacrifice underwent evolutionary paths of their own. The first phase was loosely regulated: a tribal leader or shaman would establish a sacred altar or shrine where sacrifices would take place. Anyone could offer sacrifices, and portions were sometimes offered to the chieftain. Prayers, however, were performed in groups led by the chieftain or shaman, and occurred at specific times centered around the altar. The Shaman served as an intermediary between the living world and divine (i.e. all spiritual requests must filter through him). The next phase evolved a more rigid structure: sacrifices were now controlled by the chieftain or shaman, and were centralized around seasonal holidays. Prayers were still practiced in groups led by the leader or shaman, but were more liberal in regards to timing. The final phase was highly regulated: sacrifices could only take place in a specific house of worship, they were always offered and performed by a shaman (or direct descendant of the King), they followed a specific calendar ritual, and entitlements to the shaman were strictly mandated. Prayer was now permitted in private residences by commoners, although group prayers were considered crucial.

Prayer rituals inspired emotional responses, not necessarily because a shaman expressed their importance, but because of the very nature behind these activities. For example, you watch two men handling different groups of snakes. One wears traditional street clothing, the other wears a safari uniform. The man in street clothes handles each snake a bit differently with no particular pattern. The man in the safari uniform handles each snake the exact same way. You're told one group of snakes is poisonous, the other group is not. Which man is handling the poisonous snakes? The manner in which the safari uniformed handler is behaving implies he is doing something dangerous, even though he could just as easily be a worried novice.

When this scenario is applied to religious rituals the same reaction is triggered. An authorized leader, specific clothing and location, and meticulous actions all imply importance. We understand the consequences of mishandling a poisonous snake. But we do not necessarily understand the consequences of incorrectly praying, but given the care under which the shaman is executing the ritual, we assume the worst.

Prayer studies aside, there are viable benefits to prayer and meditation. People who meditate experience lower blood-pressure, lower heart rates, and decreased anxiety during and after the ritual. The secular version would involve focusing on something positive for an extended period of time, and arguably achieving the same results. When people amidst their morning mayhem stop to pray for God to help them find their keys and then suddenly remember leaving them on the nightstand, was it a divine revelation, or simply mental clarity after taking a moment to focus?

In 1948 American psychologist B.F. Skinner conducted a behavioral experiment with pigeons. Hungry pigeons were placed in cages and delivered food via an automated mechanism at regular intervals. When the food was delivered the pigeon became aware of their own activity at that time, and would repeat the movement until the food was delivered again. Unaware that the source of the food was an automated machine, the pigeons acted as if they exhibited control over the outcome. This study was called 'Superstition in the Pigeon', and has been linked to cathartic instinct to which we associate prayer rituals.

Unfortunately not everyone has a choice when it comes to prayer. The University of San Diego's department of pediatrics and the C.H.I.L.D. (Children's Healthcare is a Legal Duty) organization in Sioux City, Iowa reviewed cases of child fatality in faith-healing sects (e.g. Pentecostalism, Christian Science) in 172 cases from 1975 – 1995. The probability of survival for each was estimated based on expected survival rates for children with similar disorders who receive medical care. 140 fatalities were from conditions for which survival rates with medical care would have exceeded 90%. 18 more had expected survival rates of better than 50%. All but 3 of the remainder would likely have had some benefit from clinical help. Unfortunately 141 of these children were left in God's hands to die, whereas medical professionals could have reduced that number to zero.

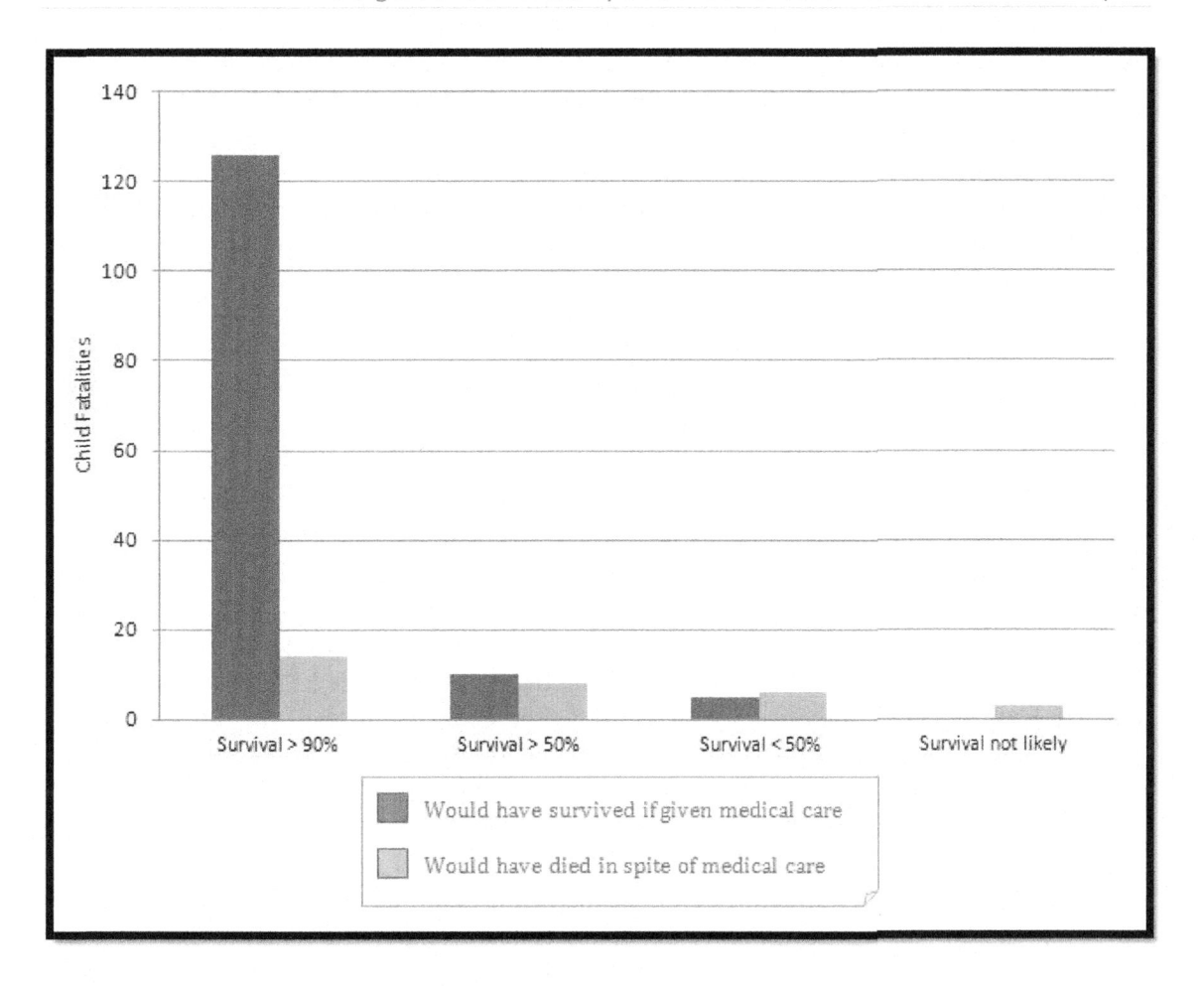

[Bar chart: X-axis categories "Survival > 90%", "Survival > 50%", "Survival < 50%", "Survival not likely"; Y-axis "Child Fatalities" 0–140. Legend: "Would have survived if given medical care" and "Would have died in spite of medical care".]

The Meaning Behind Meaning

Finding meaning is a common attribute applied to religion. Was that sudden latte craving which led me to that random coffee shop where I met my future spouse 'fate' or 'coincidence'? Regardless of our afterlife beliefs we think and act as if we have one life to live. Time spent pursuing a goal is time we can't get back, and our inability to control outcomes creates anxiety for how we spend our time. Believing in fate and meaning gives comfort that we're not wasting our life.

You've been singing since you were a child. Everyone says you have a great voice, but they're also your friends and relatives – perhaps they're a little biased. You hear about a televised singing competition where viewers vote to determine the winner, and they're holding auditions in your hometown. You show up for the audition, wait in line all day, and finally sing for the producer who will decide who gets to perform on television for the celebrity judges. You sing your favorite pop song and nail it, or so you think. The producer thanks you for your time and says they'll call back the finalists in two weeks. Two weeks comes and goes. No call. The pain of rejection sets in. Was that a sign to give up? People swear you're talented so you keep singing. A year goes by and same television show comes to your town again. You struggle with the decision whether or not to audition. Your family encourages you to go for it. You sing your heart out for a different producer this time. Two weeks comes and goes. No call. The signs are clear that you're not as good as you think you are. Would *you* continue to pursue a singing career?

We don't always consider the other half of this scenario: the decision of this dream crushing *American Idol* producer. How often do you consider the impact of your actions on other people? Maybe you hung up on a telemarketer causing him to miss his quota, which cost him his job. But maybe he found a new job which paid twice as much. Does that mean you were divinely guided to hang up on him?

There are two approaches to the fate theory: God intervenes when he deems necessary thereby temporarily suspending our freewill, or we have no freewill and everything is guided[13]. The former presents an interesting paradox. If God can divinely influence an American Idol producer to reject someone that they would have otherwise advanced, why not save a step and influence the struggling singer in the same way?

Before we address the possibility that there is no freewill, let's discuss what actually happened to pop singer Colby Caillat. She twice auditioned for American Idol and was never given the opportunity to perform for the judges. She later went on to record three albums, and win a Grammy. Were the Idol producers bad at their jobs, or perhaps they value diversity over talent and already cast someone who looked and sounded like her. The problem of no freewill rests in the interpretation of these signs.

It can be argued that Colby's Idol rejection pushed her to work harder, which is the actual reason she was eventually discovered. This renders the signs neutral and it's up to someone like Colby to interpret them (there are a fair share of American Idol contestants who are rejected for good reasons and should probably redirect their passions). Is it up to the interpreter to decipher what their signs mean, or is it up to God to continually deliver insufficient signs until they correct their path? Omnipotence should exclude the latter.

Let's take this a step further, remove ego, and ask the obvious and facetious question: is God a Colby Caillat fan? We are ultimately the centers of our own universe, so it's actually counter intuitive to our survival to gain perspective and realize that our accomplishments are relatively meaningless. From Yahweh's perspective however, some accomplishments are more meaningful than others. Perhaps Constantine the Great was given a 'real' sign at the Battle of Milvian Bridge that inspired him to legalize Christianity in the Roman Empire. But Colby Caillat's first album, good as it may be, seems like an unnecessary step to ultimately convincing the world that Jesus died for our sins.

---

[13] The theologian stance on whether or not we have freewill is still up for debate amongst Jews, Muslims, and Hindus. Christianity, on the other hand, generally accepts that we do in fact have freewill.

Religious Motivation

Religious motivation can easily turn into a 'chicken or the egg' debate. When are our actions truly inspired by religion, and when is religion simply a means for justification? This is much easier to determine on an isolated basis. For example, if someone gives up their worldly possessions because Buddha preached this as the path to enlightenment, religious influence certainly played a role in the decision. But when members of a church are convinced to drink cyanide laced punch, or fly a plane into a skyscraper, the synergetic addition of peer pressure has taken religious motivation to an overwhelming level.

Sociologist and economist Max Weber theorized a positive economical side-effect of Calvinism. The Catholic Church preached that the path to salvation lies in the fulfillment of various sacraments through clerical authority. In other words, the worshipper, with bishop approval, controlled their own destiny. The Protestant Reformation came along in the 16th century and modified this belief. They had no direct religious authority to turn to for sacrificial assurance. Calvinism took this a step further preaching that God had predetermined who would be saved and who would be damned. This motivated worshippers to do some soul searching. They looked for signs to determine whether they were among 'the elect'. Self-confidence was a common barometer for weeding out the unlucky. Even those with self doubt sought to overcome this by economic means. In other words, they worked harder and earned more money. Success in business became an unmistakably positive sign, but excessiveness and wastefulness were not. So rather than splurge, the prosperous Calvinists and Puritans invested, which boosted their fledgling American economy – the spirit of capitalism was born.

A seemingly benign aspect of religious motivation exists in our methods of *symbolism*. Idolatry and iconography were perhaps our earliest forms of marketing: statues, flags, symbols, and even sounds (e.g. gongs, bells). An iconic marble statue of Zeus in the town square sends a clear message: as long as this symbol stands untarnished, the citizens of this community endorse its meaning. Psychological studies have also attached emotions or paradigms with symbolic structure:

Circular: comfort, protection, femininity (reflected in the majority of religious symbols)

Square: strength, dependability (Shintoism)

Triangular: power, balance, masculinity (Cao Dai, Scientology; star shapes: Judaism, Druze, Thelema, Baha'i)

Vertical shapes: aggression, courage (Christianity)

Horizontal shapes: tranquility, silence, peace (relatively none)

Our affinity for symbols traces back to our tendencies towards animism, which is as relevant today as it was 200,000 years ago. When a religious symbol is disgraced we experience an emotional reaction. Fully aware of this phenomenon, when a political leader wanted to send a message, or deplete morale, they would destroy their enemy's public symbols. There is debate whether this is what was implied by the Jewish second commandment: thou shall not make for yourself a carved image, or any likeness of anything that is in heaven above. Jehovah's Witnesses take this literally and affiliate themselves with no symbols of any kind. But modern conventions favor the more archaic mindset of Bronze Age worship, which alleged that religious idols and statues truly housed the spirit of the divine. But a desecration of these forms of idolatry resonates just as profoundly as a violation on our modern symbols.

War, terrorism, and suicide cults are obvious examples of religious motivation taken to an extreme. But the religious affiliation, or lack thereof, of the leader is not always the best indicator of motivation. Adolf Hitler broke ties with the Catholic Church in his adult years, but he developed a Christian core during his adolescence as an altar boy. His disdain for Semitism grew to fruition after Germany was defeated in World War I, for which he believed the Jews were responsible. His motivations were vengeance based. It didn't take much to elevate this attitude to nation-wide acceptance. European citizens were no stranger to anti-Semitism in the 19th century, an explicable attitude when the foundation of your belief system is centered around a messiah who was supposedly indicted by Jews. Around 1860 the Catholic Church restricted Jews to the 'Jewish ghettos' in Rome. Official Catholic organizations, such as the Jesuits, banned candidates who are descended from the Jewish race unless it is clear that their father, grandfather, and great-grandfather belonged to the Catholic Church. And Catholic Churches promoted a form of 'acceptable' anti-Semitism which believed there was a Jewish conspiracy to control commercial businesses. In 2000 the Dabru Emet – a document signed by over 220 rabbis and Jewish scholars – stated, "Without the long history of Christian anti-Judaism and Christian violence against Jews, Nazi ideology could not have taken hold nor could it have been carried out." All Hitler needed was an economic depression to unite the nation under his cause. He gave German citizens a scapegoat for their weaknesses and an outlet for their frustrations in one package.

Phineas Gage was a railroad worker, circa 1845. He was known for being a kind and generous family man. An unfortunate work accident caused by a dynamite explosion forced a metal rod to pass through Phineas' left frontal cortex. He was ultimately able to think and function normally, or so it seemed. He lost complete interest in family life and eventually became a drifter. This led neurologists to believe that moral reasoning and accountability may be localized in one area of the brain.

Conformity plays a significant role how we process information, not only in the decision making process, but in our memory recall. In 1951 American psychologist Solomon Asch gave several participants the following vision test:

Exhibit 1   *Exhibit 2* (A, B, C)

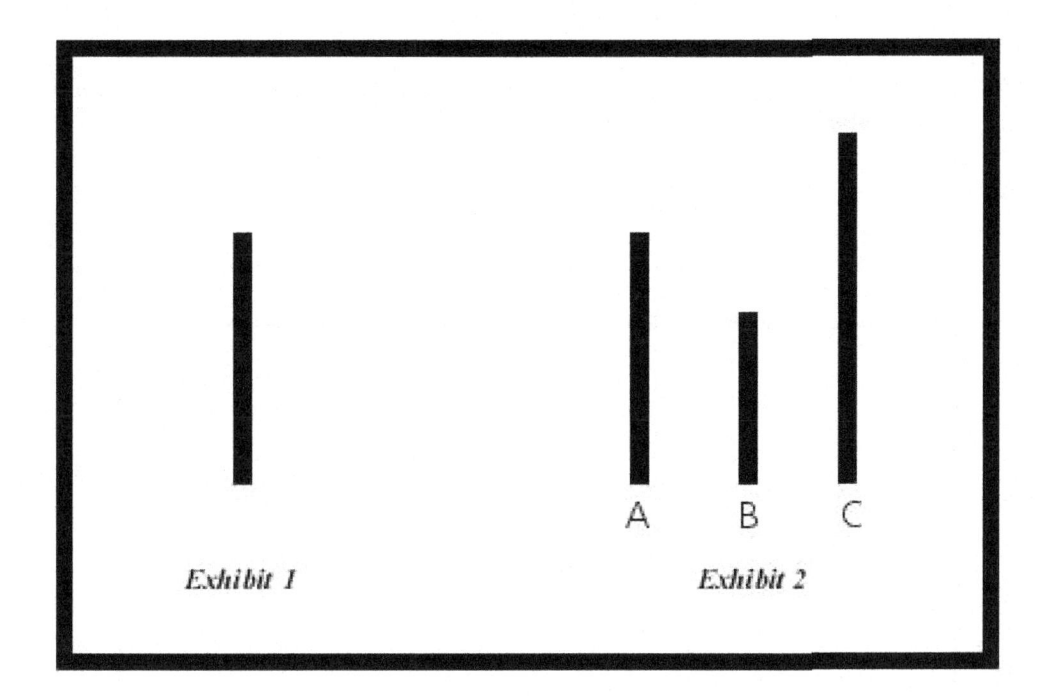

Only one of the participants was legit while the others were instructed to give an opposing response. When pseudo-subjects responded that either B or C matched *exhibit 1*, the 'actual' subject conformed to their response 32% of the time.

    A similar conformity study was conducted in 2005 by Emory University measuring the effects of peer pressure on a subject's ability to process information. The twist this time was that the opposing response came from two sources: humans and computers. The analysis in question involved similarities and differences in three-dimensional geometric shapes. Four of the subjects intentionally gave the opposite answer of the fifth subject. 41% of the time the fifth subject changed their answer to match that of their peers, consistent with Asch's study. The same experiment was then repeated with computers. The fifth subject changed his answer only 32% of the time to match the computers, demonstrating an unbalanced tendency to conform 'socially' rather than arbitrarily. The derogatory MRI measurements were evident in the amygdala and hippocampus, which are responsible for memory recall. In other words, peer pressure can literally change your memory.

    Conformity multiplies further when what is at stake is considered 'more important' and/or 'less black and white'. When conformity presents moral ramifications, the cognitive safety net of accountability is effectively removed. Nazi commanders were documented to have offered their unit a choice whether or not to participate in prisoner exterminations. Approximately 2% chose not to partake, which is to say that Nazi soldiers were not necessarily coerced into compliance, but rather felt obligated due to peer pressure.

The Milgram Experiment conducted at Yale University in 1961 put this mindset to the test. A subject was assigned the role of *teacher* (T) and told by an authority figure, the *experimenter* (E), that whenever an unseen *learner* (L) gave an incorrect answer, the teacher was to press a button that would give the learner an electric shock. The experimenter was there to supervise that the teacher did this properly. The catch, unbeknown to the teacher, was that there was no actual shock being delivered, and the learner was an actor.

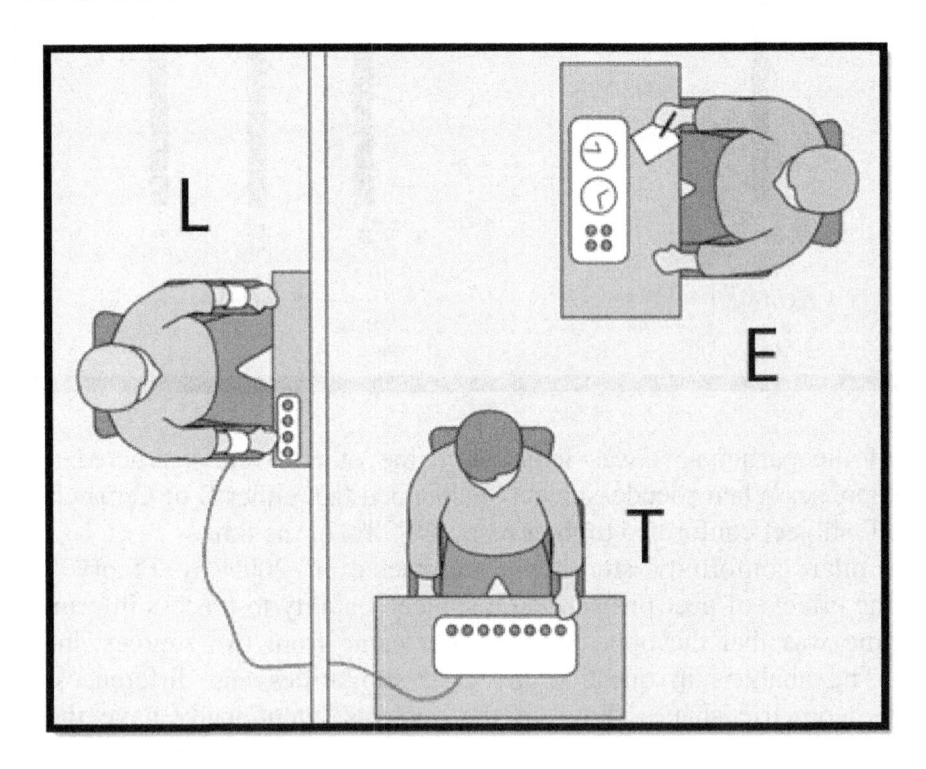

The teacher was told that the shocks started at 45 volts and would increase with every wrong answer (100 volts can potentially stop your heart). Each time he pushed the button the unseen learner would scream and beg for the teacher to stop. The voltage was increased to the point that the learner would bang on the wall, complain of a heart condition, and eventually pass out. When told to continue giving shocks 63% of the subjects delivered shocks to what they perceived to be an unconscious person until they reached a maximum of 450 volts. Results like these, and with similar experiments, demonstrate both the power of conformity as well as our tendency to dismiss accountability when instructed by an authority figure.

This behavior is evident in stock market bubbles, riots, and conspiracy cover-ups like the Penn State child sex abuse scandal in 2011. Herd mentality is an inevitable function of human nature that any like-minded social group can take advantage of. In cases of religious cult behavior, conformity has been shown to contradict survival instincts. The 39 followers of *Heaven's Gate*, the 74 members of the *Order of the Solar Temple*, and the 918 victims (303 of which were children) of the *Peoples Temple* all died of their own freewill (or at the hands of their parents), influenced by a charismatic leader who convinced them that their collective lives no longer had value. If we are not part of the group, one can only hope the religion of the leader, mainstream or cult, seeks positive benefits for those outside the congregation.

Does Religion Work?

Personal preferences aside, there's no denying that religion taps into a psychological comfort zone. Research shows that religious Americans are generally happier and less stressed than the non-religious. Religion provides a variety of stress coping tools like the belief in an afterlife (to counter our fear of death), prayer (for hope during stressful times), a social network of priests and fellow worshipers, and religion tends to discourage drug and alcohol use which reduces substance dependencies. But statistical analysis on this particular matter can be interpreted a number of ways.

To be among the religious in America is to be among the majority (around 90%). To be among the religious in the Netherlands would be a minority (around 40%). A Gallup world poll survey conducted between 2005 and 2009 has the Netherlands ranked as the 4th happiest country in the world (based on factors like overall economy, mortality rate, crime rate, heath care, etc), whereas America was ranked 14th. Religion unfortunately opens the door for depression in certain cases, like being forced to raise a child out of wedlock, a homosexual living in denial of their 'abominable' desires, or the pressure of following the tenets of a religion you no longer believe in.

Even devout clergy members (like Catholic priests Peter Kennedy and Bartholomew Brewer, or the hundreds of members of *The Clergy Project* (www.clergyproject.org): an online community for active and former clergy who no longer believe in God) have confessed a realization that they are no longer sincere believers in their faith. De-conversion can simulate a game of *Jenga* as you displace pieces of your social life, daily routines, and the promise of an afterlife. These components are interlaced throughout various sections of your brain and are difficult to undo.

Emotional attachments in general undergo the same defense mechanisms when confronted by conflicting evidence. Take red wine. During the days of prohibition, alcoholic beverages were condemned across the board in America. Shortly after that, health advocates continued their attack sighting links to blood disorders, liver damage, cancer, etc. The 1990's brought about new information that moderate consumption of red wine in particular offered health benefits like antioxidants, and strengthening tooth enamel. The research continued, suggesting that the lifestyle of the typical red wine drinker may skew the results to appear more beneficial that they really are. In other words, people who drink red wine already live healthier lifestyles, and therefore appear healthy regardless of their drinking habits. If a report came out tomorrow that sited undisputedly that red wine caused liver cancer, would you stop drinking red wine? Maybe you'd switch to white, or drink less, or ignore it completely – after all, the value of longevity is subjective if you're not happy.

Even vices with overwhelming disapproval, like cigarettes, won't guarantee that people will swap health for the anxiety relief that nicotine offers. And ever since the effects of second-hand smoke were published, American smokers have been treated almost as scantily as the pagans of the Classic era. Yet religion holds a position of entitlement regardless of who is affected. If instead of the current 20%, smokers made up 88% of the American population – like Christianity – things might have turned out differently. The theory of evolution has yet to be debunked by the scientific community, yet 46% of Americans (according to a 2012 Gallup poll) are young earth creationists (i.e. the earth is less than 10,000 years old). Imagine if 46% of Americans believed diseases were caused by malevolent spirits rather than evolving viruses. Before modern medicine they did (circa 1880 with Robert Koch's discovery of the transmission of disease by bacteria).

Perhaps the most telling indicator for the links between religion and human behavior exists in the *terror management theory*. Terror management is our instinctual anxiety geared towards the fear of death. Our management of fear is guided by two factors: self-esteem and self consciousness. Self-esteem has been defined as one's confidence in their cultural world view. In other words, the assuredness that you will live up to the standards you endorse. Self-consciousness, in the context of terror management, has been defined as one's tendency for self-examination, or, in times of stress, how much you worry. When our mortality is threatened, or if we perceive potential threats, our cultural world view becomes compromised. For example, we may all agree that civilians shouldn't be imprisoned without just cause, but in 1942 Franklin D. Roosevelt authorized the internment of some 110,000 Japanese-Americans into war relocation camps after the Pearl Harbor attack.

A study was conducted in 1989 with 22 municipal court judges in Tucson, Arizona. Half of them were exposed to a mortality salience (they were reminded of their mortality by answering questions about their own death), the other half (the control group) were not, then all told to set a bond for an accused prostitute. The control group averaged $50, a typical bond for this crime. The mortality salience group set an average a bond of $455. These results reinforced the idea of in-group solidarity and increased prejudice against those who do not fit into our world view (i.e. xenophobia: an irrational fear of foreigners – but on a smaller scale it represents those with an opposing world view in general). By comparison, our affection for religion, and all social organizations for that matter, increases during periods of anxiety.

Similar studies have been conducted to determine how terror management affects aesthetic influences. Half of an all-Christian selection was told to complete a short essay about an unpleasant, but non-death related, topic (e.g. a painful dental visit). The other half wrote an essay about what happens to them when they die. The participants were then shown two paintings, a landscape and a Christian themed piece. The mortality salient group significantly preferred the Christian artwork, but not merely as a more pleasing theme – it was deemed superior on an aesthetic level.

When we are compelled to either bond with the familiar, or repel the unfamiliar, this applies to 'ideas' as well. Our capacity for denial is an impressive defense mechanism. We are capable of shunning thoughts that are incompatible with our coveted beliefs just as easily as we can shun humans whose culture is incompatible with our own.

Who Are the Religious?

Certain fears are universal to human beings, namely our fear of the unknown. Our lack of understanding of nature, and other humans (i.e. xenophobia) has created a range of anxiety in response to 'change'. As its belief system is generally regarded as divine and 'without error', reducing change is one of the primary goals of religion. Change in one's personal life is, relatively speaking, within one's control, but change in society is not, and those who call themselves *conservatives* tend to favor a static society over an evolving one.

There are six phases we tend to undergo when confronted with, and ultimately accepting, uninvited change:
1. Hidden agenda: we are suspicious of the harbingers of the change.
2. Adversarial: we resist and attack the concepts of the change.
3. Uncertainty: we experience a transition in which we are neutral to both sides.
4. Emergent: we progress cautiously in the direction of the change.
5. Normal: we accept the change.
6. Empowerment: we recognize we are better off as a result of the change.

Conservatives rarely progress beyond phase three without a majority influence. But how do we recognize good change from bad (e.g. should we accept that the earth revolves around the sun: yes; should we quit our job because the rapture has been prophesized for next week: no)? When enough people support change our accountability towards opposition dissolves (e.g. God has yet to directly punish the millions who now work on the Sabbath, so it must be okay). But change of this nature is slow to expedite.

There are four primary fears associated with the core of this anxiety – a lack of control: fear of death, fear of suppression (i.e. loss of money, health, and/or liberty), fear of incapacitation (i.e. loss of stamina), and fear of exile. These fears stem from worry, or a lack of confidence in one's skills to overcome certain challenges. In the case of religion, these challenges encompass permanently losing everything positive that religion offers a believer: salvation in the afterlife, divine protection, confidence (associated with the comfort of having the 'answers' religion provides), and a social circle (social unity).

Fears: Lack of Control		Benefits of Religion
Death		Afterlife
Suppression	Countered	Divine protection
Incapacitation	with	Confidence
Exile		Social circle

So how are atheists able to cope without aid from these positive religious aspects? Accepting that there is *no salvation or afterlife* is misleading. When confronted with a perceived threat, our adrenaline will pump regardless of our afterlife convictions. The real difference is that some of us have a more adverse reaction to a mortality salience than others, and are prone to seek unsubstantiated support. Accepting that there is *no divine protection* is based on a simple observation: the lives of theists don't appear to be any easier than the lives of atheists. The *answers* supplied by religion, which fuels confidence, in many cases contradict logic and are unsupported by evidence (i.e. the atheist perceives them as false answers). Losing one's religious *social circle* tends to boil down to self-esteem: are my relationships grounded in our shared religion, or in 'who I am' as a person? Testing and discovering this answer often comes down to whether or not a wavering theist can go on living a lie.

On the flipside, being 'open to change' isn't without its misgivings. As social creatures we are often forced to make assumptions about other people's values. A society which undergoes an abundance of social changes can suffer from a lack of public cohesiveness. There's a reason you can leave your doors unlocked in a small town. Small town life is relatively simple and predictable compared to a bustling, fast-paced metropolis. In a small town you generally trust that the old man who waves at you from his porch is not going to someday rob you at gunpoint. Dead-bolting your front door, avoiding eye contact, and road rage are classic symptoms of too much change in a community. This is not to say that big city dwellers lack a desire for spirituality, but they are more likely to notice the chinks in religion's armor.

If religion were perfect there would be no need for denominational branching. Social and cognitive dissonance has motivated theologians to cycle through permutations of rituals and beliefs in an attempt to achieve spiritual perfection. The key to understanding religious diversity lies not in deciphering eclectic morality, or which beliefs coincide best with science and logic – it lies in the conclusion that 'God is necessary'. Once a mind has locked into the paradigm of God's essential existence, choosing which religion to follow becomes superfluous. Some tenets hold up better than others under debate, but all that's required to avoid cognitive dissonance is Isaiah 45:15 (i.e. *Truly, O God of Israel, our Savior, you work in mysterious ways*). If there is a God or Gods, then it's likely that at least one of the existing religions is accurate. And until proof can be cited for or against any of the current faiths, they're either all right or all wrong. If we are to prescribe to the former (i.e. all religions are accurate), the Schrodinger's Cat paradox consequently applies to more than just quantum mechanics[14].

[14] In 1935 Austrian physicist Erwin Schrodinger devised a thought experiment to interpret the physical state of sub-atomic matter, which simultaneously exists in two contradictory states: as particles and as waves. The analogy involves a theoretical cat trapped inside a sealed box and, depending on the speed at which a radioactive element decays, may or may not have been exposed to poisonous gas. The results of the decay cannot be known until the box is opened and the cat's mortality is observed, and until that time the cat is considered to be in a mixed state of being simultaneously alive and dead.

CHAPTER 4

RELIGIOUS BRANCHING:

Part 1: Why So Many?

"If two philosophers agree, one is not a philosopher. If two saints disagree, one is not a saint."
-Tibetan saying

So Few, Yet So Many
Corruption
Criterion of a Successful Religion
The Long Road to Christianity
The Short Road to Islam

Well over a million religions have passed through human history. Up until the Romans converted to Christianity in the late 4th century, the focus of the evolution was primarily 'deity based'. That is to say, it took somewhere in the neighborhood of 75,000 years to decide *who* to worship. A paradox of sorts has taken shape ever since then. Polytheism took a major hit, and society essentially locked in on their God. The breakdown of theistic worship is in stark contrast to the number of religious branches and denominations still in practice (i.e. there used to be thousands of gods and relatively few religions – now there are thousands of religions and relatively few gods).

Yahweh, God of the Abrahamic religions, is the outright leader. Worship towards him drapes a subservient blanket over Christianity, Islam, Judaism, and their respective branches and denominations. The million or so gods of the Hindu religion, and their respective branches, claim the next highest number of the religious population.

Lastly, Chinese Folk religion, and their supreme god Shangdi, encompass a broad enough basis that they've managed to avoid significant branching, even though the religion itself has undergone various structural transformations over the last few millennium. Yahweh, Shangdi, and the Hindu Gods – these three theistic belief systems encompass 99% of deity worship. Given the persistent theological discrepancies, data like this seems to dictate that it's not *who* you worship but *how* you worship.

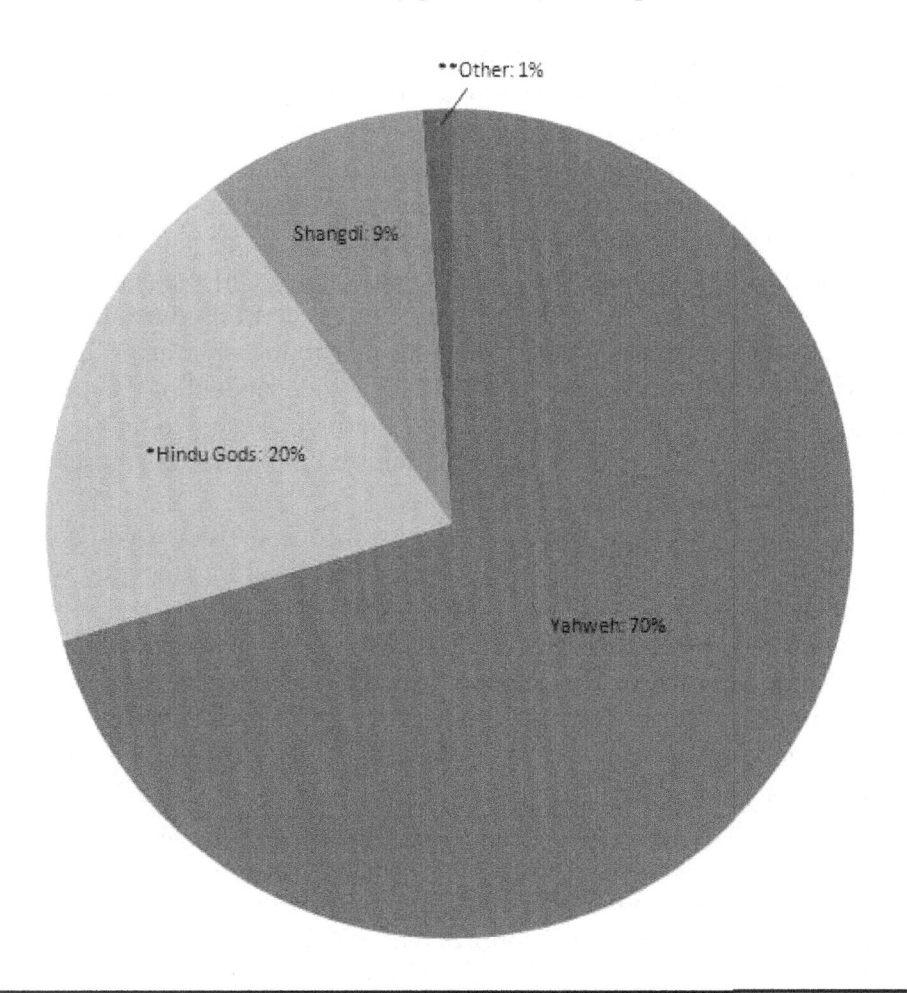

Breakdown of global deity worship

- **Other: 1%
- Shangdi: 9%
- *Hindu Gods: 20%
- Yahweh: 70%

*The most supreme of the Hindu gods are Shiva and Vishnu.
**Among these are Waheguru (Sikhism), Olorun (Yoruba), Tenri-O-no-Mikoto (Tenriko), Mazu (Mazuism), Ahura Mazda (Zoroastrianism), and many others.

Religions tend to branch for two reasons: divine inspiration or conscious restructuring. A classic example of the latter was the Orthodox Schism in 451 C.E. This division of the Christian faith involved several political issues, not the least of which was over the word "in" as it pertains to the doctrine of the trinity. Pope Leo I of Rome held that Jesus is "in" two natures: one divine and one human; Pope Dioscorus I of Alexandria would accept only "of or from" two natures, but not "in" two natures. This was primarily a result of inherent vagueness and ambiguous translations from the original Hebrew into Greek and Latin.

Divine inspiration usually involves an individual, and is regarded as one's calling regardless of their willingness to pursue this endeavor. In fact, martyrdom is widely considered a badge of honor signifying that a prophet is both humble and strong. Sunni Muslims believe Muhammad was initially distressed by his revelation, and resolved to commit suicide. Joseph Smith, founder of Mormonism, spent six years locating and translating the Book of Mormon after his encounter with the angel Moroni.

In governments where citizens are granted the right of free assembly, civilians organize and protest by means of petition, lobbying, or public display. The goal is to influence the decision makers to change inapplicable or outdated laws. Some governments suppress public opinion, but are still subject to change if the leader so chooses. Even as kings and priests doubled as political and religious authority, religion operated under a different set of rules. Religion, like living organisms, did not *replace* old beliefs with new beliefs. A new sect would form independent of the ancestral belief, and each would prosper or fail based on its own merits. And they didn't tend to form as a result of public outcry. The initial change often rested in the hands of a select few or an individual.

With regard to worship, we tend to react in one of two ways: compliance or rebellion. If properly motivated, a religious leader will rebel by changing what they see fit thus creating their own sect. To insure a 'built in' following, their faith will incorporate a majority of their former religion's beliefs. The changes often focus on the strictness or leniency of particular tenets. John Smythe was an Anglican priest who believed baptism was intended for true believers only, thereby excluding infant baptism. When the leaders of his church disagreed, he started his own church and formed the Baptist denomination.

Imagine a government that permitted narcotics for some, but deemed it illegal for others. Medicinal marijuana laws have become a source of political friction on both the federal and state level. The religious structure under the umbrella of Christianity, with the various denominations beneath it, mimics the jurisdiction of federal and state law. In America a range of creeds coexist in relative harmony. In Pakistan, Sunni-Shi'a relations have recently resulted in some 4,000 deaths primarily at the hands of sectarian groups affiliated with Al-Qaeda.

Corruption

One of the primary catalysts of religious branching is corruption. The very nature of religion is intended to create an ideal society, which can be easily tainted by the tyranny of its leaders. Corruption in religion often comes in the form of monetary excessiveness, the suppression of new ideas, and political manipulation. Dishonesty in these forms has been a seemingly unavoidable destiny for almost any position of power. So what elements are specific to religious corruption?

No society is completely immune to corruption, be it the Qin Dynasty in China or the Median Empire in Persia – two societies notorious for massive corruption – but perhaps the best documented example can be traced to medieval Europe. Religious representation generally comes in two forms: religion represented in politics, and God represented in humans. The latter defines the hierarchy of the Catholic Church whereby the Pope, followed by cardinals, bishops, priests, and deacons are direct successors to Saint Peter (whom Jesus named as the 'shepherd' of the church and is honorably recognized as the first Pope). As religion and politics were both simultaneous products of a developing society, they were merged for many thousands of years. Until the 16th century it was believed that the only way a society could function harmoniously was to overlap our 'earthly city' with the 'city of God'.

Before Judaism was permitted in the Roman Republic, their economy was on the verge of collapse. Divine intervention was thought to be their saving grace and a policy of 'emperor worship' was decreed whereby the prayers of Roman citizens were steered from the Republic as a whole to the emperor's personal well-being[15]. Rejection of the State religion at this time was tantamount to treason. This hindered the impending influence of Judaism and Christianity, which would have meant stripping the emperor of these divine offerings.

When Christianity did finally take hold, the balance of power was rarely at ease between the monarchs in medieval Europe and the Popes. One of the first steps toward separation occurred in 1,122 C.E. when the Concordat of Worms essentially diluted the King's electoral power of the Pope (as opposed to initially having autonomous power of appointment). This arrangement was aimed at limiting secular corruption, but religious corruption had just begun.

Two things happened around this time that worried the Catholic Church: Islamic aggression was rapidly encroaching on European territory, and Catharism started to flourish. The Cathars created a, now extinct, branch of Christianity similar to Manicheaism, who rejected the idea of confession, baptism, and holy Eucharist (consecrating bread and wine as the body and blood of Christ). The Inquisitions were initially established as a means to discourage Catharism, but eventually encompassed all non-Catholic faiths. The Crusades were also underway to counter the spread of Islam. By the 15th century Catholicism had a secure foothold as the dominant religion in the world. But their troubles were far from over.

It was discovered that many Catholic priests, who were supposed to be among the educated elite, were illiterate. Priests and nuns were breaking their vows of chastity

---

[15] In 1872 Sir Francis Galton conducted a prayer study which concluded that 'God doesn't answer intercessory prayers' after discovering that kings who are prayed for live shorter lives than well-to-do, but not royal, people.

and conceiving illegitimate children. Church offices were being sold to the highest bidder regardless of the buyer's background or training. And Indulgences, sometimes in the form of a financial penance, were being grossly exploited.

Catholic priest Martin Luther decided major reforms were necessary to correct these atrocities. Consequently excommunicated for his outcry, Luther's actions led to the creation of the Protestant denomination, currently the largest branch of Christianity in America. The Protestants determined that only through God and one's faith in Christ can salvation be granted, thereby rejecting the authority of the Pope. This opened wide the floodgates of religious branching.

Two major separations would lead to the Protestant boom over the next few centuries. Separation from the Pope allowed religious leaders to interpret the tenets of Bible in literally thousands of ways (approximately 41,000). And the physical separation of settlers in New England weakened the capacity by which England could govern. In 1692 John Locke, an English philosopher, published his *Letter Concerning Toleration*, which argued that individual conscience should be free from State control. This was the inspiration some hundred years later for the Bill of Rights and the clause dictating the 'wall of separation between church and state'.

Criterion of a Successful Religion

With the increase in spiritual competition, the bar was raised to achieve longevity. Religions that endure the test of time have certain attributes in common. Biology relies on fossil records to analyze extinct species. The religious texts of extinct faiths are not always easy to come by. But the specifics of dogma are not necessarily important. Religion nestles its roots in human emotion, so a successful religion needs to tap into certain intrinsic requirements.

The strict boss – Your friend works at a company run by a charismatic CEO who enforces a strict 'no tolerance' policy. The benefits at this company are amazing, but employees who fall even slightly short of their quotas are not let go – they are relocated to a branch in a third-world country where they are forced to work sweat-shop hours in a disease ridden environment and never allowed to return or have contact with their family. The employees are constantly reminded of this consequence, yet some of them still manage to fall short of their quotas. A coworker's fate is kept secret, but the employees are quite certain that those who fail are dealt with accordingly. In general, everyone does their job and appears quite happy, and this company's stock continues to rise.

Your other friend works at a company with equally appealing benefits but whose CEO is tolerant of failure. If they fall short of expectations they are given another chance. There are no threats of relocation or torture. Employees ultimately fall short in this company too, but there's no need for secrecy as the repercussions are essentially non-existent. The employees are happy, yet their stock is performing poorly.

Is fear a superior motivator? Most likely, yes, but despite this the employees at the first company are *actually* happy. One thing followers have in common is they prefer that the CEO does the dirty work. They dislike insubordinate behavior as much as the strict boss, and are content to let the enforcement of the rules play out. What isn't apparent is, despite the fact that people miss their quotas and punishment is certain, each of these employees has a special relationship with the CEO. He secretly tells everyone that he appreciates their hard work and that they are allowed to slip provided their numbers improve next quarter. This method of management encompasses the best of both worlds: employees believe their coworkers are being kept in line while secretly receiving a reassuring sense of personal entitlement.

An attempt was made to create a perfect society based on strict religious enforcement. Members of the church were expected to report other members who slipped up, potentially resulting in them being shunned from the church. They were called Puritans, and for several centuries they flourished. But the imperfection of human nature ultimately failed to live up to religious policy, and their numbers dwindled into extinction. The modern day version of this, the Amish, manage to preserve their numbers, but they're destined to remain at .07% of the American population (compared to, say, Catholics at 24%, or Baptists at 6%).

The mysterious boss – Your friend works at an animal shelter in a corrupt city. One of the laws of this city is designed to prevent animal over-population: shelters are required to randomly euthanize one animal a day. There is no supervisor at your friend's animal shelter; instead they take orders directly from the city government. You find out there are several sick animals at this shelter and ask if anyone's informed the city of this. Perhaps instead of random euthanizations they would consider prioritizing by health. Your friend says this law was made many years ago and the department set up to handle these matters no longer exists. The response they receive from the city is "this is the way it has to be". The employees have lost faith in changing this law and manage to go on without complaining.

Your other friend works at an animal shelter who abides by the same rules, only they answer to a supervisor instead of the city. Your friend says he constantly asks his supervisor why he won't bend the rules and euthanize according to health. The city never conducts inspections and never checks company paperwork. The supervisor hates this law, knows it's flawed, makes efforts to console the employees, but continues to follow the rule. The employees are constantly inventing new approaches and methods to try and convince the supervisor to do the right thing. The supervisor always seems open to suggestions, yet never changes his mind.

The potential for chaos is exponentially worse if people believe they have options. Churches are demolished by tornados, children are raped by priests, bad things happen to good people, and they go unexplained and unjustified. If a religion tried to make sense of the injustice that occurred in the world, the complaint line would have no end. Where the tides get choppy is during major economic depressions. When society loses complete confidence in their financial future the people will demand a change (*discussed further in chapter 7*). But the real beauty of mystery, in the context of religion, is that it allows for personal malleability. There are beliefs and explanations within religion that are regarded by many as extreme or amoral. Mystery (i.e. cognitive dissonance) allows believers to cope via creative justification (or creative 'interpretation'). We don't have to understand 'why' something happens but we do need to feel good about it, because what most humans are not equipped to do is condone tyranny and hypocrisy.

The old boss – You're the new accountant at a well established, very successful company. The quarterly reports are due and you are told to calculate the numbers using outdated company software. You attempt to do this and discover the software is actually incapable of performing many of the functions you require. You bring this up to your supervisor and he says the software work perfectly and that you need to figure it out. You ask an accountant in another department how she deals with this issue, and she says she secretly uses her own modern version of the software. She says all the accountants do it this way – the supervisors are happy as long as the totals add up.

The Bible (old and new testament) and the Quran go into explicit detail on slave ownership (e.g. Exodus 21:2-11, Leviticus 25:44-46, Ephesians 6:5, 1 Timothy 6:1-2), stoning unruly children (e.g. Deuteronomy 21:18-21, Leviticus 20:9), stoning your new wife if she's not a virgin (e.g. Deuteronomy 22:13-21), and polygamy (e.g. Qur'an: Sura 4 (*An-Nisa*), Ayah 3), not to mention condoning rape and murder in certain contexts (e.g. Judges 21:10-24, Numbers 31:7-18, Deuteronomy 20:10-14). These texts are considered sacred as well as socially relevant, but you would be hard pressed to find a Christian, Muslim, or Jew who would defend slavery, child abuse, domestic abuse, or polygamy.

We tend to forgive the archaic mindset of the elderly, especially if they grew up in a different culture altogether. The Bible is not only from an outdated era, it's been translated, revised, and in some cases forged. Outdated attitudes in the Bible are only addressed if they have actual power or influence. They can be sited, preached, and even condoned, but until they are *enforced* they don't really exist. Words tend to have no real power until they are put into action typically through law or vigilantism. Until that day comes we tend to let the old people rant without losing much sleep.

The last set of criteria is *proselytism*, or conversionism. With the economic potential behind religious expansion one would think the primary goal of any faith would be to grow. This is not always the case. Several religions (e.g. Zoroastrianism, Druze, Mandaeanism) actually discourage converts. Many of the older belief systems (e.g. Chinese Folk religion, Hinduism, Taoism, Confucianism) do not prescribe to a clear policy of conversionism, and therefore avoid efforts to proselytize. Some faiths do have conversion rituals in place (e.g. Judaism, Baha'i Faith, modern Buddhism) but they vary greatly from one sect to another. Rather than convert, the goal of these faiths is to educate, with the notion that a true subscriber would themselves choose to convert. It should be no surprise that the largest religions (e.g. Christianity, Islam) actively proselytize (with the exception of certain denominations). But for Christianity, their massive numbers have not accomplished unity in a pure form, rather a loose version of franchising. From the outside they appear as a cohesive unit, but within the various sects are separate beliefs and mindsets. Islam's increasing numbers have led to branching as well, but their growth seems to have exposed the weaknesses of their politics rather than its strengths. But proselytism almost always leads to growth. If Scientology existed in a time where the media was not a factor, they may have achieved much greater success. Not even a celebrity marketing campaign can overshadow the stigma of being labeled a 'cult'.

The Long Road to Christianity

For all the oppression Judaism underwent over the centuries they must have been doing something right. Once the requirement of 'being Jewish' was removed from the equation, all of Europe eventually wanted in. Contrary to biblical teachings Judaism underwent an arduous journey before it, not only became what it is today, but, actually became monotheistic *(discussed further in chapter 5)*. This too was the case for Judaism's religious brother Christianity. The only way to tell these brothers apart at the time was not necessarily by their beliefs, but by their practices. After the Roman Republic captured Jerusalem in 331 B.C.E., religious oppression inspired a transformation in the Jewish leaders. New sects were forming, one of which didn't stand out as particularly important at the time, but would ultimately become the largest religion in the world.

4th century B.C.E. – The expansion of the Roman Republic, coupled with their early economic decent, was creating a Hellenistic culture with Egyptian and Jewish influence. Religious practices were in a slump, and the time was ripe for theological branching.

40 B.C.E. – Rome installs King Herod as a client king of Judea (Herod was an Edomite by birth but called himself a Jew, and a non-practicing one at that). Judaism was unofficially allowed to flourish.

4 C.E. – Herod Antipas, Herod's son, was placed in power from 4 - 39 C.E.

6 C.E. – Zealotry, a sect of Judaism, gains popularity and creates friction between Rome and Judea (Zealotry was a political movement against Roman rule with the purpose of forcibly removing them from the Jewish Holy Land).

30 C.E. – Around this time Jesus of Nazareth was just another Jewish prophet trying to re-establish proper Jewish beliefs. But Jesus promised something the other prophets did not: his resurrection, and the imminent restoration of the 'Kingdom of God'.

33 C.E. – Jesus was put on trial for claiming to be 'king of the Jews', which was initially seen as a threat to king Herod Antipas. Herod determined Jesus was not the menace he was led to believe and sent him to Pontius Pilate, where he was then sentenced to death by crucifixion (it is debated that Pilate was reluctant to crucify Jesus, but ultimately gave in to the angry Jewish mass present during his trial – it was believed the historians at the time authored this theory to carry favor towards Rome by vilifying the Jews). Rome's failure to recognize Jesus' divinity depleted his magnitude in the eyes of many, and therefore labeled him as a false prophet. Also the worshiping of a man claiming to be the son of God bordered on idolatry, which was prohibited by Jewish law.

39 C.E. – Emperor Caligula was now claiming himself as a divinity and wanted his statue erected in the Second Temple of Jerusalem (this was considered the first open break between Rome and the Jews).

50 C.E. – During the Council of Jerusalem Jesus' followers openly reject the practice of circumcision for Gentile converts (first ritual modification).

52 C.E. – The first book of the New Testament is written: 1 Thessalonians.

64 C.E. – The Great Fire of Rome takes place (the true cause is unknown, but Emperor Neo blamed the Christians, possibly to divert the blame from his own motives to rebuild the city).

66 C.E. – The rivalry between Rome and the Jews begins:
- Greeks sacrificed birds in front of a local Jewish synagogue.
- A Temple clerk ceased Roman prayer and sacrifices.
- Jews held protests over taxation.
- Roman troops took money from the Temple in the name of Emperor Florus.
- Jews mocked the Emperor by collecting money as if Flours was poor.
- Florus responded by having Jewish citizens arrested and crucified.
- The Roman military garrison in Jerusalem was overrun by rebels who removed all Roman symbols.
- The Jewish-Roman War begins, resulting in the destruction of the Second Temple.

68 C.E – 73 C.E – The gospel of Matthew is written. Although it appears first in the New Testament, Matthew was chronologically the fifteenth book written. Matthew was also the first gospel to 'specifically' mention Jesus, as well as the first to mention any of his miracles[16].

70 C.E. – Fiscus Judaicus was instated, which was an annual tax on the Jews for upkeep of the Temple of Jupiter Capitolinus in Rome.

73 C.E. – The Jewish-Roman war comes to an end. The primary Jewish sects at the time (Zealotry, Sadducees, Essenes) were wiped out. Remaining Jews were enslaved or fled, forcing Jewish practices to be performed in secrecy. This widened the divide between the only remaining Jewish sects: Pharasees (eventually becoming Rabbinic Judaism) and Christianity. Jesus' prophecy for the restoration of the 'Kingdom of God' (i.e. heaven on earth) now seemed inaccessible.

98 C.E. – Christians are exempt from paying the Fiscus Judaicus tax under Emperor Nerva. Jews did not participate in the Imperial Cult (prayers for the well-being of the Emperor) as the tax was considered their imperial offering, but Christians who did not participate in this practice were subject to persecution.

110 C.E. – Christians revise the Sabbath from Sunday or Sat night, strictly to Sunday (second ritual modification).

132 C.E. – Emperor Hadrian threatened to rebuild Jerusalem as a pagan city dedicated to the Roman Gods.

132 - 135 C.E. – Simon bar Kochba (believed by some to be the Jewish messiah) led a revolt, for which most Christians did not take part. The Jews were ultimately defeated. Bar Kochba, in comparison to Jesus, was a more militaristic messiah, which better suited the mold of a descendant of the war god Yahweh, whereas Jesus was observably non-violent.

190 C.E. – Pope Victor openly rejects the practice of preparation for Passover known as Quartodecimanism (third ritual modification).

200 – 220 C.E. – Rabbi Judah Yehudah haNasi edits together the Mishna (oral Torah) and creates Rabbinic Judaism.

    Before Christianity was legalized by Emperor Constantine certain religious distinctions became evident over the next century. Judaism was based on being

---

[16] The miraculous claims of Jesus were recorded in a manner consistent with 'legendary' characters (i.e. actual people who were believed to have performed amazing or supernatural feats). The first books written in the New Testament referred to Jesus in vague terms. His miracles were not documented until he was more prominently highlighted in the gospel of Matthew and beyond. This chronology is typical of legends in that the supernatural aspects grew over time, contrary to what would be expected: the most memorable aspects of Jesus (virgin birth, healing the sick, resurrection, etc.) should have been mentioned immediately.

descended from Abraham (those marked by circumcision) and held a quasi-intimate stature as the 'religion of the Jews'. Their theology was a reflection of their heritage: enslaved, persecuted, oppressed, and displaced. Now they had something unique and personal that would inspire future generations through unity and perseverance. Christianity reflected the other side of this coin. It was designed to expand as it allowed for conversion, and seen as a 'religion of all people'. This created a noticeable dissonance around Judaism as they professed that Yahweh was the one and only God, but restricted worship to a birth right. Christianity essentially replaced the Temple of Jerusalem, which Jews considered tantamount to their worship, with a new covenant of Jesus Christ. This led to Christian apathy over the destruction of the Temple. Lastly, Judaism focuses on how you live 'this life' properly; whereas Christianity focuses on proper living for the afterlife (i.e. gnosticism). Christianity had officially graduated from a Jewish sect to an entirely separate religion. But Christianity was no longer able to share in the newly found benevolence that Judaism was able to achieve with the Roman Empire. They carved a much different path of acceptance through Emperor Constantine.

Constantine's mother was Christian and of low social standing, providing the future Emperor with a humble foundation. He was a gifted politician and served as an officer in the Roman army. He would quickly rise up through the ranks and eventually change history.

285 C.E. – Constantine is given the governorship of Dalmatia in Croatia.

303 C.E. – Constantine witnesses instances of the 'Great Persecution' of Christians under the leadership of Emperor Diocletian[17].

306 C.E. – Constantine is granted the title of Caesar of Britain, Gaul, and Spain.

312 C.E. - During the *Battle of Milvian Bridge* (the fourth battle in the civil rivalry between Constantine and Emperor Maxentius) Constantine was said to have looked up to the sun before the battle and saw a cross of light above it, and with it the Greek words translating to "With this sign you will conquer". He told his army to adjourn their shields with the Christian cross. Constantine – whose army was outnumbered 2 to 1 – emerged victorious, decapitated Maxentius, and reclaimed Emperorship in the West.

313 C.E. – Constantine, with support from Licinius (Caesar of the East), organized the Edict of Milan and legalized Christianity.

321 C.E. – Sunday is declared an official day of rest.

323 C.E. – Constantine bans Christians from participating in pagan sacrifices.

---

[17] Historians estimate that the most intense period of the Great Persecution was between 303 – 311 C.E. where as many as 3,000 Christians were executed under Roman authority.

324 – 330 C.E. – As Roman architecture was themed toward Greek Gods, Constantinople was erected at Byzantium as a new imperial 'Christian themed' capital.

331 C.E. – 50 Christian bibles are delivered to the Church of Constantinople.

337 C.E. – Constantine ordered the destruction of pagan temples in Rome.

363 – 375 C.E. – Paganism was tolerated and approached restoration under the rulership of Julian the Apostate, Jovian, Valens and Valentinian.

378 C.E. – Theodosius was appointed co-Augustus of the East Roman Empire.

380 C.E. – Theodosius, along with Emperor Gratian and his son Valentinian, declare Christianity as the state religion of the Roman Empire. Pagan sacrifices and rituals are officially banned.

381 – 476 C.E. – Pagan persecution continued until the fall of the Roman Empire and beyond.

After nearly 300 years the tables were officially turned on paganism. But the irony of religious branching, in contrast with obstinacy, is the extreme nature of religion. In other words, it is clear from history that a single religion will never satisfy everyone. This is not necessarily a function of the belief systems as much as it is a reflection of sociology. Liberals and conservatives will always exist; therefore religion will always struggle with evolution and perseverance.

The Short Road to Islam

The evolution of Islam was not nearly as dense as its cousin faiths Christianity and Judaism. The groundwork of monotheism and prophet worship had been laid out. Pre-Islam Arabia was much like pre-Christian Rome; only instead of worshipping the gods of Greek Mythology they worshipped a muddled pantheon of new and renamed Mesopotamian and Canaanite deities (approximately 360 in total) with Hubal at the top. Amongst this pantheon was their creator god Allah, but he was not their supreme deity, and certainly not the one and only. Judaism and Christianity had already blazed a monotheistic path, which primed the Middle-East for further religious evolution. But, like many matters of faith, it was ultimately accomplished through force.

610 C.E. – At the age of 40 Muhammad receives the oral Qur'an from the angel Gabriel, who had previously visited several important biblical figures, like the prophet Daniel and the Virgin Mary.

613 C.E. – Muhammad begins preaching Islam to the masses and gains a spectrum of displaced followers who disrupted the polytheistic climate in Mecca. Muhammad descended from royalty and was protected, but several of his followers (mostly slaves) were persecuted and killed.

616 – 619 C.E. – The leaders of the Makhzum and Banu Abd-Shams clans declared a boycott against the Banu Hashim (Muhammad's clan) to persuade them to remove their protection. It succeeded in limiting, but not stopping, his preaching.

619 C.E. – Muhammad's Uncle, and clan leader, dies. Leadership of the Banu Hashim is passed on to Muhammad's rival Abu Lahab, who removed Muhammad's protection. Muhammad then gained alternative security through the Banu Nawfal clan.

621 – 622 C.E. - Muhammad gains support through some influential Arabs in the town of Yathrib (Medina) 200 miles from Mecca. They saw potential in Islam as a means to gain power in Mecca. Pagan converts within Medina, along with many Meccan Muslims, immigrated to Medina to join their cause.

623 – 632 C.E. – 14 battles and invasions are waged in the name of Islam, concluding with the surrendering of the city of Taif and the destruction of their pagan idols.

632 C.E. – Muhammad dies, and a series of Caliphs govern the Muslim occupied territory.

    From here a massive Muslim campaign of war ensues lasting some 800 years, but Islamic conversions were actually discouraged to prolong the collection of jizya (a tax on non-Muslims). Persecution of non-Muslims – ranging from taxes to violence – would continue to be the case until modern times, resulting in a massive expansion of their faith, and a depletion of Pagans, Jews, Christians, and Zoroastrians. Along the way Islam experienced milder branching as compared to Christianity. This was more a result of outside influences (e.g. magic, reincarnation) than the catalyst of political corruption (e.g. the papacy in Rome). But a lack of religious and political diversity would come with its own costs (*discussed further in chapter 7*).
    A religious society as a whole must implement certain safeguards if they want to minimize religious branching; the top of the list being a strong military. If another nation conquers you, chances are their ruler practices a different religion and will persecute those of a different faith. For all the faults of the Catholic Church, they appreciate the power of social and scientific adaptation. They ignored Darwin's theory for 90 years before finally stating in 1950 that, "it's okay to form scientific opinions, as long as they don't contradict the Bible". 57 years later they ultimately accepted the principles of evolution as well as the theory of the big bang. In the same year, to the relief of grieving

parents, the Church published its evolved view that God's mercy will save un-baptized infants from Limbo.

Islam's success lies in its suppression rather than its charm, which only works in an environment of economic equality. The prosperity of the west, although seemingly unrelated, is plaguing extremist Muslims with the same mentality that motivated the Nazis. If the terrorism continues it's only a matter of time before they suffer the same fate.

CHAPTER 5

RELIGIOUS BRANCHING:

Part 2: What's the Difference?

"I've never understood how God could expect His creatures to pick the one true religion by faith—it strikes me as a sloppy way to run a universe."
-Robert A. Heinlein

General Similarities

Prophets

Texts

The Window of Opportunity

If you switched religions, but kept all the names and terms the same, you might not know the difference. With the possible exception of being denied certain foods, beverages, and potential clothing restrictions, the tenets tend to parallel each other. They all preach the same basic moral principles – some gender exclusions aside – like honesty, moderation, charity, and devotion (with the exception of Buddhism which allows dual worship). For all the war and hate involved with religious disputes the similarities far outweigh the differences. But even the slightest variance in belief can warrant the creation of a new sect.

There are several base aspects that nearly all religions have in common. The more menial involve features like exclusivity to reduce outside influence and establish solidarity. A more unstable characteristic is the answering of the 'unanswerable', like "why are we here?" As emotionally satisfying as "to serve God" may sound, it's still an empty explanation. Why would an omnipotent creator have an ego that demands one of his creations worship him or her? In the days before monotheism this might have made sense, as there was an implied competition amongst the Gods for supremacy. Without true understanding there's virtually no difference between "to serve God" versus "to serve supernovas" (astronomy's explanation for our molecular make-up). Even evolution is an empty explanation for biological diversity unless you understand the details.

Among the most significant attributes that religions have in common is the manner by which they achieve humility: personal sacrifice has been a monumentally effective tool with multi-faceted benefits from the religious perspective. It originates on the base level with belief itself. A man is raised in an environment free of religious influence. He makes a conscious decision not to drink alcohol or eat meat, he is honest, hardworking, regularly donates to charity, and is considered by his peers to be a model citizen by all accounts. Another man is raised in a religious environment and, according to the tenets of his faith, is required to act in the same manner as the first man. If religion were truly about creating a harmonious society, both men would receive salvation. But this is not the case because the requirement for salvation of any theistic religion is, at the very least, the belief in their deity. The actual behavior is secondary to intent. There's more value in the sacrifice one makes for their faith rather than a proactive lifestyle that happens to correlate with their tenets.

Why does sacrifice work: how many economies have a foundation built on charity? Socialism taken to an extreme will collapse unless a majority of its citizens pull their weight. Our innate sense of integrity tells us that anything worth having is worth sacrificing for. Belief in divine justice is a mental requirement for gnostic religions, so if a follower suffers in their physical life, righteousness will balance their fate via salvation in the afterlife. If a religion came along that offered eternal life, divine guidance, and spiritual fulfillment, and required that you change nothing about your current lifestyle, it would be about as convincing as a weight loss plan that allowed you to eat anything in any portion[18].

We tend to look back on human and animal sacrifices as barbaric rituals. The intent behind this practice was similar to the passing of the collection plate at church. Before there was currency, a universally acknowledged item of value was livestock, or, even more so, someone's virgin daughter. This was the ultimate sign of humility and appreciation that a tribe as a whole could offer their god. By comparison, it's far less emotionally taxing to donate 10% of your income, yet we look upon our 'blood thirsty' ancestors as ignorant and immoral rather than devout. The reality is that blood sacrifices exist at the militaristic base of every theological tree – they either still continue, have evolved a more refined substitute (e.g. almsgiving), or have been symbolically excused (e.g. Jesus' crucifixion as atonement for our sins).

There are several other methods common to a majority of religions in which personal sacrifice is ritualized. The most popular among these involves food. Thousands

---

[18] The core of the Thelema religion is to follow your 'true will' and "do what thou wilt". The bad news is they have no concept of Heaven, and therefore no salvation in the afterlife.

of years ago, when societies were rarely afforded the luxury of pickiness, rules weren't arbitrarily applied to food. Religious association simply provided an efficient way to reduce sickness among the public. Knowledge of bacteria and modern food regulations reduces the need for dogmatic 'warnings', but prior to contemporary farming techniques the pig was one of the most disease ridden forms of livestock[19]. In the sea, shellfish earned a harmful reputation due to their proclivity to absorb bacterial contaminants. In Hinduism, the cow, which was used for dairy products, tilling fields, and its excrement for fertilizer, was more valuable alive than dead, especially among a culture that readily embraced a vegetarian diet. Fasting is also a common tool for honing discipline amongst worshippers, usually as a way to pay homage to a meaningful religious event.

Physical appearance is another resource for control, generally in the form of clothing. For men, it tends to be symbolic as well as a means of cultural identity. Women, on the other hand, were seen as the source of sexual temptation. If there was less visible skin, there would be fewer extramarital affairs. Unfortunately, the stifling of sexuality in women didn't stop at ones appearance. In much of tribal Africa and in some Sunni Islamic practices female genital mutilation is commonplace. The explanations revolve around unsubstantiated health benefits, but the reality produces a range of results, depending on the extent of the disfigurement, from reduced sexual pleasure to making the act of intercourse nearly impossible. This ritual is primarily rooted in 'culture' rather than religious dogma, which may lend hope to its eventual demise.

Afterlife beliefs tend to fall in one of three categories: transition to a spiritual or existential existence, reincarnation, or simply unknown. There is a relatively even split between belief in a spiritual afterlife (heaven, hell, purgatory) verses reincarnation. The details surrounding a spiritual world vary greatly from one religion to the next, from being judged based on your earthly devotion, to enduring the equivalent of a heavenly oral exam (as with the Egyptian religion). Proto-indo Iranian religions have a near monopoly on belief in reincarnation. Afterlife beliefs in reincarnation have also been traced to ancient Greece through Orphism, as well as Norse mythology of northern Europe (ultimately replaced by Christianity). Several of the indigenous African faiths, like that of the Serer and Yoruba, also believe in reincarnation. Both seek to enforce a motivation for altruism, and as deity worship was influenced by society's needs, afterlife beliefs dig a bit deeper.

Spiritual domains of salvation and punishment are relatively straightforward in their conception, but reincarnation may tap into something more uninhibited. Psychiatrist Ian Stevenson is one amongst many scholars who have conducted studies on children (generally between ages 3 – 7) who claim to have memories from a past life. These memories include having a different name, names of people they've never met, descriptions of places they've never been, and details about historical events (like wars). Valid or not, it's likely this sort of phenomenon led to the origins of a belief in reincarnation.

---

[19] Christopher Hitches (author of "God is Not Great") argues that the modern aversion to pork is grounded in our rejection of human sacrifices, which ties into the similarities between pig and human flesh.

Prophets

The prophets of religion also bare various similarities. The understanding and appreciation of a prophet's life and teachings sometimes takes priority over God itself. They sought the goal of creating a prospering society, but their methods were a bit of a paradox: they were humble and peaceful (e.g. Siddhartha the Buddha, Jesus) or they believed in force (e.g. Simon bar Kochba, Muhammad). They were often hyper-sensitive to suffering and corruption, and felt pressured to change this. Many went through a period of 'revelation' resulting in the realization of their religious purpose in life. Sometimes this revelation was quickly realized, like Joseph Smith (LDS) after he was visited by an angel. Sometimes it took years, like Vardhamana Mahavira who went into seclusion for 13 years before returning with the principles of Jainism.

When a social leader utilizes force to inspire a cause, and dies in battle, they are considered war heroes. When they use passive protest, and die at the hands of a government, they are martyrs. Almost all prophets, to some extent, were martyrs – some by choice (like Bab with Babism), and some by circumstance (like Thomas Cranmer with Anglicanism). Martyrdom is often not enough to solidify a new belief system into society. Typically an inspired government leader will take the reins of promoting the cause; sometimes through legislation, sometimes via warfare.

One thing almost no prophet has been is female. Queen Victoria ruled England in the 19th century, Joan of Arc led the French army in the 15th century, but there has been only one noteworthy female prophet in history. In 1838, at the age of 40, Nakayama Miki founded the Japanese religion Tenrikyo quite by accident (*discussed further in chapter 8*).

The less mainstream religions could be the musings of another kind of prophet. They may exhibit materialism, grandiose claims, promiscuity, glibness, impulsiveness, and apathy. Their personal history may involve a range of psychological problems. These are widely considered to be false prophets, or cult leaders.

Prophets weren't always a prerequisite of religion, especially in polytheism. Primitive religion was often determined by committee, with final approval from the tribal chieftain, albeit passed down and revised over generations. In the primitive era of polytheism the line between humans and deities was clear: mortals lived on earth, immortals lived in the heavens (in some cultures animals were the possible exception as some were believed to possess spiritual powers). After written language developed, the line became blurred. Mythology fashioned mortals with supernatural tendencies – Bronze Age superheroes with deity fathers and human mothers. Sometimes these demigods were champions of war, sometimes they were chosen to spread the gospel of their immortal fathers, but their purpose was always divinely motivated.

If the life of a prophet dates back far enough, historical recordings tend to become exaggerated. The birth and death of a prophet or deity, for example, tends to be of particular importance. According to scripture a generous number of prophets (mortal or eternal) entered into existence by means of a **miraculous birth**.

3,000 B.C.E. – Egyptian mythology: The deity Horus was conceived by means of an immaculate conception after his mother Isis retrieved all the dismembered body parts of her murdered husband Orisis, and resurrected him in order to impregnate her.

1,500 B.C.E. – Mycenaean/Greek mythology: The Greek god Dyonisus was born prematurely from the womb of a dying mortal mother, rescued by his father Zeus, and carried to full term in Zeus' thigh, thereby credited with a distinctive 'double birth'.

1,500 B.C.E. – Zoroastrianism: Some traditions claim the prophet Zoroaster was conceived by a shaft of light unto his virgin mother Dughdova.

1,250 B.C.E. – Chinese mythology: The cultural hero Houji was supernaturally conceived when his formerly barren mother stepped in a footprint left by the supreme god Shangdi.

1,250 B.C.E. – Phrygian/Greek mythology: The Phrygian semi-deity Attis was born of the discarded phallus of daemon Adgistis, which sprouted an almond tree, where Nana, daughter of the river god Sangarius, picked an almond and laid it in her bosom.

1,200 B.C.E. – Aztec mythology: The deity Huitzilopochtli was born of a mother who bore many Aztec gods, but his immaculate conception was a result of a ball of feathers that fell on his mother while she was sweeping a temple.

900 B.C.E. – Greek mythology: The Greek hero Perseus was the son of Danae, mortal daughter of the King of Argos, who was impregnated by Zeus, manifesting himself to her in a shower of gold.

771 B.C.E. – Roman mythology: Twin heroes Romulus and Remus were born of a mortal mother sworn to chastity until she was impregnated by Mars, the god of war (some myths believe the father to be the demi-god Hercules).

623 B.C.E. – Buddhism: Guatama Buddha's mother Queen Maya was said to have conceived him miraculously while dreaming of a white elephant.

550 B.C.E. – Hinduism: On July 18, 3228 B.C.E. the Hindu deity Krishna was born without sexual union, rather the divine mental transmission of the god Vasudeva to the womb of demi-goddess Devaki at the stroke of midnight while imprisoned together.

80 B.C.E. – Mithraism: The Persian god Mithra was depicted as being born from a rock on December 25th.

6 – 4 B.C.E. – Christianity: The Christian prophet Jesus of Nazareth was prophesized by the angel Gabriel, and immaculately conceived in the virgin womb of Mary by the Holy Spirit of Yahweh.

800 C.E. – Japanese folklore: The mother of the Japanese folk hero Kintaro was said to be impregnated by a clap of thunder sent from a red dragon.

1,440 C.E. – Sufism: The Indian poet Kabir was said to be born of a virgin widow through the palm of her hand.

The legend behind the 'death' associated with various prophets and disciples integrates the supernatural as well, the common theme being **resurrection**. Sometimes the resurrection happens to the prophet, and sometimes they are caused by the prophet. The dates below correspond to the time the event was recorded.

650 B.C.E. – Greek mythology: The Greek poet Aristeas' dead body disappeared from inside a locked fuller's shop where he suddenly dropped dead, only to reappear seven years later to write the poem *The Arimaspeia*.

600 B.C.E. – Judaism: The Jewish prophet Elijah resurrected the son of Zarephath's widow:

> 1 Kings 17: 22 – 23
> *And the Lord heard the voice of Elijah; and the soul of the child came into him again, and he revived. And Elijah took the child, and brought him down out of the chamber into the house, and delivered him unto his mother: and Elijah said, See, thy son liveth.*

Elijah also raised a Shunammite's son from the dead:

> 2 Kings 4: 34
> *And he went up and lay on the child, and put his mouth on his mouth, his eyes on his eyes, and his hands on his hands; and he stretched himself out on the child, and the flesh of the child became warm.*

62 C.E. – Christianity: Saint Peter resurrected Tabitha from the dead:

> Acts 9: 40
> *Peter asked everyone to leave the room. He knelt and prayed. Then he turned to the body and said, "Tabitha, arise!" Tabitha opened her eyes, and when she saw Peter, she sat up.*

62 C.E. – Christianity: The apostle Paul raised Eutychus from the dead:

> Acts 20: 10 – 11
> *And Paul went down, and fell on him, and embracing him said, Trouble not yourselves; for his life is in him. When he therefore was come up again, and had broken bread, and eaten, and talked a long while, even till break of day, so he departed.*

70 C.E. – Christianity: The bodies of many dead saints were raised upon the death of Jesus Christ, and three days later Jesus himself was resurrected.

> Matthew 27: 50 – 53
> *And when Jesus had cried out again in a loud voice, he gave up his spirit. At that moment the curtain of the temple was torn in two from top to bottom. The earth shook and the rocks split. The tombs broke open and the bodies of many holy people who had died were raised to life. They came out of the tombs, and after Jesus' resurrection they went into the holy city and appeared to many people.*

220 C.E. – Judaism: Some 200 years after Rabbi Judah died he would visit the home of Sefer Chassidim for Shabbat every week until he was discovered.

1,518 C.E. – Sufism: The Indian religious leader Kabir was said to have returned to settle the controversy amongst his followers over whether or not to cremate his body, which was suddenly replaced by flowers.

1,895 C.E. – Hinduism: guru Lahiri Mahasaya told his followers he would rise again after his death, and did so after being cremated, appearing to three of his followers in three separate cities.

Miracles and fulfilled prophecies often accompany the life of the prophet, or, in some cases, assisted in the promulgation of a particular faith. A study from the *Pew Research Center* in 2010 showed that 79% of Americans, even those who don't regularly attend religious services, believe in miracles. Whether this belief stems from an innate yearning for hope, or a lack of perspective regarding coincidences, it sheds light on the power behind a belief system that proposes to harness the supernatural.

15th century B.C.E. – Zoroastrianism: In addition to his miraculous birth, Zoroaster was believed to have healed the blind, cured disease, and control weather.

13th century B.C.E. – Judaism: Moses was believed to have extracted water from a rock, commanded a series of 10 supernatural plagues upon the Egyptians (e.g. swarms of locusts and frogs), as well as parting the Red Sea.

6th century B.C.E. – Buddhism: Gautama Buddha was believed to have been conceived without intercourse, and had no physical need for sleep or food.

500 B.C.E. – Zoroastrianism and Baha'i Faith: Baha'u'llah, prophet of the Baha'i Faith, claims to be the prophesized messiah from Zoroastrian scriptures (as well as similar prophecies in Buddhism and Hinduism).

> Farvardin Yasht 13: 129
> *He shall be the victorious benefactor by name and world-renovator by name. He is benefactor because he will benefit the entire physical world; he is world-renovator because he will establish the physical living existence indestructible. He will oppose the evil of the progeny of the biped and withstand the enmity produced by the faithful.*

30 C.E. – Christianity: In addition to his miraculous birth and death, as well as prophecies of both, Jesus was believed to have cured lepers and the blind, resurrected the dead, as well as numerous examples of control over nature (e.g. water into wine).

527 C.E. – Buddhism: Ichadon, the Korean King's grand secretary, prophesized that his execution would result in a miracle that would convince the court officials of Buddhism's power, thereby convincing the King to adopt Buddhism as the national religion. The day he was executed the earth shook, the sun darkened, and flowers rained from the sky. Buddhism was made the state religion during the reign of next ruler King Chinhung 7 years later.

630 C.E. – Islam: Muhammad was believed to have 'split the moon' in response to the Quraysh's persecution of Muslims.

Moral living standards alone won't always grab the attention of the masses, not without prominent marketing. The morals and lessons of religion didn't necessarily convey concepts foreign to society. Survival was enhanced due to advances in technology, not advances in morality. Yet these prophets didn't teach society about the concept of zero, or how to build a bridge. In other words, they did not offer us 'revealed wisdom', as was the case with other historical figures like Socrates or Aristotle[20]. The moral teachings of prophets with memorable births, miraculous powers during their life, and resurrected deaths were elevated in their importance because they were considered 'sacred' – directly from the mind of God.

---

[20] If the authenticity of a historical figure is in question, the 'revealed wisdom' of our scientific forefathers serves as proof of their existence in that this knowledge originated from the mind of an actual person. The 'who' is actually less important than 'what they revealed'. Religious prophets operate counter to this concept: their teachings, although important, are reiterations of existing beliefs, and the supernatural details of their life elevate the significance of their words.

Texts

The evolution of religious texts occurs on two primary levels. The first, and most direct example of pure evolution, is a natural function of linguistics. As language evolved and religion spread to foreign regions, translations were necessary to preserve the original context, but metaphoric representation often resulted in ambiguous interpretations. Sometimes the changes were based on presumed cultural biases (e.g. after being adopted by the Roman Empire, it was believed the name *Jehoshua* denoted an overt Hebrew connotation, thus Christian scripture ultimately translated this name to *Jesus*). The next level of scripture evolution existed in the emulation of stories and ethics. The texts of extinct religions bare similarities with the texts of contemporary religions, not necessarily in their writing structure, but in their mythology.

With no followers left to defend their honor, the texts of extinct religions are less subject to ridicule and viewed primarily as archeological. It begins with the religion of the Egyptians written on papyrus in 2,300 B.C.E., which describes their ritualistic practices and mythology through stories. *Atra-Hasis*, the text of the Sumerians, was written around 2,150 B.C.E. on clay tablets, and goes into detail on their god's hierarchical expectations (e.g. God gives power to the King, and the King administers God's will). The *Epic of Gilgamesh* was an ambitious Mesopotamian poem written on stone tablets around 2,000 B.C.E., which were said to have influenced some of the stories of the Old Testament. The *Enuma Elis*, another Mesopotamian creation, focuses on the supremacy of their god Marduk (once a minor deity) over the other gods in the Babylonian pantheon. It was recorded onto seven clay tablets around 1,750 B.C.E. and features a creation story similar to the version from Abrahamic religions.

More in-depth research has been devoted to religions still in practice, even those whose archaic essence has endured, like that of the Vedic Religion. The *Rigveda* was written in an Indo-Aryan language around 1,400 B.C.E. and, in addition to including germane Hindu prayers, contains poetic accounts of cosmology and religious Vedic hymns. As religions of this area and period were primarily oral, it wasn't until the 6th century B.C.E. that the 16 members of the Vedic priesthood canonized it into the version we have today.

The *Avesta,* from the Zoroastrian faith, was the first religious text to incorporate the miraculous life of a prophet. It was complied in two parts: the Old Avesta and Young Avesta. The *Old Avesta* was originally written in the Avestan language (probably Gathic or Old Avestan) which comprised the *Gathas* (17 hymns thought to be composed by Zoroaster himself) and the *Yasna* c. 1,500 B.C.E. The *Young Avesta* entered its written form (probably in the extinct Parthian language) around 500 B.C.E., but vanished (likely the result of a fire caused by the troops of Alexander). It primarily consisted of their repeated prayers, and thus existed in the minds of Zoroastrian priests. It then underwent a series of four major oral transmissions throughout Iran over the course of the next 800 years. The Young Avesta was finally documented in writing once in the 3rd century, and again in the 4th century, which yielded 21 volumes. These were eventually deemed as flawed translations and ultimately corrected throughout the 9th and 10th centuries.

The *Tanakh* of the Jewish faith led an equally dubious journey. Its first five books (the Torah) were composed from 950 - 450 B.C.E. utilizing the newly developed Aramiac alphabet, which evolved into Hebrew, and was scribed by at least four independent, anonymous authors, revised and rearranged by a redactor (*discussed later in the chapter*). According to German biblical scholar Martin Noth and Frank Moore Cross, the next five books (Deuteronomy, Joshua, Judges, Samuel, and Kings) are considered to be the work of a single anonymous historian whose work 'retroactively' coincided with historical events. Deuteronomy in particular was thoroughly revised to emphasize the Hebrews' lack of commitment to Yahweh and the Babylonian conquest of Jerusalem as their punishment. The remaining four books of the Nevi'im portion were authored, edited and revised in various order by numerous scribes (many anonymous) between the 6th – 2nd centuries B.C.E. The 11 books of the Ketuvim portion were authored by various prophets (some anonymous) during the 7th – 2nd centuries B.C.E. There are three disputed theories regarding the canonization of these books.

1. The *Men of the Great Assembly* (120 prophets and scribes) compiled the books around 450 B.C.E., and it has remained unchanged ever since.
2. The Torah (450 BCE), Nevi'im (200 BCE), and Ketuvin (100 BCE) were compiled by the *Council of Jamnia* around 90 C.E.
3. The books were canonized by the Hasmonean Dynasty in Judea c 100 B.C.E.

The Christian *Bible* is comprised of two parts: the Old Testament (the *Tanakh*), and the New Testament. The authorship of the gospels of *Mark* and *John* are generally undisputed as being written by Mark the Evangelist and John the Apostle. The gospel of *Matthew* sources to Mark, plus a hypothetical collection of Jesus' sayings written in Greek (known as the Q source). The gospels of *Luke* and *Acts* feature unusual fluctuations in tense and context, which has lead scholars, like Rebecca Denova, to conclude its authorship as an anonymous non-eyewitness (known as the L source). The *Pauline Epistles* (14 books) were written by the Apostle Paul from 50 - 60 C.E., with the exception of the gospel of *Titus*, which is argued to have been written as late as 200 C.E. The remaining 9 books were written by various authors, most of them identifiable, except for *Hebrews* (anonymous) and *Revelations* (disputed authorship).

The *Qur'an* of Islam was written in Arabic most likely during Muhammad's lifetime (610 – 632 CE) by as many as 48 scribes (as Muhammad was believed to be illiterate). Its unusual poetic-prose style devoid of chronology or thematic structure is considered to be "unachievable by humans" as it was said to be inspired by Allah verbally via the angel Gabriel. Ali ibn Abu Talib had a version of the Qur'an six months after Muhammad's death, but this version was believed to have been altered (e.g. the potential manipulation of words pertaining to Ali's rights as the first caliph) and therefore was not accepted[21]. Memory and most oral accounts of the Qur'an were lost when 700 Muslims died in the Battle of Yamawa in 633 C.E. Abu Bakr, the elected Caliph, ordered that the scattered versions of the text (on palm-leaf stalks, thin white stones, and from men who memorized it) be canonized by Zaid ibn Thabit, Muhammad's primary scribe. This task was described by Zaid ibn Thabit in these words:

> "...if [Abu Bakr] had ordered me to shift one of the mountains, it would not have been harder for me than what he had ordered me concerning the collection of the Qur'an."

It was ultimately completed by 650 C.E., and then translated into one specific form of Arabic three years later. Evolution of the Arabic language would further alter the Qur'an over the next three centuries.

The story behind the authorship of Taoism's *Tao Te Ching*, was, by contrast, very straight forward. It was written in Chinese Calligraphy sometime between the 6th and 4th century B.C.E. by Laozi and contains 81 brief chapters of ambiguous, singular ideas in a poetic style. It makes no miraculous claims, but does present the Chinese creation myth.

The texts of prophet based religions (i.e. Avesta, Tanakh, Bible, Qur'an) tend to ascribe their written word as absolute law, free of error or cause for change. It wasn't until the 17th century that Moses' authorship of the *Torah* was challenged, along with the likelihood that he never actually existed. Separate authorships, known as the *documentary hypothesis*, explain the various repetitions, shifts in linguistic style, tense, and inconsistencies. For example, the chronicle of the great flood has two distinct accounts:

> Genesis 6: 19 - 20
> *You are to bring into the ark two of all living creatures, male and female, to keep them alive with you. <u>Two of every kind</u> of bird, of every kind of animal and of every kind of creature that moves along the ground will come to you to be kept alive.*

> Genesis 7: 2
> *Of every clean beast you shall take to you <u>by sevens</u>, the male and his female: and of beasts that are not clean by two, the male and his female.*

Judas' death in the New Testament also has two distinct versions:

---

[21] Disputes over this version of the Qur'an and Ali ibn Abu Talib's rights as the first Caliph is what ultimately led to the great Sunni-Shi'a schism within the Islamic faith.

Matthew 27: 5
And he threw the pieces of silver into the sanctuary and departed; and he went away and <u>hanged himself</u>.

Acts 1: 18
Now this man acquired a field with the price of his wickedness; and falling headlong, he burst open in the middle and all <u>his bowels gushed out</u>.

The discrepancy between "pairs" of animals and "sevens", as well as Judas' "hanging" versus "falling", has inspired various justifications, the more benign involving the preservation of the 'tradition' of these separate manuscripts taking priority over 'consistency' during their canonization.

The various religious texts often share similarities, not necessarily in the way that Abrahamic religions share specific gospels, or in structure or belief, but in their stories.

Battle Story

A common element in polytheistic mythology involves an epic battle between the ruler of a pantheon and either a serpent or dragon, which sometimes predates the creation story.

Egyptian: Ra vs. Apep (serpent from the Nile)
Mesopotamian: Marduk vs. Tiamat (sea serpent, chaos goddess of the ocean)
Canaanite: El Elyon vs. Lothan (seven-headed sea serpent)
Greek: Zeus vs. Typhon (hundred-headed serpent)
Germanic: Thor vs. <u>Jörmungandr</u> (sea serpent)
Vedic: Indra vs. Vrtra (dragon of the drought)
Zoroastrian: <u>Kərəsāspa</u>, vs. <u>Aži Dahāka</u> (three-headed dragon)
Judaism: Yahweh vs. Leviathan (sea serpent)

Creation Story

1,750 B.C.E. – Mesopotamian (Enuma Elis): Marduk creates the firmament, the earth, the stars, the sea, man to serve him, plants and animals, and ends in a period of rest.

550 B.C.E. – Judaism / Christianity (Genesis): In six days Yahweh created light, sea, land, sun, moon, stars, fish, fowl, man and other land creatures. On the seventh day God rested.

Garden of Eden

2,150 B.C.E. – Sumerian (Erudi Genesis): Enki (patron god of the city of Eriduand) and Ninhursag (mother goddess) lived in Dilmun, the site where creation occurred and where sickness and death were unknown.

2,000 B.C.E. – Mesopotamian (Epic of Gilgamesh): Shamhat (the woman) tempts Enkidu (the man) with food, covers his nakedness, and must leave his former realm unable to return.

550 B.C.E. – Judaism / Christianity (Genesis): Adam and Eve are the first humans in paradise. Satan (in the form of a snake) tempts Eve from the Tree of Knowledge, which leads to original sin and the fall of mankind.

500 B.C.E. – Greek Mythology: The Garden of Hesperides was a blissful garden where a single tree of immortality sprouted golden apples.

Great Flood

2,000 B.C.E. – Mesopotamian (Epic of Gilgamesh): Ea (god of crafts) commands Utnapishtim to build a boat in preparation for an impending flood because Enlil (lord of the storm) has rejected mankind. The storm lasts 6 days and 6 nights.

1,650 B.C.E. – Sumerian: Enki (lord of the underworld sea) instructs Ziusudra to build a large boat for an impending flood for a storm that lasts 7 days.

700 B.C.E. – Hinduism (Satapatha Brahmana): The Matsya Avatar of Vishnu warns Manu of an impending flood and to build a large boat.

550 B.C.E. – Judaism / Christianity (Genesis): Yahweh tells Noah to build an ark for an impending flood to erase the wickedness of mankind. The storm lasts 40 days and 40 nights.

Tower of Babel

600 B.C.E. – Sumerian (Schoyen Collection): Etemenanki was an 'actual' 7-story ziggurat dedicated to Marduk in the city of Babylon. Alexander the Great destroyed the decaying tower in 331 BC in a failed attempt to rebuild it.

550 B.C.E. – Judaism / Christianity (Genesis): The survivors of the great flood built a tower in Shinar that will reach heaven. Yahweh curses their ability to communicate, forcing them to speak different languages, which prevents the completion of the tower.

632 C.E. – Islam (Qur'an): Pharaoh asks Haman to build him a tower so that he can mount up to heaven and confront the God of Moses.

Laws from on high

1,500 B.C.E. – Mycenaean Mythology: Dionysus and Bacchus (sons of Zeus) received the laws of the land written on two stone tablets.

1,000 B.C.E. (approx) – Zoroastrian (Avesta): Zoroaster received the "Book of the Law" from God on a mountain.

800 B.C.E. – Greek Mythology (Odyssey): Minos (a mythical King of Crete) received sacred laws from Zeus on a mountain.

600 B.C.E. – Judaism (Tanakh): Moses received the Ten Commandments on two stone tablets from Yahweh atop Mount Sinai.

End Times

500 B.C.E. – Zoroastrian (Bahman Yasht): Good will eventually triumph over evil, resulting in a comet striking the earth and a mass resurrection of the dead, who will then be judged by means of wading through a river of molten metal. The righteous will wade through unharmed and achieve immortality. The wicked will be burned as the river flows into hell where it will annihilate the ruler of the underworld Angra Mainyu.

400 B.C.E. – Judaism (Tanakh): God will restore the House of David (Jewish law) and return the Jewish people to the Land of Israel where a Jewish Messiah will usher in an age of justice and peace. The dead will be resurrected and the heavens and earth will be rebuilt.

60 C.E. – Christianity (Old and New Testament): At some unknown time natural disasters and Armageddon will occur on a worldwide scale preceding the return of Jesus to earth in human form. The dead will be resurrected and the righteous will ascend with Jesus into Heaven, leaving the wicked to remain and suffer the wrath.

Much of the Old Testament spans a period of time when polytheism was still evolving into monotheism in the Semitic region. Controversy surrounds the origin of Yahweh, and how or why he replaced El Elyon in the Canaanite religion. Some sources depict Yahweh as one of El Elyon's 70 sons. Some believe he was borrowed from the pantheon of the Edomites. According to the German biblical scholar Julius Wellhausen it took approximately 500 years (from 950 – 450 B.C.E.) to finalize the content of the first five books. The beginning of this period marks the official origin of Judaism. At that point it had adopted many followers, but the Torah itself was still a work in progress in the hands of at least four sources: Yahwist, Elohist, Deuteronomist, Priestly, as well as Redactor (editors). Their accounts paint an ambiguous picture of monotheism, which contradicts archeological polytheistic evidence.

The portions written by the Yahwist were believed to have been written first (950 B.C.E.). They display a rich, narrative style and reflect a personally accessible version of Yahweh. The overall theme is essentially an account of Israeli society, Abraham, and an introduction to who Yahweh is. The portions written by the Elohist were next (850 B.C.E.) and were in a slightly less eloquent style. Here, Yahweh is accessible only through the dreams and visions of prophets (Abraham, Jacob, Joseph, and Moses). There is increased focus on the 'fear of God', covenant, and Israel's goal to be a religious nation of priests. In the Deuteronomist portions (600 B.C.E.) the tone darkens depicting historic lessons that suffering is deserved for those who are not loyal to Yahweh[22]. Finally, the Priestly portions (500 B.C.E.), written in a dry, legalistic style, grew darker still – Yahweh was distant, unmerciful, and approachable only through the priesthood. Ritual was depicted as a priority: covenant of circumcision, dietary laws, Sabbaths, and the strictness of tabernacle worship.

As monotheism took hold over the span of the authorships, four primary gods dominated Canaanite worship: El Elyon (Elohim, god most high), Asherah (Asharte, Goddess of the sea, queen of heaven, El Elyon's wife and likely Yahweh's mother), Ba'al (god of storms and fertility, likely Yahweh's brother) whose cult worshippers were in fierce competition with the followers of the fourth god Yahweh. The context of Ba'al tends to be as an example of a 'false god' no longer deserving of worship, occurring several times throughout the Old Testament. Theologian Francesca Stavrakopoulou argues that, due to artwork of the period, Asherah was dually worshipped in the temples of Jerusalem as Yahweh's wife rather than his mother. The archeological pottery art depicts a polytheistic context with Yahweh and Asherah, leading Stavrakopoulou to conclude that such references were edited out of the Bible once the Hebrew canons approached solidification. What we have are passages such as these, which implies Moses' polytheistic worship after escaping Egyptian slavery:

Exodus 15:11
Who among the Gods is like you, Lord?

Exodus 18:11
Now I know that the Lord is greater than all other gods, for he did this to those who had treated Israel arrogantly.

---

[22] Given its variant linguistic style, timely unveiling, and the context of the reactionary reforms surrounding its discovery, the general consensus amongst biblical scholars was that the book of Deuteronomy was a forgery.

As well a movement from polytheism with King Hezekiah of Judah and his abolishment of idolatry and devotion to Yahweh:

> 2 Kings 18:4
> *He removed the high places, smashed the sacred stones and cut down the Asherah poles. He broke into pieces the bronze snake Moses had made, for up to that time the Israelites had been burning incense to it (and he called it Nehushtan).*

Eventually resulting in the outright denial of polytheistic roots:

> Isaiah 44:6
> *Thus says the Lord, the King of Israel and his Redeemer, the Lord of hosts: "I am the first and I am the last; besides me there is no god."*

El Elyon, on the other hand – or some version of his name – occurs some 2,570 times in the Hebrew Bible. The ambiguity of translations (including random shifts to the plural tense: e.g. Gods) make it difficult to discern whether these references are just labeling semantics, or a separate deity entirely. Nevertheless, El Elyon was absorbed by Yahweh, and Asherah and Ba'al were abolished from worship initially by King Hezekiah and again by King Josiah in 622 B.C.E. But polytheism would rear its head in another 40 years, and the scriptures would be modified to incorporate this (*discussed further in chapter 6*).

The Window of Opportunity

The transition to monotheism was an arduous process taking the better part of a century to rectify in the Near East (Middle East) alone. The collapse of the Roman Empire led to the western migration of Judaism, yet it essentially stopped there. Like an animal who flourishes in a particular climate, monotheism almost exclusively branched from Judaism, and nowhere else. The Abrahamic religions never took a strong hold in the east. The disbursement of religious beliefs (excluding vague categorizations such as "general spirituality" or "unsure") is demonstrated here:

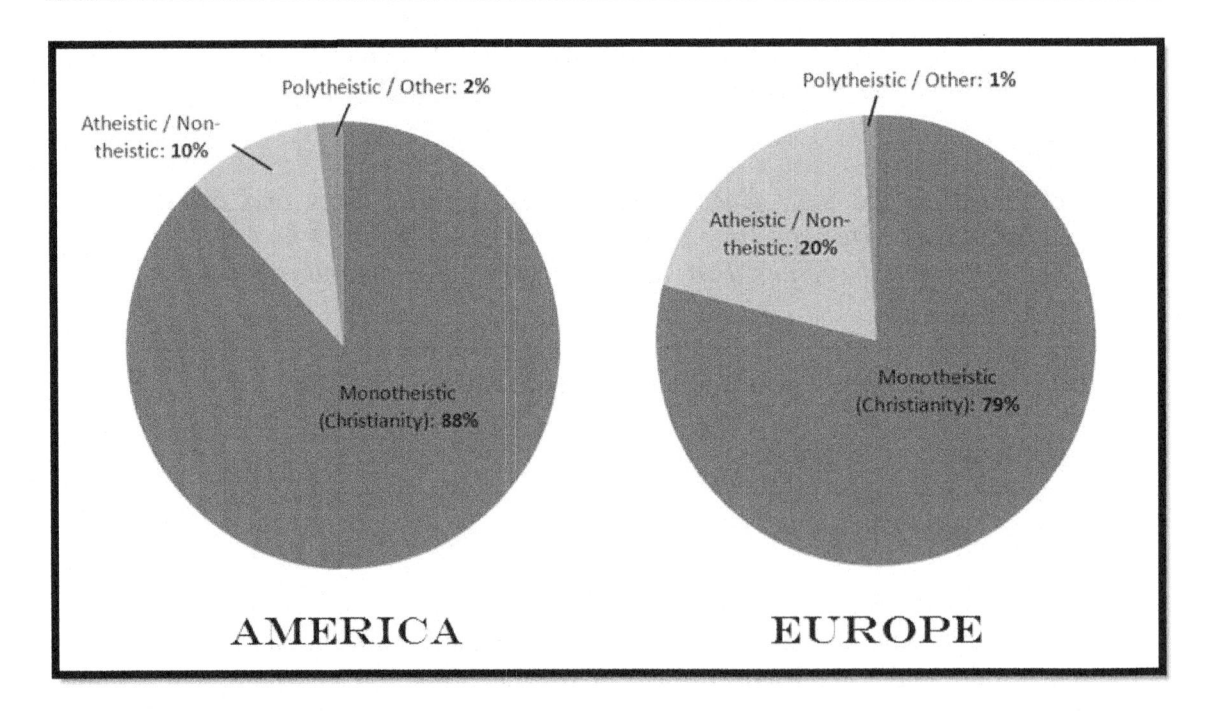

AMERICA

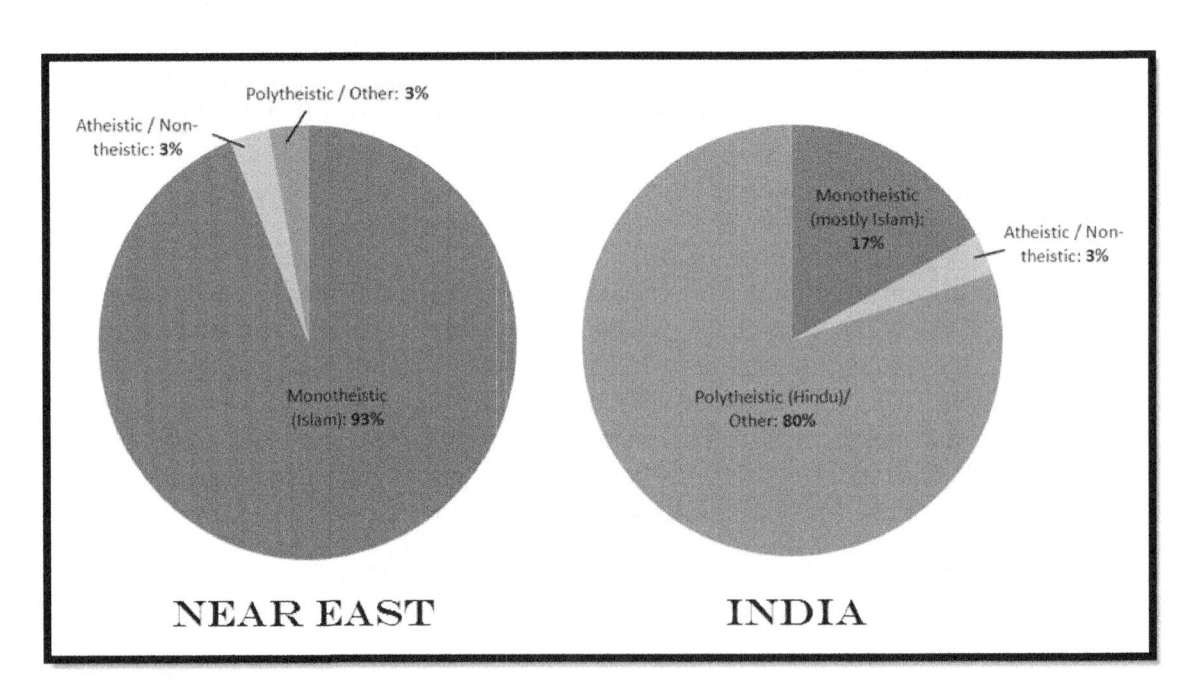

- Monotheistic (Christianity): **88%**
- Atheistic / Non-theistic: **10%**
- Polytheistic / Other: **2%**

EUROPE

- Monotheistic (Christianity): **79%**
- Atheistic / Non-theistic: **20%**
- Polytheistic / Other: **1%**

NEAR EAST

- Monotheistic (Islam): **93%**
- Atheistic / Non-theistic: **3%**
- Polytheistic / Other: **3%**

INDIA

- Polytheistic (Hindu) / Other: **80%**
- Monotheistic (mostly Islam): **17%**
- Atheistic / Non-theistic: **3%**

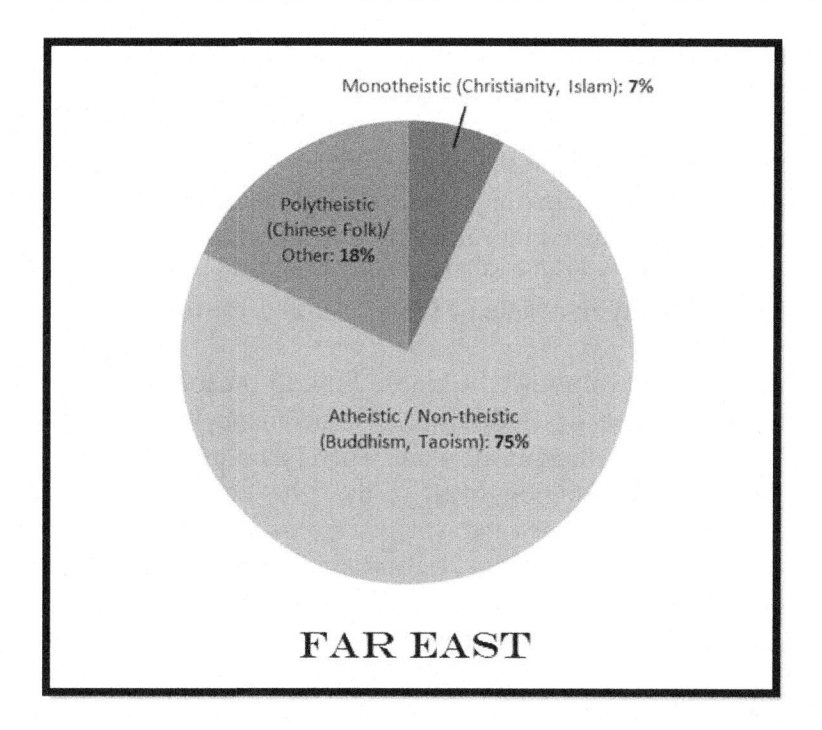

Pie Chart: FAR EAST
- Monotheistic (Christianity, Islam): **7%**
- Polytheistic (Chinese Folk)/Other: **18%**
- Atheistic / Non-theistic (Buddhism, Taoism): **75%**

The primarily monotheistic regions (America, Europe, and the Near East) demonstrate a relatively similar demographic spread. The polytheistic belief of Hinduism dominates India, which isolates their unique partition of worship. But how do we explain the seemingly 'non-theistic' beliefs of China and the Far East? Feng Shui (the Chinese system of geomancy and astrology), which is heavily driven by spiritual harmony and perceived life forces, dates back to 4,000 B.C.E. and encompasses a wide range of contemporary support. Our tendency to view the world around us through an empathetic filter results in our inherent spirituality, but in East Asia the 'god' portion never fully caught on the way it did in the rest of the world.

There are two approaches to explaining this. The first involves our definition of religion. Buddhism, Confucianism, and Taoism are primarily a guide for establishing harmony with the forces of the universe. Their tenets are vague as well as their theistic beliefs, but their purpose for guiding its followers to create an ideal society coincides with almost any religion. Their version of God does not have a human face, but is nonetheless an eternal force that created the universe and influences its path. Their version of prayer, or meditation, is more a method to coincide with spiritual energy rather than sway it. Their afterlife ranges from reincarnation to an ambiguous fusion with 'reality'. The political powers of religion still exist as a catalyst for unification, but a personal god does not. Initially established by the indigenous Chinese Folk mythology, many of their religions are non-exclusive. In other words, the worshipper is allowed to 'moonlight' by following additional faiths. There were no inherent weaknesses in their non-theistic beliefs in terms of morality or social accord, and therefore no motivation to evolve toward monotheism.

The second approach is the result of a window of opportunity shaped by our utilization of warfare. War has been the primary means by which religious beliefs thrive or go extinct. For some 5,000 years this window for change was opened, and the leaders of the world, whether they realized it or not, had the opportunity to shape religious belief to the extent that their armies could muster. This window is just now starting to close leaving the religions of today in a state of limbo, waiting for the next wave of influence to develop.

The Far East's window allowed Chinese Folk to prosper initially, followed by a wave of reform in the guise of Buddhism, Confucianism, and Taoism (6th century B.C.E.), which brought about an agnostic slant. Then Islam and Christianity made recent attempts to penetrate Asia's religious wall in the 19th century, but never resulted in overwhelming conversions. And now the window is closing.

The same could be said for India. They started with a Vedic influence, which led to Hinduism (9th century B.C.E.). Then Buddhism arose, but was essentially bastardized and sent eastward in search of a home. Then Islam came forcibly from the north (11th – 14th centuries C.E.), had at least a foot in the door, but ultimately retreated from whence it came. And now their window is closing. So what changed and who, if anyone, changed it? How could something as 'devoid of ethics' as warfare suddenly become encumbered by rules and limitations. Apparently this was exactly what happened, and the man at the helm was Adolf Hitler. The so-called 'poster child for atheism' was indirectly accountable for hindering the most effective method by which religions evolved (*discussed further in chapter 6*).

CHAPTER 6

WAR:

What is it Good For?

"The belief in a supernatural source of evil is not necessary; men are quite capable of every wickedness."

- Joseph Conrad

NATO and the Media
The First Armies
How Religion Shaped War
How War Shaped Religion
Xeno–Dichotomy
Warfare and Judaism

Until the late 18th century government and religious beliefs were essentially one in the same. It was a preverbal crap shoot whether the ruler of a nation would be tolerant of religions that differed from their own. If they weren't, and your government was overthrown, your freedom to worship your desired faith was in jeopardy.

War determined governments, and governments determined religion, for a period. To date, many nations practice a separation of church and state (e.g. United States, Australia, Brazil, India, Turkey, Japan, Mexico, most of Europe). State authority does not necessarily dictate religious persecution in these nations. But war too has evolved. At the conclusion of World War II the alliances of NATO helped to suppress excessive militaristic activity. The reign of the warmonger was dwindling and a semi-universal cultural was established that bound the economic super-powers in an agreement on the ethics of warfare. The window of opportunity to 'claim your territory' was closing, and the spread of religion by force was coming to an end.

The hindrance created by the alliances would be compounded by the expansion of media coverage. An example of this is the sociological reaction to the war in Vietnam, the first American war to receive extensive media coverage. World War II and the Korean War received relatively optimistic exposure, encouraging support and admiration from American citizens. But the devastation and reality of the Vietnam War became more than just a newspaper headline. Anti-war protests and counter-culture movements became a major theme throughout America and Europe.

1965 – Alice Herz and Norman Morrison (separate occasions) set them self on fire in protest.
1968 – A protest turns into a riot outside the US Embassy in London (86 injured).
1969 – WUO (Weather Underground Organization) bombs a Chicago statue.
1970 – WUO detonates a bomb at the Park Police Station in San Francisco (1 killed).
1970 – Kent State shootings in Ohio (4 killed).
1970 – Jackson State protest in Mississippi (2 killed, 12 injured).
1970 – WUO detonates a bomb in NYC Police Headquarters.
1970 – Sterling Hall bombing in Wisconsin (1 killed, 3 injured).
1970 – The Chicano Moratorium riot in Los Angeles (2 killed).
1971 – WUO detonates a bomb in the Washington Capital.
1971 – The NY Times and Washington Post published the top secret *Pentagon Papers* revealing much higher casualty rates than the publicly released government statistics.
1972 – WUO detonates a bomb in a Pentagon bathroom.

American support for the Vietnam War peaked at 59% in 1966, but plummeted to 28% five years later. Society's attitude changed, and government's engagement in warfare would change with it. The militaristic window opened with the formation of the first armies and started closing in 1949. This period of roughly 5,000 years has essentially shaped the demographic of religious worship.

The First Armies

Is war an inevitable function of society, or did it evolve over time? Professor Lawrence H. Keeley from the University of Illinois wrote that societies who frequently traded with one another engage in more wars with one another. In fact the mortality rate due to warfare (as with the Jivaro tribe in Peru) could be as high as 60% (compared to modern rates around 1%). There were, of course, violent Paleolithic rivalries over territory, but this was nothing like the 'luxury' of warfare that a thriving society could afford. Chieftains didn't see building a proper military as a viable option until a large enough percentage of their population was 'expendable'. After the Neolithic population explosion (around 10,000 B.C.E.) this percentage was in the neighborhood of 15 - 20%.

Armies were being developed, but territory wars were relatively rare by modern standards. Territorialism was driven by an instinctual moral distrust of the unfamiliar. Religion sought to tighten those within your tribe, and, by repercussion, distance you from outsiders, thereby increasing the territorial impulse.

The first large scale battles of any kind didn't occur until 40,000 – 30,000 B.C.E. The most notable wasn't until 14,000 B.C.E. in Egypt, and even this is disputed whether it was legitimately militaristic in nature. The population increase due to improved agricultural techniques coincided with improved weapons (e.g. a proficient bow and arrow in 12,000 B.C.E.). Evidence of tangible historic warfare traces back to around 3,000 B.C.E. At this time armies numbered from 1,000 – 10,000 and comprised approximately 10% of the societal population. Every millennium these numbers would essentially double. One of the most powerful armies of its time was in Egypt c. 5,000 B.C.E. Military recruitment for training started as early as the age of five. Without religion as a binding cause, citizens may have migrated east to avoid losing their sons to warfare.

If the populace had the option of leaving or hiding to avoid serving in the military, how could one's loyalty be tested? 'Rite of passage' rituals were an effective tool for determining allegiance. The practice of circumcision dates back some 15,000 years, predating most structured religious beliefs. If you were willing to allow a stranger to sever the foreskin of your 8-day-old son's penis because your religion decrees it, you were likely to allow him to serve in the military for the same reason.

How Religion Shaped War

In ancient Rome, augurs would read the will of the Gods to the people, which often included declarations of expansionism. This was essentially all it took to justify warfare to the commoners a few thousand years ago, and sometimes even less than that. But there's a glaring fundamental problem with war in the name of religion: if wars are for a cause, and each cause is subjective to those who are affected by it, how can morality be determined? This is a dangerous mindset in that it removes the 'affects' of a cause entirely.

Around 1920 German anthropologist Franz Boas established a principle known as *cultural relativism*, which is the understanding that there are no universal or absolute moral standards. The environmental and economic aspects of one society (e.g. the practice of polygamy amongst herding and horticultural societies) may dictate an opposing code of morality compared to a dissimilar society. This concept is illustrated in the following analogy.

You discover your friend just died after eating a strange fruit. You tell the leader of your tribe that this fruit is poisonous. Your leader announces a new law than anyone seen with this fruit will be imprisoned (i.e. it could be used to poison an enemy). You come across a neighboring tribe who ration mass amounts of this fruit. You tell your leader what you've discovered and he announces to this tribe that they have one full day to destroy the entirety of their poisonous fruit supply. They refuse, and your leader responds with a military offensive. After wiping out their entire population you discover a medical journal that describes how this tribe suffered from a rare skin disease for which applying this fruit is the only known cure.

If you believe the impact of this analogy relies on hyperbole, the soursop (or guanabana) grows in tropical Central America. The seeds are toxic, but if you remove them the fruit contains antimicrobial ingredients that can clear up fungal infections, bacterial infections, intestinal parasites, as well as treating cancer.

Was it morally correct to declare war on this tribe? Is declaring war on a society who practices 'illegal' rituals any different? The answer is usually dressed up in a proactive disguise in which war is intended as a defense for what would be an inevitable foreign offense (e.g. the Crusades). When Yahweh commanded the Jews to *"...not leave alive anything that breathes. But you shall utterly destroy them: the Hittite and the Amorite, the Canaanite and the Perizzite, the Hivite and the Jebusite, as the Lord your God has commanded you,"* (Deuteronomy 20:16-17) this was carried out under the assumption that morality is dictated by religion, which is the covenant of a perfect God. If there is only one perfect God, we're left with an unanswerable question of which God, as well as which denomination of belief.

How War Shaped Religion

As religious development transitioned from the *Neolithic* phase and entered the *Dionysian* phase, or war god phase, it became clear where religious motivation was headed. During the Neolithic period, our survival depended on mastering the mysteries of agriculture. Success in that realm led to an increase in population, affording government leaders the ability to build armies and claim additional territory, as well as defend their own. Survival now depended on mastering the 'mysteries of war'.

In the days of polytheism, when territorial expansion was particularly in vogue, warfare often determined the supreme deity of a pantheon. To compare it to contemporary football, each tribe represented a football team, and the neighboring tribes make up a single chiefdom called the NFL. To play in the NFL you follow the same rules (or religion). Instead of representing cities, each tribe represented a specific deity. The most powerful tribe put their deity in charge, until he or she was defeated and replaced by another. For example, in Mesopotamia c. 1,750 B.C.E. the army of Marduk, the sun god of Babylon, was victorious over the army of Enil, lord of the storm in Nippur, resulting in his supremacy over the pantheon. When one god could finally be agreed upon, it united the chiefdom and increased their loyalty to a common cause. This gave rise to monotheism leading to the Abrahamic religions.

Xeno-Dichotomy

When President Eisenhower, a recently baptized Presbyterian, signed a bill in 1954 to add the words "under God" to the pledge of allegiance, he was most likely oblivious that he was demonstrating a prime example of *xeno-dichotomy*. The prefix *xeno* means foreigners, and *dichotomy*, in this context, refers to a rebellious and opposing viewpoint. By 1954 the cold war between America and the Soviet Union was firmly established, and America's campaign to demonize Communism dominated the media and was now officially part of our public school system. America was, for the most part, non-secular, and, even though Russia's policy of State Atheism varied over the years, Communists were considered 'godless'. Adding "under God" to our pledge was a sub-conscious reminder that Americans had their beliefs, and Communists believed the opposite, which gave us an additional reason to remain bonded as a nation to ensure our longevity.

As with biological evolution, whereby a prey evolves in accordance with its primary predator (e.g. Murex snails evolved thick shells and spines to avoid being eaten by crabs and fish), religion seeks out methods of adaptation, although these methods tend to resist conformity and instead promote xenophobia. A quasi-secular example was observed when African-Americans were stripped of their culture during the slave trades[23]. Rather than adopting the attitude, "if you can't beat them, join them," *xeno-dichotomy* observes an opposing retort: "if you can't beat them, magnify their differences". This is often secularly demonstrated via new government policy, or, non-secularly, new beliefs or rituals.

The primary example of this surrounds the Abrahamic religions. The origins of Judaism came out of a reactionary attitude in Israel circa 950 B.C.E., which was essentially a society of cultural orphans. Periods of crisis can inspire societal bonds, and when there is a lack of culture to bond over, one is created. In other words, Israel was suppressed from establishing a solid cultural foundation due to the revolving door of military occupation, so they established a religious foundation to compensate: monotheism. The fact that they gravitated toward Yahweh, a 'war' god, did not necessarily indicate their proficiency for war, rather their desire to 'become' proficient. The more damage their culture sustained due to foreign oppression, the more they gravitated toward a faith no one else understood, a faith solidified when the Babylonians destroyed their temple in 586 B.C.E. The Torah was canonized just over 100 years later. Jerusalem's history of religious influence is perhaps the most turbulent of any nation in history.

Before 1,550 B.C.E. – Canaanite religion
1,550 B.C.E. – Egyptian religion under pharaoh Ahmose I

---

[23] The depletion of African culture due to slavery led to their development of the Gullah language, spiritual music (which would evolve into jazz and blues), and rebellious forms of witchcraft based religions like Myalism and Vodou.

1,178 B.C.E. – Canaanite religion under the Jebusite tribe
    957 B.C.E. – *Temple built by King Solomon*
    928 B.C.E. – *Temple sacked by Sheshonk of Egypt*
    835 B.C.E. – *Temple rebuilt by King Jehoash*
    701 B.C.E. – *Temple stripped by Sennacherib of Assyria*
622 B.C.E. – Judaism under King Josiah
586 B.C.E. – Mesopotamian religion under the Babylonians and Nebuchadnezzar II (temple destroyed)
538 B.C.E. – Zoroastrianism or Judaism under the Persian king Cyrus the Great (religious freedom was permitted) – *Temple rebuilt*
    332 B.C.E – *Temple nearly destroyed by Alexander of Mecedonia*
331 B.C.E. – Greek mythology under Alexander the Great
37 B.C.E. – Judaism under the Roman installed leadership of King Herod
    70 C.E. – *Temple destroyed during the Roman Siege of Jerusalem*
135 C.E. – Hellenistic religion under Emperor Hadrian after the Bar Kokhba revolt
391 C.E. – Christianity under the Roman Empire and Theodosius I
614 C.E. – Zoroastrianism under the Persian Sassanid army and Ardashir I
629 C.E. – Christianity under the Romans and Heraclius
638 C.E. – Islam, Judaism, or Christianity under the Arabs and Umar al-Khattab (religious freedom was permitted)
    691 C.E. – *The Muslims construct the Islamic Dome of the Rock on the old Temple site*
996 C.E. – Shi'a Islam, Judaism, or Christianity under Al-Hakim (Jews and Christians paid a tax)
1007 C.E. – Islam (Al-Hakim allows Sunni Islam and persecutes Jews and Christians)
1012 C.E. – Shi'a Islam, Judaism, or Christianity (Al-Hakim reverts to his prior beliefs)
1099 C.E. – Christianity as a result of the Roman Crusades
1187 C.E. – Islam, Judaism, Christianity or under Sultan Saladin of Egypt and Syria (non-Islamic persecution was unofficially rife)
1517 C.E. – Judaism, Christianity, or Islam under the Ottoman Turks and Suleiman the Magnificent (religious freedom was permitted, but Judaism prospered)
1948 C.E. – Religious turmoil between the Jews and Muslims during the Arab-Israeli War
1967 C.E. – Judaism in the west, Islam in the east

    Granted, the Jews were not known for sitting back idly while their religion slipped through their fingers, but the political instability illustrates their plight as the pawns in Europe and Asia's ongoing war games[24]. But why was Israel the most popular military target in the Middle-East, possibly the world? These reasons may have factored into their cultural mindset if they possessed a valuable resource like gold reserves, or a

---

[24] An ongoing historical comparison has been made between the plight of the Jews in Israel and the American Indians via European conquest.

major shipping port. If you consider the factors that actually guided ancient military expansion, it wasn't anything Jerusalem had, but what others lacked. It was largely based on *climate,* but not theirs – Russia's and Africa's.

There were four major economic powers in the world during the Bronze Age: the Roman Empire, the Persian Empire, India, and China. When their own government leaders weren't battling for civil supremacy, they were motivated to expand. But it wasn't always as simple as a skirmish over common borders.

China's expansion options* *India's expansion options***

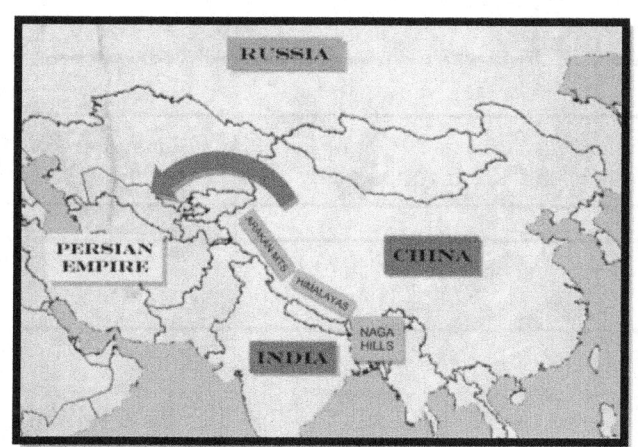

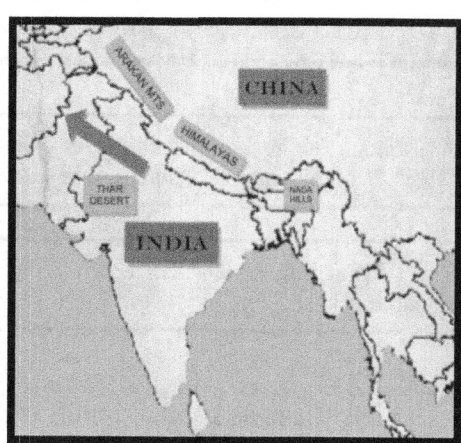

*China's options to expand were relatively limited. India was primarily off the table due to environmental obstacles (e.g. Himalayas, Arakan Mts, Naga Hills). China's chief military conquest was during the Mongol invasions of the 13th century (they expanded as far west as Turkey). Long distance military campaigns were expensive and difficult to maintain, and their borders receded back to their original state about a century later due to peasant revolts and the black plague epidemic.

**India's expansion was directed west beyond the Thar Desert resulting in three notable India-Persian confrontations between 484 – 1191 CE (the White Hun Invasion, the Conquest of Sindh, and the Battle of Tarain), a relatively modest amount by Middle-Eastern standards.

The Roman Empire's expansion options *The Persian Empire's expansion options**

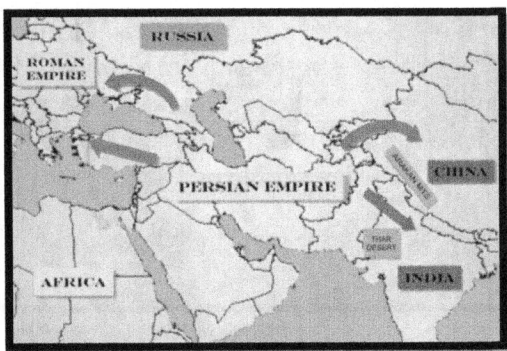

*The Roman Empire had two routes of expansion into the Persian Empire, resulting in many territorial conflicts, beginning around 200 B.C.E and continuing through the Crusades.

**The Persian Empire had the most options of the four, but the bulk of their efforts were in defense against the Roman Empire.

The purpose of examining expansion routes isn't to understand where military efforts were concentrated as much as understanding where they were 'not' concentrated. Two regions, Africa and Russia, could have reduced military conflict between the Roman and Persian Empires by adding additional expansion options. The tundra of Russia and the deserts of Africa (specifically the Sahara Desert) offered little in the way of agricultural opportunity (Tsardom wasn't established in Russia until 1,547 C.E., and the Russian Empire not established until 1,721 C.E.). Thus an epic military rivalry ensued between the Romans and Persians. What region was caught in the center of this military tug-of-war? The Levant (i.e. Israel). Jerusalem was a victim of geography.

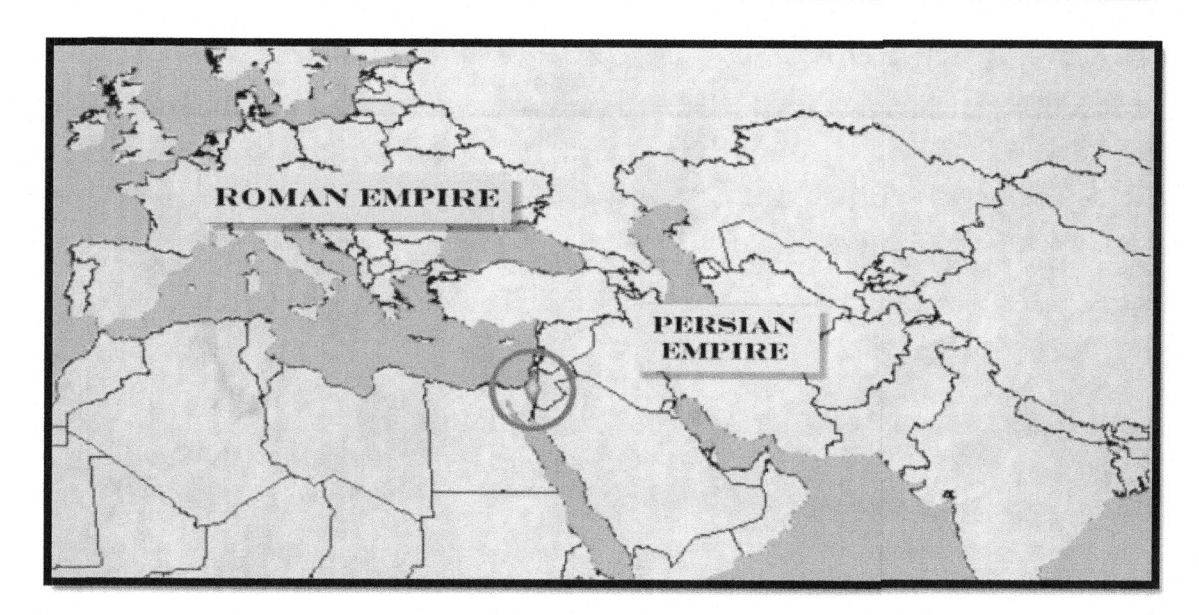

When these opposing forces practice incompatible faiths (i.e. Christianity versus Arabian mythology) a rivalry faith evolved. If you're the Roman Empire, your military opponents share your religion only 50% of the time. And if you're the Assyrian or Sassanid Empires (Persian), major battles are reserved for opponents of opposing religious 50% of the time as well.

Wars against opposing religious forces: **Roman Empire**

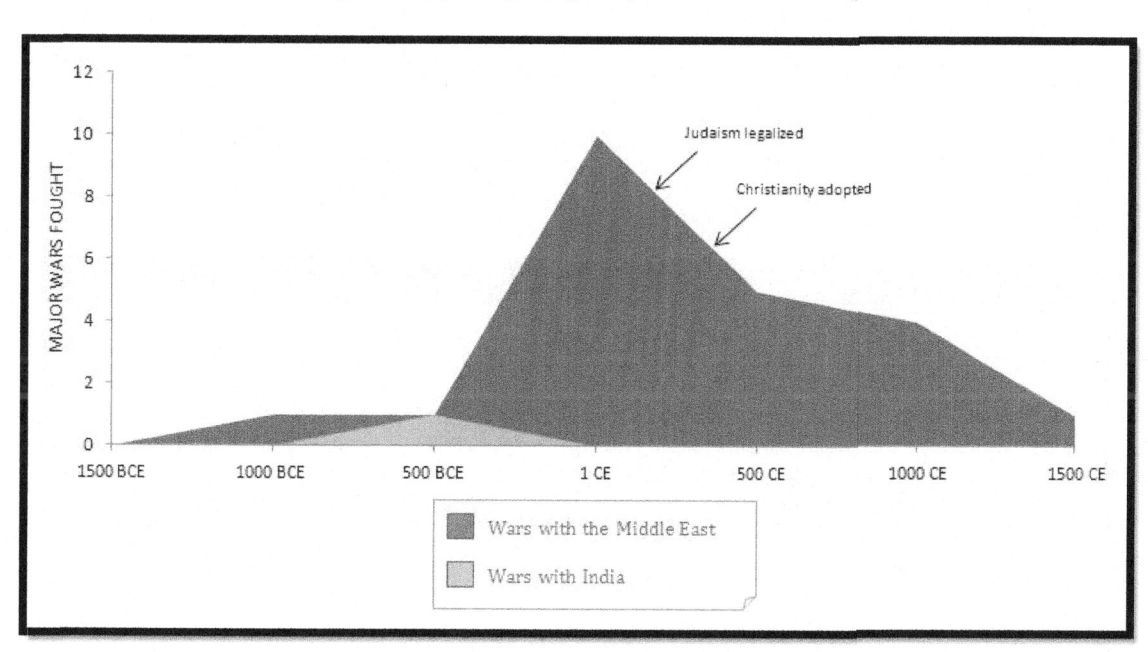

Wars against opposing religious forces: **Middle-East**

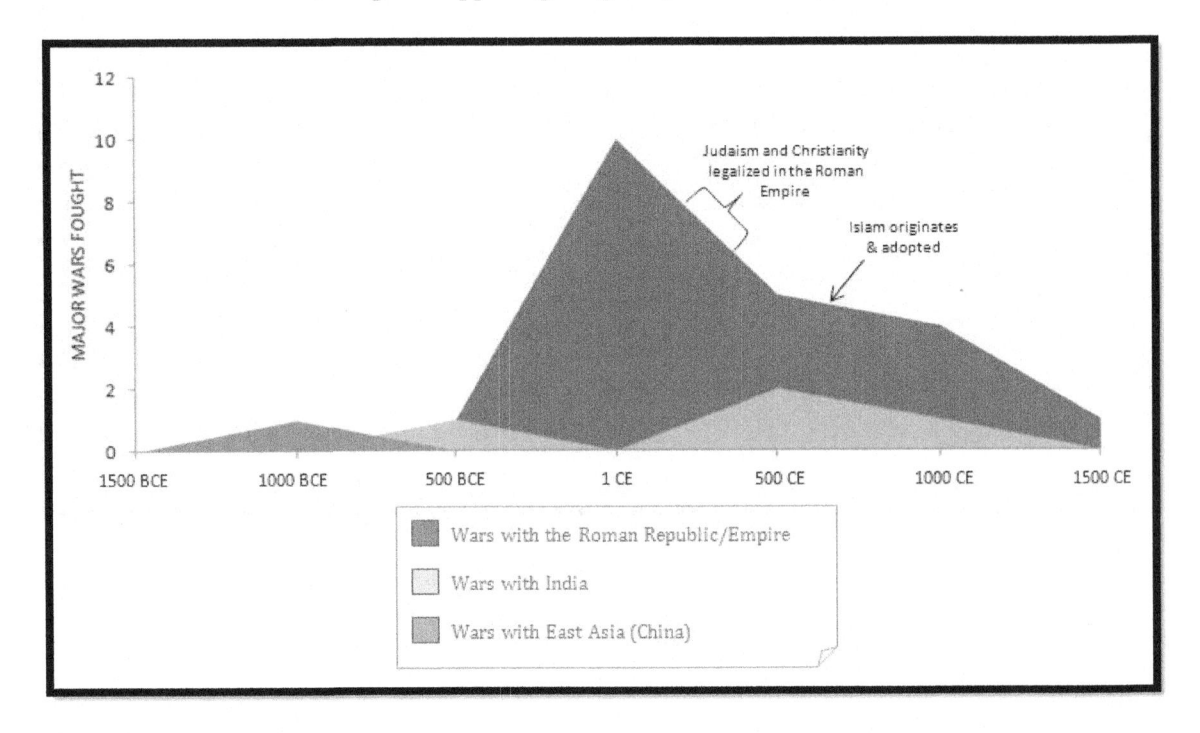

[Chart: Major Wars Fought vs. time from 1500 BCE to 1500 CE, showing Wars with the Roman Republic/Empire, Wars with India, and Wars with East Asia (China). Annotations: "Judaism and Christianity legalized in the Roman Empire" and "Islam originates & adopted".]

    Xeno-dichotomy is a semi-conscious military tactic used to unify morale against a specific opposition. Israel countered their war-ridden culture with Judaism. After Christianity became the Roman Empire's version of Judaism, and after some 16 wars over the course of a millennium, Islam spawned as a theological rival to its Roman predecessor.

    China provides another example of xeno-dichotomy with Confucianism and Taoism. Although similar in scope there are political differences between the two philosophies that had nothing to do with false prophets or which God reigned supreme.

Confucianism	Taoism
Embrace wealth	Greed leads to corruption
Man should use nature	Man should become one with nature
Ritualistic	Rituals cause confusion
Pro hierarchy	Pro equality
Pro government	Power leads to corruption
Seek harmony within society	Seek harmony within one's self

The various leaders that established the Dynasties of China engaged in an unprecedented amount of warfare to claim superiority, and their authority determined which philosophy was promoted or appointed.

141 B.C.E. – Confucianism is adopted by Emperor Wu of the western Han Dynasty
  20 battles fought from 133 B.C.E. – 194 C.E.
194 C.E. – Taoism received support from Emperor Cao Cao of the eastern Han Dynasty
  26 battles fought from 194 – 219 C.E.
220 – 265 C.E. – The Three Kingdoms are established: Wei in the north (Cao Cao), Shu in the west (Liu Bei), Wu in the east (Sun Quan)
  13 battles fought from 222 – 263 C.E.
265 – 420 C.E. – Confucianism begins to weaken as Buddhism, which is closely tied into Taoism, starts to flourish
  9 battles fought from 280 – 416 C.E.
420 – 618 C.E. – Neo-Daoism (a blend of Taoism & Confucianism) received support from Emperor Wen of Liu Song (though he leaned toward Confucianism)
  4 battles fought from 439 – 617 C.E.
606 C.E. – Emperor Yang of Sui supports Confucian education
618 C.E. – Buddhism and Taoism are adopted by Li Yuan who claimed Laozi (founder of Taoism) was their decedent
  11 battles fought from 621 – 689 C.E.
722 C.E. – Neo-Confucianism evolves
  6 battles fought from 745 – 817 C.E.
845 C.E. - Taoism adopted by Emperor Wuzong of the Tang Dynasty (even Buddhists were persecuted)

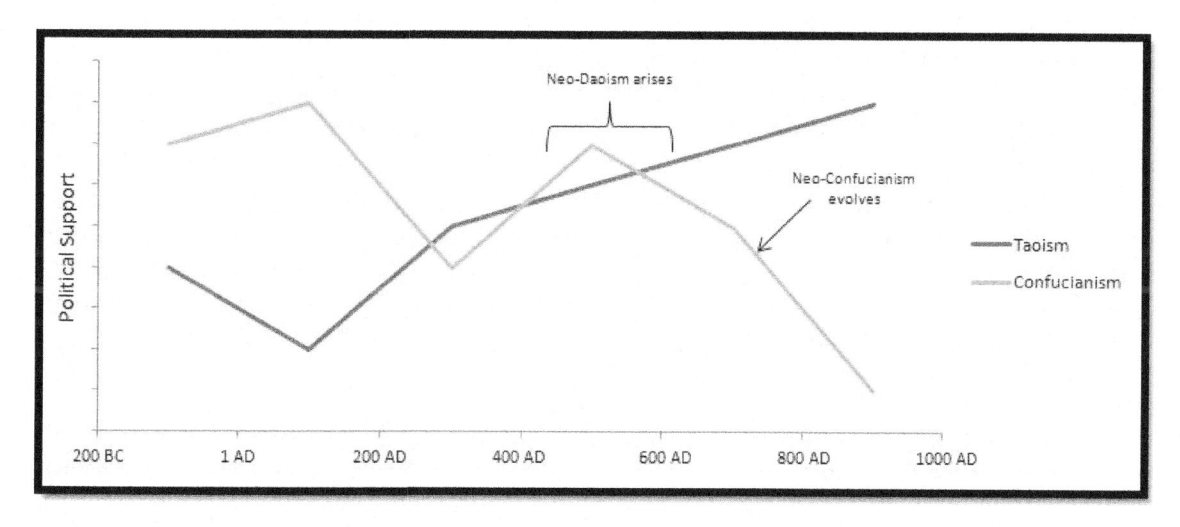

Taoism vs. Confucianism

As political support for Confucianism declined after the fall of Neo-Daoism, Confucianism evolved into Neo-Confucianism, which maintained the same differences with Taoism but made one critical change. Rather than embrace the spiritual facets of the prospering philosophies of Taoism and Buddhism, it chose to distance itself further by rejecting all aspects dealing with the supernatural and instead established a solid foundation in reality. This, however, did not aid its recovery. To date, Taoists outnumber Confucians 66 to 1.

Xeno-dichotomy, in general, is a theme within a majority of religions. It accounts for religious origins (i.e. the subconscious desire for change), as well as public acceptance of these beliefs. This consistency is demonstrated within all the four economic leaders. The Roman Empire's adoption of Christianity (monotheism) is consistent with their military rivalry with the polytheistic Persians. The Persian's adoption of Islam is consistent with their military rivalry with the Romans, which countered Christianity. The Chinese adoption of the non-theistic philosophies (i.e. Taoism, Confucianism, and Buddhism) is consistent with their rampant civil war, and a desire to move away from theistic hierarchy and balance out the political turmoil. The Indian adoption of Hinduism even shows consistency with the migration of Aryans and Asians into their culture, which may have inspired the origins of their religiously enforced caste system.

Warfare and Judaism

Like all religious evolution, change never comes without a fight. The sequence of events that dictated the pace of the transition from polytheism to monotheism in Israel played out in a serendipitous chain of military actions. The consensus of biblical scholars places Jewish accounts of the exodus around 1,200 B.C.E.[25] The first mention of Yahweh probably arose around this time as a proposed agent of freedom for these Jews, which formed a dubious mix with the current 'God most High' El Elyon of the Canaanite religion. But once David took over the throne in Judah (*via warfare*) in 1,010 B.C.E. peace settled in, and the collective need to worship a 'war' god like Yahweh was replaced with desires of family life (i.e. the worship of Asherah the mother goddess, and Ba'al the fertility god).

Amidst this quagmire of henotheism the unofficial establishment of Judaism began with the first authors of the Torah and their independent accounts of the culture of that time (the Yahwist and the Elohist). An impending attack from the east around 722 B.C.E. prompted the outcry of three prophets – Isaiah, Amos, and Hosea – who were stringent supporters of sole worship to Yahweh. Their counsel went unobserved and

---

[25] Contrary to Biblical documentation, warfare, rather than slavery, was the catalyst for the suppression of Hebrew culture circa 1,000 B.C.E. In addition to the mismatched chronology of the proposed enslavement with the construction of the pyramids (c. 2,600 – 1,800 B.C.E.), no confirmed evidence has been found for the exodus of the estimated 2 million people who migrated across the Sinai, or the actual enslavement of any Jews in Egypt.

Jerusalem was captured (*via warfare*) by the Assyrians. An account of these three prophets lived on in Hebrew scripture and influenced Josiah, who would become king in 641 B.C.E. Assyria's domination was eventually crippled by *civil war*, and opened a door of religious opportunity. The timely discovery of the book of Deuteronomy in 622 B.C.E., which proclaimed the suffering Yahweh would unleash upon those who denounced his exclusive covenant, was the justification Josiah needed to demolish polytheism (*via genocide*). But it wouldn't last. Babylon's attack on Israel in 586 B.C.E. was imminent, as warned by the prophet Jeremiah, and a fleeting public devotion to Yahweh was blamed. The beliefs of the Mesopotamians would both hinder and influence Judaism (*via warfare*), shaping its canons to reflect a more consistent version of monotheism than what actually occurred.

If religion exists within the minds of those who follow it, warfare's impact on religious evolution creates a deep parallel with phylogenetics. Religious belief becomes the gene, the believers become the carriers, and the armies become the forces of change. But what's to say of religion that persists regardless of leadership influences? Can the seeds of religion be planted and prosper without central nourishment? Displaced belief was perhaps the only thing keeping Zoroastrianism, Judaism, and the Baha'i Faith alive for selected periods throughout history. This is a primary difference between theological and biological evolution. A hungry predator can detect its prey based on sight, smell, and sound – government leaders cannot. Religious beliefs garnish the luxury of existing in secrecy within the worshipper. Religious practices, on the other hand, require a degree of subtlety to elude the senses of would be persecutors. Depending on the duration and intensity of the oppression, preserving a faith for future generations must be chaperoned with great care.

CHAPTER 7

ECONOMICS:

Expensive Bibles Sell Better

"No one would remember the Good Samaritan if he'd only had good intentions; he had money as well."
- Margaret Thatcher

How the Economy Influences Religion
Economy in the Roman Empire
Economy in the Near East
Economy in China
Economy in India
The Economic Paradox of Islam

As effective as war can be to spread and stifle religion, this is merely a forceful intervention. If a rehabilitated drug addict encounters depression, they may resort to drastic measures to change their state. If an economic depression befalls a nation, they too may resort to drastic measures. A crumbling economy is a sign of weak or inefficient leadership, and a society's religion is often a product of its leadership. Using history as a guide, it would appear that money can't always buy religion, but poverty can.

Terror management is put to the test in times of social depression. Society members can become competitive as the demand for resources increases. But if some semblance of leadership can prevail, people can be easily united under a common goal – especially if an antagonist can be singled out[26]. As awareness of our mortality increases (e.g. during an economic recession) our preference in leadership styles change. Charismatic leaders (i.e. those who reinforce your self-esteem) suddenly have an advantage over 'relationship-oriented' leaders, which seems counter-intuitive to survival. This could lead to near unanimous support of the Nazi political party, or it could lead to the collective embracing of a new religion; either way, change is a must. In the opposite scenario – an economic surge – societies tend to cling to what works. Even if they have no tangible connection to the results, presidents will be re-elected, CEO's will keep their jobs, and budding religions will be largely disregarded. After periods of social crisis, spiritual revivals and movements are particularly abundant. The situation in which this is best demonstrated is with the four economic powers of the world and their subsequent religious majority. This includes the Roman Empire (Europe) with Christianity, the Near East with Islam, the Far East (China) with Taoism, and India with Hinduism.

A prime example of this is demonstrated during the reign of the Romans. The **Roman Republic and Roman Empire** suffered three major economic depressions in their tenure. The first was the downfall of the Republic from 133 – 27 B.C.E. The second was a period of military anarchy and near collapse of the Roman Empire from 235 – 284 C.E. The third economic blow was during a final decline from 395 – 476 C.E. There were two major religious influences that came in contact with Roman territory across these periods: Judaism and Christianity.

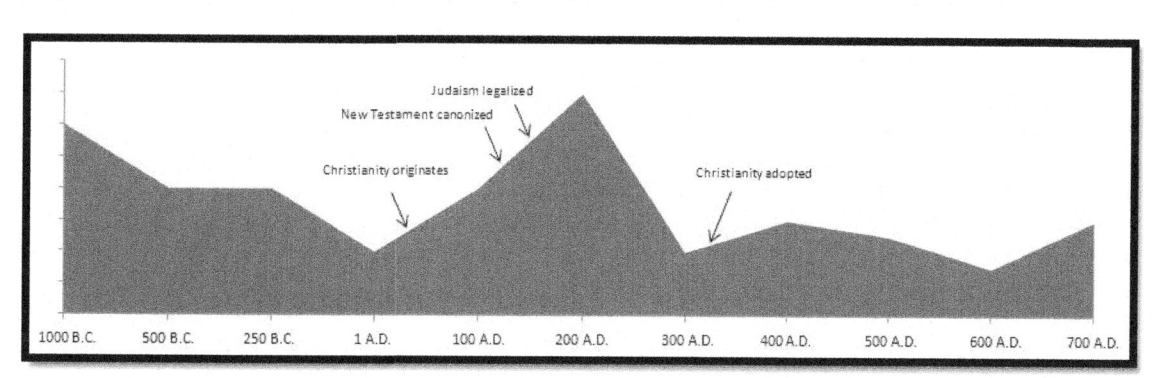

Economic fluctuations of the Roman Republic/Empire

Christianity originated around 33 C.E in the Levant region, which was under Roman occupancy at the time. This occurred in the early phase of an economic surge, and it would be another century before its gospels were compiled into the Bible. By this time the economy continued to climb, and Judaism was finally allowed to prosper. But shortly after the Jews were granted Roman citizenship the economy took a turn. Soldier

---

[26] George W Bush's approval rating jumped 39% (from 51% on Sept 10, 2001 to 90% on Sept 21, 2011) after the antagonists were revealed for the 9/11 terrorist attack.

revolts, inflation, and a major smallpox outbreak would overshadow all religious reforms. In 305 C.E. the economy bottomed out and Constantine took leadership in the West. Christianity, after nearly 300 years of persecution, was legalized. 80 years later it was adopted as the state religion by Theodosius I.

The **Near East**, specifically the Assyrian Empire, was the largest and most thriving economy in the world from 1,365 – 605 B.C.E. Judaism and Zoroastrianism developed during this period to challenge the polytheistic religions of the time, but these were religions structured around heritage. Unlike many religions they did not seek to convert but rather inform, which kept their numbers low regardless of political influence. The Assyrians suffered some territorial losses to Persia and Rome in the centuries to come, but they remained a stable economic force. Meanwhile, Judaism and Christianity gained recognition in the West, but the Middle-East was still wading about in a quagmire of polytheism. A stalemate of warfare between the Persian and Roman Empires, lasting some 5 centuries, severely weakened these powers and left the Middle East in a damaged economic state. Around this time Islam developed, and its well timed arrival almost immediately bred new life into the Arabs leading to both a militaristic and economic surge[27]. But a seemingly unpredictable crutch would eventually evolve in the Islamic economy that would unveil a key fiscal disadvantage (*discussed later in the chapter*).

Economic fluctuations of the Near East

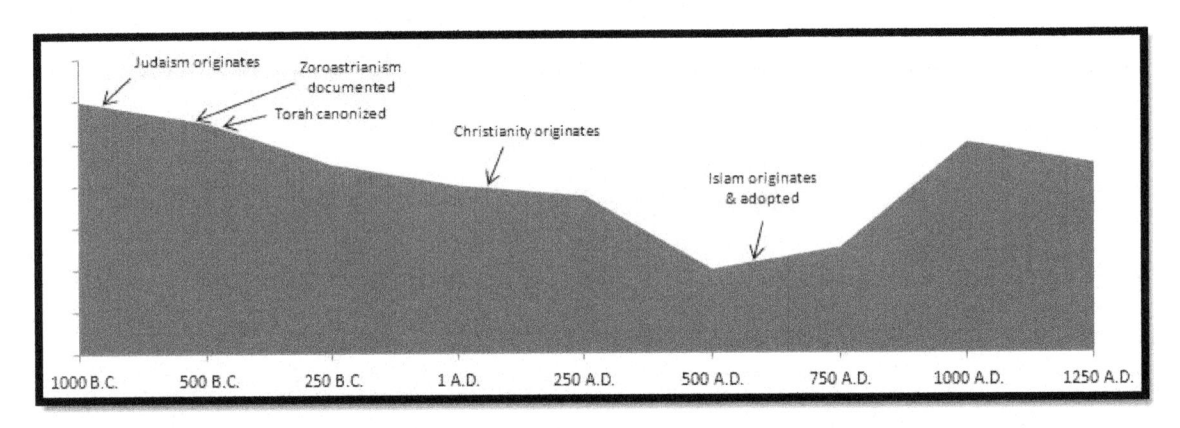

The economy in **China** and eastern Asia had one major recession and three major religious developments. The latter consisted of Taoism, Confucianism, and Buddhism. The recession came after China's Golden Age with the collapse of the Han

---

[27] The Romans and Persians shared parallel religious circumstances: evolving polytheism in the East and West was initially influenced by Judaism, the pioneer of monotheism – after an economic downturn Christianity was adopted in the West, and a similar economic decline in the East, 200 years later, opened the door for Islam.

Dynasty in 220 C.E., a period plagued by warfare and major losses in tax revenue. The three afore mentioned religions influences came during a period of relative economic stability contrasted by massive civil war. Literally hundreds of philosophies emerged during a 300 year period. The collapse of the Han opened the door for reforms, and, until this point, Confucianism was the forerunner as it received political support during the Han Dynasty. But acceptance during an economic peak produced a doubtful foundation. Cao Cao would not only establish policies that stopped the bleeding of the economic depression, he also supported Taoism. Meanwhile, Buddhism would have to wait another 400 years before political support would gradually boost its fellowship. Taoism was fortunate enough to climb its way out of the economic valley and claim early domination in the East, steering Confucianism down an uncertain path, eventually resulting in its evolution into Neo-Confucianism.

Economic fluctuations of East Asia (China)

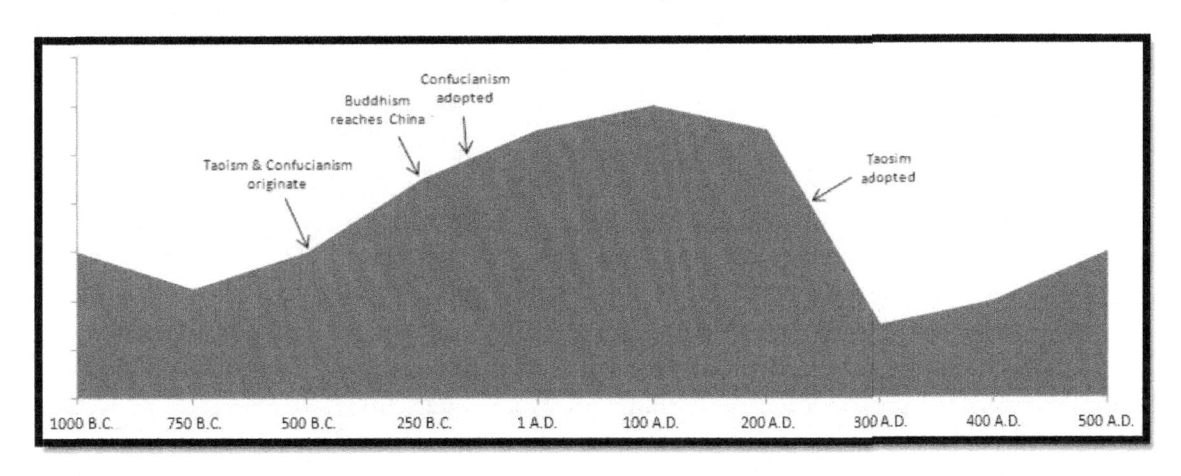

India's development was unique in that it is essentially devoid of significant economic recessions. They were a dominant economic force prior to 1,800 B.C.E., and experienced a 'Golden Age' lasting well over a millennium (200 B.C.E. – 1,200 C.E.) in which they had the largest economy in the world. Their chief religious schools of thought (Hinduism, Buddhism, Jainism) follow the pattern of the other cultures to an extent, but not enough to draw significant conclusions about a fiscal impact on Hinduism's overwhelming domination. What stands out about Hinduism is that it is a rare example of a relatively smooth evolution, one that incorporated its divergent branches. In other words, Hinduism broadened to allow for evolutionary changes. In fact, the Śrauta branch of modern Hinduism retains much of the traditional Vedic beliefs. Reactionary belief systems, like Buddhism and Jainism, were a much stricter departure from traditional Vedic customs, including a more dramatic agnostic philosophy. Hinduism, however, actually incorporated all 33 of the Vedic deities into a massively expanded pantheon, and allowed for an ambiguous agnostic overview. Animal sacrifices, which were removed from Hindu rituals, were already on a decline in the Vedic culture.

Economic fluctuations of India

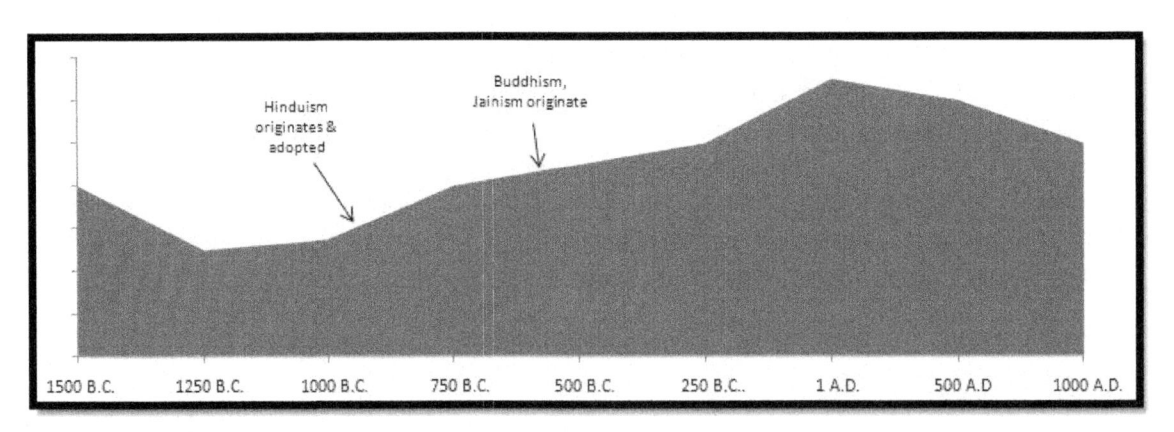

[Graph showing economic fluctuations from 1500 B.C. to 1000 A.D., with annotations "Hinduism originates & adopted" around 1000 B.C. and "Buddhism, Jainism originate" around 500 B.C.]

The most perceptible change in that era was adoption of the jati caste system around the time of the southern migration of Aryan nomads. Dating back to around 1,000 B.C.E, the reasons for incorporating this social construct are debatable, and may not even tie into religion if it weren't for the privileged position of religious leaders. At the top of the hierarchy are the *Bhramin* (priests), followed by *Kshatryia* (warriors, rulers), *Viasya* (merchants, landowners, minor officials), *Sudra* (commoners, servants), and finally *Pariah* (outcastes, "untouchables"). There is support for the notion that the caste system was part of the Vedic heritage, but was never actually enforced. The Hindu advent of 'karma' promoted individual accountability and provided an altruistic scapegoat by which it could be imposed. In other words, those suppressed by the caste system we given hope for an improved 'next life' via reincarnation. Impending economic backlash aside, those with the incentive and authority to reform the caste system were few and far between.

The Economic Paradox of Islam

Perhaps one of the most ironic outcomes of religious history rests in the rise and fall of the Middle East. Islam caught on with a fury, and, within 20 years of its origin, Caliph Umar led Muslim armies on a series of conquests that would continue for another 800 years. Islam experienced massive gains in territory and religious conversions, significant enough to motivate the Catholic Crusades. They experienced a 'Golden Age' between 750 – 1250 C.E. Their economic strength was soon rivaling their military strength. Their naval technology was advancing and they established trade routes throughout Asia, Africa, and Europe. They developed breakthroughs in medicine, and experienced an agricultural revolution whereby farming techniques were adapted to sustain a bevy of new crops from around the continent. But by 1,250 C.E. the impact of the Crusades and Genghis Kahn had the Muslims on the defensive. Forces in India recouped and drove out the Islamic armies. Their conquests came to a halt, but their accomplishments left a permanent mark in history. Islam would become the second largest religion in the world behind Christianity. In 1453 the Ottoman Empire arose and united the entire region under one ruler, and would continue to do so for the next 400 years. But Europe was gaining on the Middle East and eventually surpassed them in almost all categories: territory, economics, art, and technology. The Middle East was forced to watch its western neighbors establish and thrive during the industrial revolution. Then a turning point: oil. In 1908 it was discovered that in Persia (and later in Saudi Arabia) existed the world's largest reserve of crude oil. Muslim nations were primed to recapture their economic glory.

To date, Turkey has the 17th highest ranking economy, the highest of any Muslim dominated nation. They have a relatively diverse economy driven by industry, agriculture and tourism, and a poverty rate around 17% (slightly higher than the United States). But, unlike many Islamic countries, Turkey's government is not bound by *Shiria Law*. The next highest GNP of any Islamic nation, which is bound by the tenets of the Qur'an, belongs to the oil capital of the world Saudi Arabia at 19th. Saudi's poverty rate (whose statistics have been suppressed by their government) is around 25%. If we travel further down the Islamic GNP rankings we'll find Iran at 23rd, Egypt at 39th, and Iraq at 57th. Even India and its caste system (with 30% below the poverty line) has the 10th highest ranking economy. Mexico has a devastatingly high poverty rate at 51% yet maintains the 14th highest economy. The nations of the Middle East have robust petroleum reserves and thriving tourism. How is this possible?

The Middle East's recent economic woes have been a major topic of discussion, and the consensus is relatively consistent. Islam, like many religions, addresses economics in its dogma. Its aspirations were noble, aiming to limit corruption and preserve equality. Two primary covenants of their faith have been the center of economic focus. The first deals with *riba* (interest / usury on bank loans). Here is but one of several verses in the Qur'an on this topic:

Chapter 2: 276
Allah does not bless usury, and He causes charitable deeds to prosper, and Allah does not love any ungrateful sinner.

According to the Qur'an money itself has no intrinsic value; it exists by law, not by nature, and to make money from money is an 'unnatural' way to achieve wealth. Charging interest places an aberrant value on money, rather than value on the asset money can acquire. If a debt goes bad it's up to God to determine what failed, and the burden of risk rests equally on both the borrower and the lender.

The second covenant deals with inheritance and partnership, and is broken down in detail several times in the Qur'an:

Chapter 4: 12
You shall get half of what your wives leave, if they die childless. But if they do have children, your share shall then be a quarter of what they leave after carrying out any will made by the deceased or payment of any debt owed by her. And they (your wives) shall have a quarter of what you leave, if you die childless. But in case you have children, they shall then get one-eighth of what you leave, after carrying out any will made by you or payment of any debt owed by you (the deceased). And if a man or a woman is made an heir on account of his [or her] kalalah relationship [with the deceased] and he [or she] has one brother or sister, the brother and sister shall each receive a sixth and if they be more than two, they shall then share in one-third, after carrying out any will that had been made by the deceased or payment of any debt owed by him – without harming anyone. This is a command from Allah and Allah is all-knowing, most forbearing.

Pre-Islam, women were often excluded from inheritances as almost all estates were passed on to the son. Islam sought to rectify this by including all members of the family in an inheritance, which included business ventures. A partnership must dissolve if a partner dies or becomes incapacitated (this is relatively standard in economic practices resulting in a customary execution of renewed contracts). Islamic inheritance dictates that an estate be divided amongst all members of the family, including uncles and cousins.

The economic Achilles heel of these covenants was exposed around the 17th century, about 100 years before the industrial revolution. Europe and America were taking advantage of economic corporations, which allowed for the disbursement of risk across multiple active investors. Adding business partners in Islam became an inheritance nightmare as long-term business tenure would be dispersed amongst literally dozens of ill-equipped owners, and was made exponentially worse when polygamy was in practice. This resulted in businesses remaining small (usually two partners), which often over-personalized company practices. This issue was compounded when trade opportunities arose with Europe in the 18th century. Business ventures went international creating two sets of partnership laws, which left Islamic investors at a legal disadvantage.

When it came to usury, the balance of risk across both the borrower and lender has stately intentions, but the reality was that fewer loans were being issued. This also makes modern investment opportunities – like hedging, futures, day trading, and credit cards – very difficult, as well as earning the label of 'illegal gambling' in the eyes of Allah. Islam was essentially responsible for both the rise to greatness and the decline to mediocrity due quite simply to economic evolution contrasted against an overambitious adherence to archaic tenets.

Both Christianity and Judaism have similar verses in their texts, to list but a few:

Exodus 22: 25
If you lend money to any of My people who are poor among you, you shall not be like a moneylender to him; you shall not charge him interest.

Deuteronomy 23: 19
You shall not charge interest to your brother – interest on money or food or anything that is lent out at interest.

Europe also had partnership laws in the Middle Ages which shadowed Islamic beliefs. The problem was that, due in part to the ineptness of the government during the Dark Ages, these laws were rarely enforced. By the 10th century these partnership laws were all but forgotten. Regarding the Old Testament's ban on usury, authorities realized the weakness of corrupt usury policies and created legislation to regulate it. The Christian and Jewish community justified these biblical verses in a less than creative fashion: they ignored them. So in the 1960s Islamic banking created a loop-hole around riba through profit and loss sharing between the borrow and lender known as *Mudarabha*, but given the West's 500 year head start, the impotence of Muslim economics remains magnified.

What does the future hold for Islamic nations? This was put to the test in 1979 during the Iranian Revolution when high hopes after an oil boom resulted only in increased inflation (primarily due to Arab oil embargos), compounded by Reza Shah's incorporation of 'western' policies. What if your neighbor was running a successful business while you were barely making ends meet? Your friend finds out the secret to his business model and shows you how it works. It makes sense and seems likely that you can copy this model and accomplish the same. Another friend tells you it's a lie, and that he actually makes money by utilizing corruption and exploitation. This is how the west was portrayed to the Islamic people, and this was the direction the Shah was steering the entire nation. Despite the Reza's efforts to dress up western culture in presentable attire, the Iranian public demonstrated the power of religion and xenophobia when they chose to keep their oppressed economy rather than sample a thriving foreign influence.

Part of the ongoing political strategy in unifying Islamic followers involved demonizing those who believed what was counter to their theology, in this case the competing Abrahamic religions: Judaism and Christianity. Judaism was an ancient theology of slaves who have been oppressed since their origin. Christianity, the more culturally accessible revision, was an elitist theology and a tool of a power hungry and corrupt clergy. Muhammad arrives several centuries later to set mankind on the proper path by establishing peace and equality amongst the regulars of society. Yet the reality is that a majority of his followers live in poverty in contrast to Westerners who live oppression free, indulgent lifestyles.

The government in Iran was overthrown in 1979, and a devout Shi'a Muslim Ruhollah Khomeini rose to power to the overwhelming support of Iranian citizens. A lack of strict adherence to Islamic law was determined as the reason for the Middle-

East's current economic dilemma. It was the Biblical story from 586 B.C.E. of prophet Jeremiah and the capturing of Jerusalem all over again. Only this time, instead of Yahweh using the Babylonians as his instrument of destruction against the wavering devotion of the Jews, the punishment was economic repression for a lack of strict Islamic commitment via the leadership of the Shah. Ironically enough, according to a majority of economic scholars, the truth was the exact opposite. They couldn't declare war on America without inviting their own demise, but they could terrorize Israel and take American hostages. Islam has hand-cuffed its development by outlawing fundamental rights and imprisoning public information into the hands of rulers who are openly guided by their religious tenets. 30 years later we're still plagued by terrorism and an extremist regime, which leads us to the critical question: when will Islam evolve?

CHAPTER 8

COMPARISON:

The Stats

"The idea that God is an oversized white male with a flowing beard who sits in the sky and tallies the fall of every sparrow is ludicrous. But if by 'God' one means the set of physical laws that govern the universe, then clearly there is such a God. This God is emotionally unsatisfying... it does not make much sense to pray to the law of gravity."

- Carl Sagan

Far East Religions
Indo Iranian Religions
Near East Religions
Indo European Religions
Indigenous Religions

Statistical analysis aids in establishing perspective, and when applied to religion it seeks to consolidate the decision making process when we ultimately prepare to choose 'which one is right'. As dry and tedious as statistics often are, the information offered in this chapter is best represented via categorization. The evolution of the various theological branches and denominations are more easily compared and contrasted when expedited through grouping and labels, along with tree graphs and timelines; although a brief summary of each religion's origin or overview accompanies the stats.

The religions of the world have been categorized by the region or civilization responsible for their origin: Far East, Indo Iranian, Near East (subdivided into three branches: Judaism, Christianity, and Islam), Indo European, and Indigenous. Each of these families was founded by a theological forefather, so to speak, which gave birth to its forthcoming beliefs. In the Far East it was the *Chinese Folk religion*, the Indo Iranians had *Proto-Indo Iranian religion*, the Near East had the *Mesopotamian* and *Egyptian religions*, and the Indo Europeans had the *Minoan religion*. These five belief systems laid the groundwork for essentially all of our mainstream religious beliefs.

Certain statistics are grounded in history and surveys, such as *date of origination*, *region founded*, *deity* (or deities), *prophet* (or teacher), *sects* or *denominations*, and *number of followers*. *From which theology did a religion evolve* treads on ambiguous ground, but is historically quantifiable and significant (as with *which theology did a religion branch into*). *Religious rituals* are tangible in terms of measurability and often most practical when comparing and contrasting religious beliefs (i.e. what am I required to do if I intend to follow this religion?).

Religious belief, although subject to interpretation, often defines a religion's character. These beliefs tend to focus on two areas: what happened in history, and what this teaches us. Historical viewpoints are often based on mythology and prophets (i.e. the history of the Gods, and the life of their prophets). Interpreting 'what we were taught' begins to incorporate rituals, and our 'purpose for living'. This is often where dispute arises. The two most popular rebuttals to a belief system has been to 'reinterpret' what we were taught, or establish an entirely new religious history. Religiously, our 'purpose for living' generally falls in one of three schools of thought: Eastern, Vedic, or Abrahamic.

The Eastern school is divided amongst three dominant orders: Taoism, Confucianism, and Shintoism. They are primarily based on a submission to our refined social instincts. Reactions to the violence and destruction of war inspired an aversion to the rampant egocentric political behavior. This influenced a departure from ego and a movement to elevate society through individual guidance without the need for spiritual worship. A departure from this mode, demonstrated in Shintoism, encompasses a mystic approach influenced by the expansion of Buddhism.

Taoism: Living in compliance with *wu-wei* (action without intent: understanding facts will naturally determine your course) and *Tao* (balance in accordance with nature).

Confucianism: Fulfill your role in society through honesty, humanity, and ancestral appreciation.

Shintoism: Perform purity rituals to achieve peace in the afterlife.

The Vedic school is comprised of the dharmic faiths (Hinduism, Buddhism) and Zoroastrianism. Both are fusions of Far Eastern and Near Eastern schools of thought, with the dharmic leaning towards a more humanist approach. The movement toward gnosticism (emphasis on the spiritual world over the material) is also apparent.

Dharmic: Avoid suffering to achieve enlightenment and be released from re-birth.

Zoroastrian: We are prone to good and evil, and through freewill must collectively choose good in order to unite all of humanity.

The Abrahamic school is centered around Judaism, Christianity, and Islam. The lines are drawn more distinctly in regards to 'action' and 'result', but only Christianity and Islam demonstrate a full movement toward gnosticism.

Judaism: Obey the Ten Commandments to achieve fulfillment in your earthly life.

Christianity: Salvation from sin is only possibly through accepting Jesus Christ.

Islam: Submit to the will of Allah through the Five Pillars (testimony, prayer, alms-giving, fasting, and pilgrimage).

The evolution of beliefs from east to west, which once flowed more evenly from loose (east) to rigid (west), is now peppered with global influences that blur the overall pattern. But the remnants of history are still evident.

Also critical to the evolution of a religion are its various means of support and opposition. Religion has proven time and time again to be a tool of authority, and the will of authority is subject to change over time[28]. History has demonstrated that the will of an individual can affect the lives of many, and religious belief is no exception.

---

[28] Authority doesn't necessarily have to change hands to promote political instability. Al-Hakim, the third Fatmid caliph of Shi'a Islam, was a rampant anti-Sunni Muslim and prohibited many of their rituals, at least during his first 11 years in power. He then gained some unexpected sympathy, displacing his hatred of the Sunni towards the Jews and Christians and banned their religious holidays. Staying true to his moniker as the 'Mad Caliph', he reverted back to his original hatred of the Sunni 5 years later.

The Evolution of Religion

Main categorizations: Tree of evolution

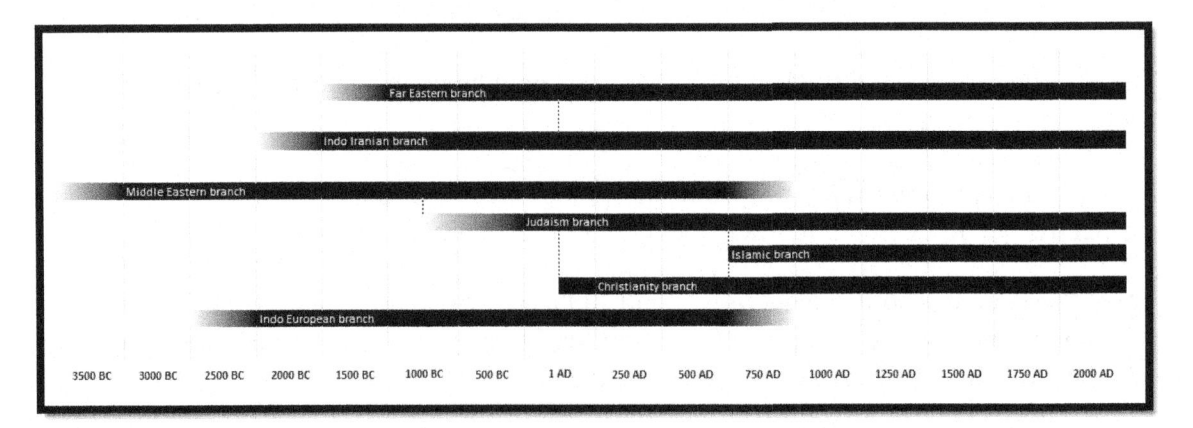

FAR EAST RELIGIONS

The theology of this region has, merely as a product of geography, isolated itself from a majority of the world. Early marine trade with India added a pinch of external influence, but their religious roadway was paved with little assistance. This would gradually change over time as Christianity was documented to enter China as early as the 7th century, but missionary work, rather than warfare, was their primary means to accomplish infiltration.

Categorically this family of religions includes only Taoic and Shenism theology. Taoic focuses on the flow of the universe (the concept of Tao, or 'The Way'). Shenism is more deity centric and mythological. The primary focus of Far East religions tends to center itself on societal harmony rather than spiritual subservience.

The religions categorized in this family are as follows:

Religion	Date originated	Current followers
Chinese Folk Religion (Shenism)	1,250 B.C.E.	450 million
Wonderism	675 B.C.E.	*extinct*
Taoism (Daoism)	475 B.C.E.	400 million
Confucianism	470 B.C.E.	6 million
Mohism	470 B.C.E.	*extinct*
Shintoism	712 C.E.	4 million
Mazuism	960 C.E.	160 million
Cao Dai	1,926 C.E.	3 million

Far East religions: Tree of evolution

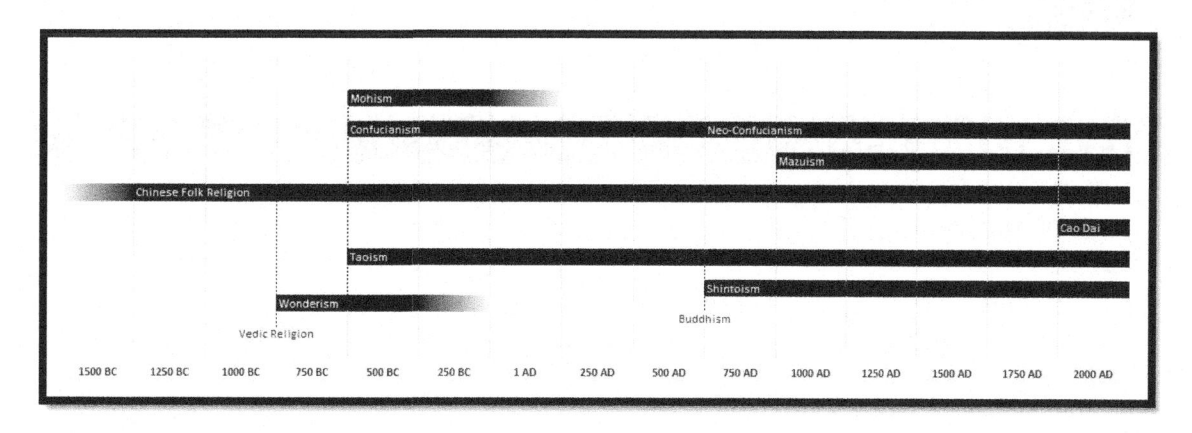

CHINESE FOLK RELIGION (SHENISM)

Date originated: 1,250 B.C.E. (possibly as early as 4,000 B.C.E.)
Region founded: China
Branched into: Wonderism, Confucianism, Mohism, Taoism, Mazuism
Deity: Shangdi (in addition to 100's of gods and goddesses)
Current followers: 450 million
Denominations: Shamanism, Animism
Rituals: food and wine sacrifices
Misc: animal sacrifice (no longer practiced), ancestor worship

Chinese Folk religion as it's know today officially originated around 1,250 B.C.E. with the composition on the oracle bones during the Shang Dynasty. The exact date of origin is unknown, but cultural celebrations depicted in artifacts suggest it may date back to 4,000 B.C.E.

Year	Support	Opposition
221 B.C.E.		The Qin Dynasty adopted Legalism as its official government philosophy and suppressed all other philosophical schools.
141 B.C.E.		Emperor Wu made Confucianism the official State ideology in China.
845 C.E.		Tang emperor Wuzong outlaws all foreign religion in support of Taoism.
1,864 C.E.		The Taiping Rebellion in southern China resulted in the replacement of

Confucianism, Buddhism, and Chinese Folk religion with Christianity.

WONDERISM

Date originated: 675 B.C.E.
Region founded: East China
Evolved from: Chinese Folk religion, Vedic religion
Branched into: Taoism
Deity: polytheistic
Current followers: extinct

Wonderism is a term coined by French sinologist Terrien de Lacouperie as a means to describe the fusion of theology of sea traders from the Indian Ocean (Vedic religion) who settled in eastern China (Folk religion), which would later evolve into Taoism (Daoism).

Year	Support	Opposition
221 B.C.E.		The Qin Dynasty adopted Legalism as its official government philosophy and suppressed all other philosophical schools.
141 B.C.E.		Emperor Wu made Confucianism the official State ideology in China.

TAOISM (DAOISM)

Date originated: 475 B.C.E.
Region founded: China
Evolved from: Chinese Folk religion, Wonderism
Branched into: Shintoism, Cao Dai
Deity: varies

Prophet / Teacher: Lao-tze (Laozi)
Current followers: 400 million
Denominations: Religious (Daojiao), Philosophical (Daojia)
Rituals: food sacrifices, t'ai chi
Misc: Ying and Yang, astrology (fortune-telling)

Taoism (modernly: Daoism) is generally considered agnostic in that God (or the Tao) is defined as incomprehensible (e.g. "The Tao that can be told is not the eternal Tao"). However, Taoism retains sparse belief in certain deities from Chinese Folk mythology, such as Yu Di (Jade Emperor). The Celestial Masters sect recognized Laozi and the *Three Pure Ones* (Wuji, Taiji, Laingyi) at the top of their pantheon.

Year	Support	Opposition
221 B.C.E.		The Qin Dynasty adopted Legalism as its official government philosophy and suppressed all other philosophical schools.
141 B.C.E.		Emperor Wu made Confucianism the official State ideology in China.
142 C.E.	Zhang Daoling starts a movement to spread Taoism.	
220 C.E.	Cao Cao, emperor of Wei, officially recognized Laozi as a divinity.	
492 C.E.	The Shangqing movement elevated the awareness of Taoism.	
731 C.E.	The Shangqing School gains official status in China through Li Yuan.	
845 C.E.	Tang emperor Wuzong outlaws all foreign religion in support of Taoism.	
1,222 C.E.	The Quanzhen School received tax exempt status from Genghis Kahn.	
1,782 C.E.		The Qianlong Emperor excluded Taoist works in the imperial library.

CONFUCIANISM

Date originated: 470 B.C.E.
Region founded: China
Evolved from: Chinese Folk religion
Branched into: Neo-Confucianism
Deity: non-theistic (Shangdi, the god of folk religion, is considered to be heaven)
Prophet / Teacher: Confucius
Current followers: 6 million
Denominations: Han, Contemporary, Japanese, Vietnamese, Singapore
Misc: women subservience, ancestor worship

Confucianism's 'non-theistic' nature has spawned debate over whether it should be classified as a religion or simply an ethical system.

Year	Support	Opposition
221 B.C.E.		The Qin Dynasty adopted Legalism as its official government philosophy and suppressed all other philosophical schools.
141 B.C.E.	Emperor Wu made Confucianism the official State ideology in China.	
606 C.E.	Emperor Yang supports Confucian education.	
618 C.E.		Li Yuan installed the already growing influence of Buddhism and Taoism as the ruling doctrines.
772 C.E.		Buddhist and Taoist growth leads to Confucianism becoming Neo-Confucianism, which eliminated the 'mystical' influences of Buddhism and Taoism.
845 C.E.		Tang emperor Wuzong of China outlaws all foreign religion in support

Year	Support	Opposition
1,241 C.E.	Emperor Lizong adopted the Confucian "Four Books" as part of the civil service scholarly requirement.	of Taoism.
1,864 C.E.		The Taiping Rebellion in southern China resulted in the replacement of Confucianism, Buddhism, and Chinese Folk religion with Christianity.
1,905 C.E.		The examination system is abolished marking the end of official Confucianism.
1,912 C.E.		'New Culture' intellectuals lead a revolt against Confucianism.

MOHISM

Date originated: circa 470 B.C.E.
Region founded: China
Evolved from: Chinese Folk religion
Branched into: Taoism (absorbed by)
Deity: Tian (the concept of Heaven and celestial justice)
Prophet / Teacher: Mozi
Current followers: extinct
Rituals: animal sacrifices (disputed)
Misc: impartial caring

Mohism was seen as a rival to Confucianism, and likely disappeared due to its overly impartial and utilitarianism take on society.

Year	Support	Opposition
221 B.C.E.		The Qin Dynasty adopted Legalism as its official government philosophy and suppressed all other philosophical schools.
141 B.C.E.		Emperor Wu made Confucianism the official State ideology in China.

SHINTOISM

Date originated: 712 C.E. (possibly as early as 500 B.C.E.)
Region founded: Japan
Evolved from: Buddhism, Taoism
Deity: Izanagi (in addition to millions of gods and goddesses)
Current followers: 4 million
Denominations: 5 branches (Shrine, Imperial Household, Folk, Sect, Old), nearly 100 sects
Prayer rituals: daily
Other rituals: Omairi (shrine ritual), Harae (offerings), Misogi (water purification), Kagura (dance ritual)
Misc: shrines

The recorded history of Shintoism dates back to an ancient chronicle known as the Kojiki composed in 712 C.E., but cultural evidence points to primal origins nearly a millennium prior. Shintoism has an amicable relationship with Buddhism, to the point of creating its own Buddhist pantheon of over 3,000 deities.

Year	Support	Opposition
1,868 C.E.	The Japanese government utilizes shrine worship to mobilize imperial loyalty.	
1,945 C.E.		The imperial era came to an end after World War II and State religious influence ceased.

MAZUISM

Date originated: 960 C.E.
Region founded: southern China
Evolved from: Chinese Folk religion
Deity: Mazu
Prophet / Teacher: Lin Moniang

Current followers: 160 million

Mazu is the 'Ancient Mother' (goddess of sailors) of the Chinese Folk pantheon.

Year	Support	Opposition
1,864 C.E.		The Taiping Rebellion in southern China resulted in the replacement of Confucianism, Buddhism, and Chinese Folk religion with Christianity.

CAO DAI

Date originated: 1,926 C.E.
Region founded: Vietnam
Evolved from: Buddhism, Taoism, Confucianism
Deity: Cao Dai (God), Tao, and Mother Buddha
Prophet / Teacher: Phạm Công Tắc
Current followers: 3 million
Denominations: 6 sects
Prayer rituals: daily
Other rituals: meditation
Food restrictions: vegetarianism
Alcohol restrictions: none
Clothing restrictions: none
Misc: non-violence

Phạm Công Tắc and two other colleagues aspired to contact spiritual entities. They received messages from spirits, saints, and eventually God. A year later 18 mediums were chosen by God to spread his teachings, and Phạm Công Tắc was considered the most important.

Year	Support	Opposition
1,975 C.E.	After the fall of Saigon, the incoming Communist government proscribed the practice of Cao Dai.	

INDO IRANIAN RELIGIONS

This family differs from Near-Eastern religions in that they migrated east rather than west, and encompass a significantly higher tendency towards agnosticism. Two dominate branches evolved from their prehistoric Iranian parent: Hinduism (dharmic) and Zoroastrianism. The Hindu partition held a more agnostic stance, and typically defined their 'wheel of life' through reincarnation, whereas the Zoroastrian side took a quasi-monotheistic route and a belief in Heaven and Hell.

The religions categorized in this family are as follows:

Religion	Date originated	Current followers
Vedic Religion	1,500 B.C.E.	*extinct*
Hinduism	900 B.C.E.	1 billion
Zoroastrianism	600 B.C.E.	150,000
Buddhism	563 B.C.E.	500 million
Jainism	557 B.C.E.	4.2 million
Mazdakism	500 B.C.E.	50,000
Mithraism	80 B.C.E.	*extinct*
Sikhism	1,469 C.E.	30 million
Tenrikyo	1,838 C.E.	2 million
Brahma Kumaris	1,932 C.E.	825,000
Scientology	1,952 C.E.	50,000

Indo Iranian religions: Tree of evolution

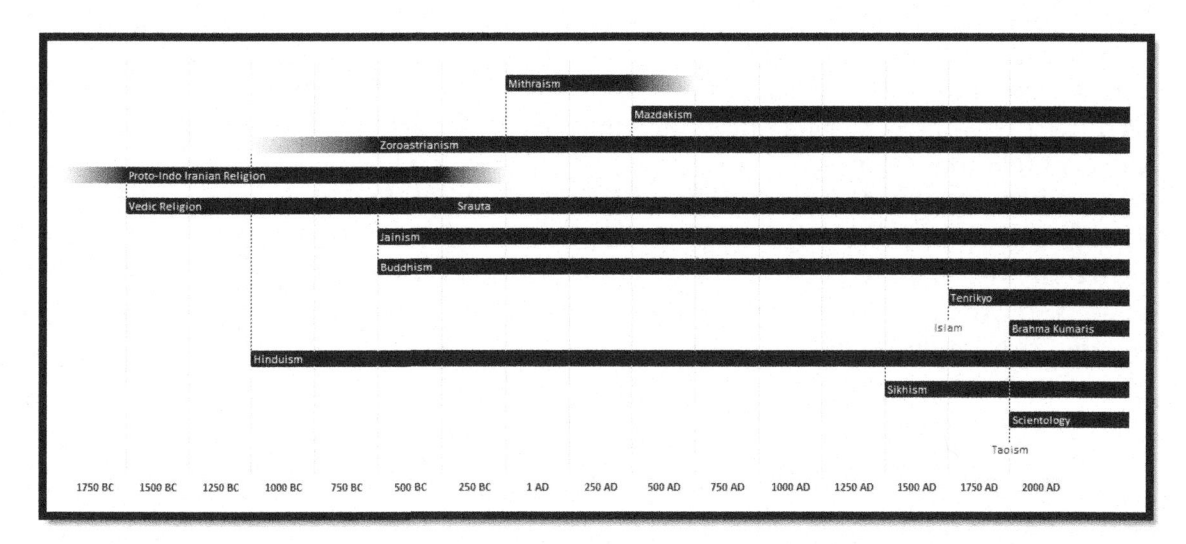

VEDIC RELIGION

Date originated: circa 1,500 B.C.E.
Region founded: northern India
Evolved from: proto-indo Iranian religion
Branched into: Hinduism, Buddhism, Jainism
Deity: Indra (in addition to 32 gods and goddesses)
Current followers: extinct
Prayer rituals: chanting of hymns
Other rituals: Agnistoma (consumption and sacrifice of Soma)
Misc: Purushamedha (symbolic human sacrifice), animal sacrifice, yoga

The transition from Vedic religion into Hinduism started around 900 B.C.E. and ended around 500 B.C.E., retaining the majority of its original tenets in the Śrauta branch.

HINDUISM

Date originated: 900 B.C.E.
Region founded: India
Evolved from: Vedic religion
Branched into: Sikhism, Brahma Kumaris
Deity: varies – Shiva, Vishnu (in addition to 330 million gods and goddesses)
Current followers: 1 billion
Denominations: Bhakti, Vaishnavism, Shaivism, Shaktism, Smartism, Puranas, Śrauta
Prayer rituals: morning prayer after bathing
Other rituals: cremation
Food restrictions: no beef
Alcohol restrictions: in moderation
Misc: caste system, reincarnation, karma, yoga

Hinduism borders on being agnostic, ultimately worshipping Brahman: the unchanging reality amidst and beyond the world. The Vedas (Vedic texts) lists 33 deities followed by the Sanskrit word *koti*, which can mean "class" or a number equal to 10 million, which multiplied by 33 yields 330 million gods. It is also said to symbolize "infinity", indicating infinite forms of God.

Year	Support	Opposition
800 C.E.	Several Hindu philosophers influence Jain persecution and forcible conversions.	
1,001 – 1,398 C.E.		The gradual Muslim conquest of India results in a massive conversion to Islam.
1,775 C.E.	The Marathas (Indian warrior caste) end Islamic rule in India, and Hinduism makes a comeback.	

ZOROASTRIANISM

Date originated: 600 B.C.E. (possibly as early as 1,500 B.C.E.)

Region founded: Persia (Iran)
Evolved from: proto-indo Iranian religion
Branched into: Mazdakism, Mithraism
Deity: Ahura Mazda (illuminating wisdom), Angra Mainyu (destructive spirit)
Prophet / Teacher: Zoroaster (Zarathushtra)
Current followers: 150,000
Denominations: Parsis, Quadimis, Faslis
Prayer rituals: before meals
Other rituals: Navjote (girdle initiation), Barashnum (nine-night purification ritual)
Alcohol restrictions: in moderation
Clothing restrictions: head covering, sedreh and kushti (girdle)

With Ahura Mazda being the primary god of worship and supreme creator, Zoroastrianism is the first of the Proto-Indo Iranian family to delve into a form of monotheism, which likely predated Judaism. Unlike Abrahamic afterlife beliefs, Zoroastrian hell is reformative (punishment fits the crime) rather than detrimental (e.g. Christianity).

Year	Support	Opposition
539 B.C.E.	Cyrus the Great of the Persian Empire invades Mesopotamia, permitting a Zoroastrian influence.	
330 B.C.E.		Alexander the Great of Macedonia invades Persia, and many Zoroastrian texts are destroyed.
228 C.E.	Ardashir comes into power and promotes Zoroastrianism in Iran	
651 C.E.		Persia is overthrown by Muslim Arabs.
750 – 1,258 C.E.		Gradual persecution of non-Muslims slowly coverts the majority of Zoroastrians to Islam.

BUDDHISM

Date originated: 563 B.C.E.
Region founded: Magadha (eastern India)
Evolved from: Vedic religion
Branched into: Shintoism, Cao Dai, Tenrikyo
Deity: non-theistic
Prophet / Teacher: Siddhartha Gautama (Buddha)
Current followers: 500 million
Denominations: Theravada (16 sects), Mahayana (28 sects), Vajrayana (24 sects), Sthaviravāda (11 sects), Mahāsāmghika (9 sects)
Prayer rituals: meditation
Other rituals: bowing, pilgrimage, offerings, chanting
Food restrictions: primarily vegetarian, in moderation
Alcohol restrictions: in moderation
Misc: karma, non-violence, yoga

Born into royalty, Siddhartha Gautama exposed himself to the lives of the commoners and their suffering. This compelled him to embark on a quest, which ultimately inspired the 'Four Noble Truths', the heart of Buddhism. During its origin, Buddhism was little more than a 'cleansed' branch of Hinduism without the caste system. It wasn't until its acceptance in China that it developed an estranged identity.

Year	Support	Opposition
261 B.C.E.	The Mauryan emperor Asoka sent emissaries to countries outside of India to spread Buddhism.	
185 B.C.E		Pusyamitra Sunga of the Sunga Dynasty (northern India) authorized the destruction of Buddhist monasteries and killing of 1000's of Buddhist monks.
180 B.C.E.	Demetrius of Bactria (Afghanistan) invades and conquers north-east India and allows Buddhism to expand.	
534 C.E.	King Chinhung of Korea makes Buddhism the official state religion.	
540 C.E.		Buddhism weakens north of India after the Hephthalite invasion.
618 - 845 C.E.	The Tang Dynasty (north and east China) was open to foreign	

	influenced, and Buddhism flourished.	
711 C.E.		Muhammad bin Qasim's invasion of Sindh (Pakistan) sought to replace Buddhism with Islam.
845 C.E.		Tang emperor Wuzong of China outlaws all foreign religion in support of Taoism.
1,001 – 1,398 C.E.		The gradual Muslim conquest of India results in millions of Buddhist casualties.
1,127 – 1,279 C.E.	The Song Dynasty (east China) allows Buddhism to prosper.	
1,275 C.E.	The reign of the Mongols north of India created a surge in Buddhism.	
1,864 C.E.		The Taiping Rebellion in southern China resulted in the replacement of Confucianism, Buddhism, and Chinese Folk religion with Christianity.

JAINISM

Date originated: 557 B.C.E.
Region founded: India
Evolved from: Vedic religion
Deity: non-theistic in regards to a creator (believe in demi-gods that are not to be worshipped)
Prophet / Teacher: Vardhamana Mahavira
Current followers: 4.2 million
Denominations: 8 sects
Prayer rituals: non-material, non-request (gesture of respect)
Other rituals: meditation

Food restrictions: lacto-vegetarian, no night meals, fasting (Santhara)
Alcohol restrictions: no fermented beverages
Clothing restrictions: simple attire
Misc: reincarnation, karma, non-violence, celibacy

Vardhamana Mahavira was born into royalty, but renounced his kingdom and family and went into seclusion for 13 years where he meditated and cleansed himself of all pleasures. Upon his return he devoted the remainder of his life to the preaching of Jainism. The origins of Jainism are lengthy and difficult to trace, which hindered the impact of its influence.

Year	Support	Opposition
170 B.C.E.	Emperor Kharavela of Kaligna (East India) propagates Jainism.	
800 C.E.		Several Hindu philosophers influence Jain persecution and forcible conversions.
1,130 C.E.		Minister Brahmana Basava and the Hoysala king Vishnuvardhana overtook temples, and tortured and converted many Jain worshipers.
1,001 – 1,398 C.E.		The gradual Muslim conquest of India results in a massive conversion to Islam.

MAZDAKISM

Date originated: 500 B.C.E.
Region founded: Persia
Evolved from: Zoroastrianism
Deity: Ahura Mazda (illuminating wisdom), Angra Mainyu (destructive spirit)
Prophet / Teacher: Mazdak
Current followers: 50,000
Prayer rituals: before meals
Food restrictions: vegetarianism
Alcohol restrictions: in moderation
Misc: non-violence, early form of Communism

Mazdak philosophers took Zoroastrianism in a hedonistic direction with the pursuit and fulfillment of life's pleasures.

Year	Support	Opposition
500 C.E.	King Kavadh of Persia converts to and sponsors Mazdakism, stifling Zoroastrian worship.	
529 C.E.		Hephthalite pressure leads to a murderous campaign against the Mazdakis, restoring Zoroastrianism.

MITHRAISM

Date originated: 80 B.C.E.
Region founded: Rome / Greece
Evolved from: Zoroastrianism
Deity: Mithra
Current followers: extinct
Prayer rituals: unknown
Other rituals: 7 grades of initiation
Food restrictions: unknown
Misc: men only

Zoroastrian mythology migrated through to the Roman Republic to inspire this mysterious following. Mithraism was perhaps the first recognized 'cult' with its underground temple worship, initiation rituals, and explicit membership.

Year	Support	Opposition
394 C.E.		Theodosius of Rome forbade non-Christian worship, all but putting an end to Mithraism.

SIKHISM

Date originated: 1,469 C.E.
Region founded: Pakistan
Evolved from: Hinduism
Deity: Waheguru
Prophet / Teacher: Guru Nanak
Current followers: 30 million
Denominations: 15 sects
Prayer rituals: morning prayer after bathing, before and after eating
Other rituals: cremation, baptism, meditation
Food restrictions: can only eat meat of an animal slaughtered via 'Jhatka'
Alcohol restrictions: no alcohol, drugs, or tobacco
Clothing restrictions: men wear turbans
Misc: reincarnation, cutting hair is forbidden

Guru Nanak had a vision at the age of 30 from which he concluded that both Hinduism and Islam were the wrong paths to God. From there Nanak embarked on several major journeys to spread the principles of the Sikhism.

Year	Support	Opposition
1,699 C.E.	The Khalsa (army of God) is established and many Muslim and Mughal territories are conquered.	
1,799 C.E.	Maharaja Ranjit Singh captures Lahore in Pakistan establishing the Sikh Kingdom of Punjab.	
1,947 C.E.		The Anglo-Sikh wars result in the partition of British India resulting in the death and displacement of millions of Sikhs.

TENRIKYO

Date originated: 1,838 C.E.
Region founded: Japan
Evolved from: Buddhism, Christianity
Deity: Tenri-O-no-Mikoto
Prophet / Teacher: Nakayama Miki
Current followers: 2 million
Prayer rituals: twice daily
Misc: reincarnation

Originally set on becoming a Buddhist nun, Miki became a medium for God at the age of 40 after taking part in a Shugendo exorcism ceremony. 'God the Parent' (Tenri-O-no-Mikoto) spoke through her saying, "I am God of origin, God in truth. There is causality in this residence. At this time I have descended here to save all humankind. I wish to receive Miki as the shrine of God."

Year	Support	Opposition
1,872 C.E.	Tenrikyo is authorized by the Japanese government as one of the official 13 Shinto Sects.	

BRAHMA KUMARIS

Date originated: 1,932 C.E.
Region founded: India
Evolved from: Hinduism, Islam
Deity: Shiva (same as the Abrahamic god)
Prophet / Teacher: Lekhraj Kripalani
Current followers: 825,000
Prayer rituals: daily
Other rituals: Raja yoga
Food restrictions: lacto-vegetarian
Alcohol restrictions: no alcohol or tobacco

Clothing restrictions: generally white (symbolizing purity)
Misc: reincarnation, karma

Lekhraj Kripalani was a jewel supplier in Pakistan until he started having visions at age 50 whereby his business partner Sevak Ram became the manifestation of the god Shiva. Together they started a spiritual organization, but Sevek left 10 years later allowing Lakhraj to assume complete control.

SCIENTOLOGY

Date originated: 1,952 C.E.
Region founded: New Jersey, USA
Evolved from: Hinduism, Taoism
Deity: Xenu
Prophet / Teacher: L. Ron Hubbard
Current followers: 50,000 (200,000 at its peak)
Misc: auditing of engrams (traumatic subconscious memories), aversion to psychiatry

Scientology bares similarities to Hinduism in that their life cycle beliefs are analogous to reincarnation. Hubbard was said to have also been influenced by William Durant, author of *The Story of Philosophy*.

Year	Support	Opposition
1,990 C.E. - present		A negative portrayal by the media led to government investigations and mass criticism.

NEAR-EAST RELIGIONS

The Near-East is the primary source of modern day western religion. The original belief systems having gone extinct, what prevails today, with the exception of a handful of off-shoots, are the Abrahamic religions (i.e. Judaism, Christianity, and Islam).

Similarities aside, these three faiths have essentially been poised as competitors since their founding.

The religions categorized in this family are as follows:

Judaism branch

Religion	Date originated	Current followers
Mesopotamian Religion	3,750 B.C.E.	*extinct*
Egyptian Religion	3,500 B.C.E.	*extinct*
Sumerian Religion	3,500 B.C.E.	*extinct*
Canaanite Religion	2,500 B.C.E.	*extinct*
Edomite Religion	1,000 B.C.E.	*extinct*
Judaism (Pharisees)	950 B.C.E.	13.4 million
Sadducees	200 B.C.E.	*extinct*
Essenes	200 B.C.E.	*extinct*
Zealotry	6 C.E.	*extinct*
Elcasaites	220 C.E.	*extinct*
Mandaeanism / Sabian	904 C.E.	*endangered*
Thelema	1,904 C.E.	5,000
Wiccan	1,954 C.E.	800,000

Christianity branch

Religion	Date originated	Current followers
Christianity	30 C.E.	2.2 billion
Catholicism	200 C.E.	1.2 billion
Manichaeism	228 C.E.	*extinct*
Oriental Orthodoxy	451 C.E.	82 million
Eastern Orthodoxy	1,054 C.E.	230 million
Lutheranism	1,521 C.E.	75 million
Anabaptist	1,525 C.E.	5 million
Calvinism (Reformed)	1,536 C.E.	75 million
Anglicanism (Episcopal)	1,549 C.E.	85 million
Puritanism	1,558 C.E.	*extinct*
Presbyterianism	1,592 C.E.	40 million
Baptists	1,609 C.E.	100 million
Quakers	1,647 C.E.	400,000
Evangelicalism (Pietism)	1,675 C.E.	80 million
Amish / Mennonites	1,693 C.E.	250,000
Methodism	1,729 C.E.	75 million
Mormonism	1,830 C.E.	14.1 million

Seventh-day Adventism	1,840 C.E.	17 million
Jehovah's Witnesses	1,870 C.E.	7.5 million
Pentecostalism	1,900 C.E.	279 million

Islamic branch

Religion	Date originated	Current followers
Islam	610 C.E.	1.3 billion
Sunni Islam	661 C.E.	1.1 billion
Shi'a Islam	661 C.E.	200 million
Sufism	850 C.E.	7.5 million
Druze	1,017 C.E.	1 million
Babism	1,844 C.E.	*endangered*
Baha'i Faith	1,863 C.E.	6 million
Ahmadiyya	1,889 C.E.	10 million

Near East religions (Judaism branch): Tree of evolution

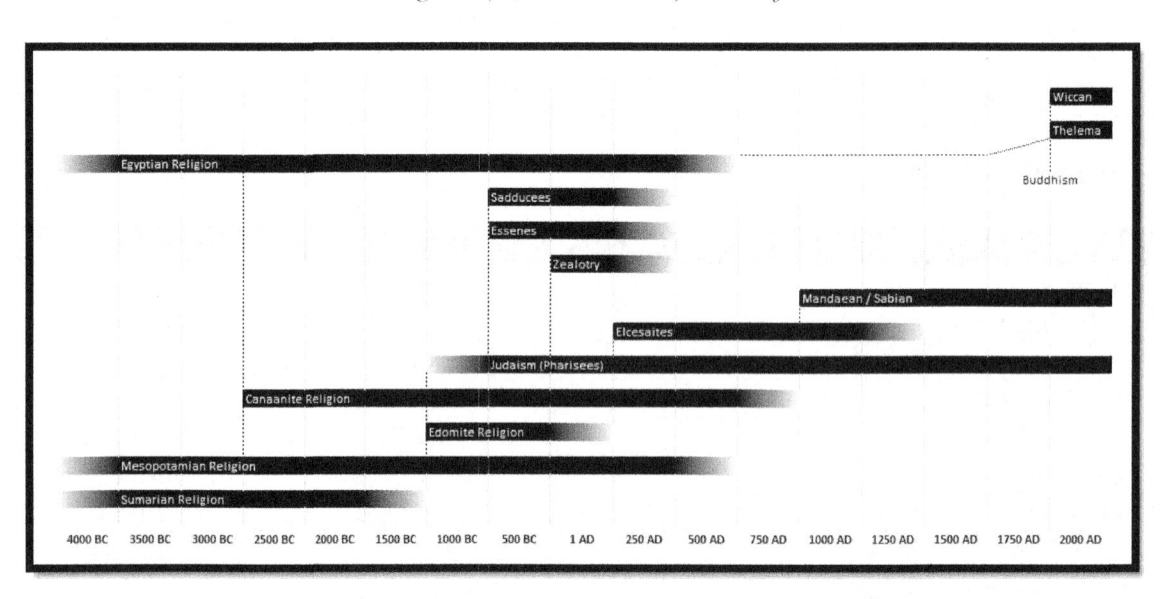

MESOPOTAMIAN RELIGION

Date originated: circa 3,750 B.C.E.
Region founded: Mesopotamia (Iraq)
Branched into: Canaanite religion, Edomite religion
Deity: Marduk (in addition to over 2,400 gods and goddesses)
Current followers: extinct

Once viewed as amicable equals, around 1,750 B.C.E. the cult of Marduk (worshipped primarily in Babylon) eclipsed the cult of Enlil (Lord of the Storm, worshipped primarily in Nippur) resulting in Marduk's supremacy over the Mesopotamian pantheon.

Year	Support	Opposition
1,307 – 1,077 B.C.E.	Much of Syria and the Mediterranean coastal regions fall to the Assyrian Empire.	
934 - 841 B.C.E.	The Neo-Assyrian Empire conquers the entirety of the Canaanite region.	
604 B.C.E.	The Babylonians under King Nebuchadnezzar conquer Jerusalem.	
539 B.C.E.		Cyrus the Great of the Persian Empire invades Mesopotamia crippling the religion with Zoroastrian influence.
330 B.C.E.		Alexander the Great of Macedonia overthrew the Persians and brought a Hellenistic influence.
100 C.E.		Judaism and Christianity spread throughout the Roman Empire.

EGYPTIAN RELIGION

Date originated: circa 3,500 B.C.E.
Region founded: Egypt
Branched into: Canaanite religion, Thelema
Deity: Ra, Amun, Atum (in addition to over 2,000 gods and goddesses)
Current followers: extinct
Rituals: morning offering at temples, circumcision
Misc: magic, animal cults, burial or tomb mummification

Egyptian mythology is thought to have influenced many Roman religious concepts during the 4th century, like the Egyptian perception of the afterlife: Elysium (described in Homer's Odyssey), Hell from Duat (Egyptian underworld), and the iconography of Mary from the goddess Isis (mother of Horus).

Year	Support	Opposition
1,650 B.C.E.		The Theban Pharaohs promote their God Amun over Ra.
1,600 B.C.E.	The Nubians absorb Egyptian religion, adopting Amun as their supreme God.	
1,344 B.C.E.		Pharaoh Akhenaten (Amenhotep IV) abolishes the worship of all other Gods accept for the sun-disk Aten (first documented practice of monotheistic worship in history).
1,335 B.C.E.	Akhenaten's successors restore polytheism and Amun's supremacy.	
1,000 B.C.E.		Egyptian reign grew weaker, and the Goddess Isis becomes the most popular.
305 B.C.E.		Ptolemy Lagides takes over and merges Hellenistic worship in with traditional Egyptian worship.
350 C.E.		As Egypt grew significantly weaker Christian emperors replace Egyptian temples and icons with their own.

SUMERIAN RELIGION

Date originated: circa 3,500 B.C.E.
Region founded: southern Mesopotamia (Iraq)
Deity: An, Enlil (in addition to over 3,600 gods and goddesses)
Current followers: extinct

Due to their proximity, the Sumerian religion shared much of its mythology with Mesopotamia including deities like Enlil, Nanna, Ninlil, as well as developing counterparts with the Mesopotamian pantheon (e.g. An and Anu, and Inanna and Ishtar).

Year	Support	Opposition
2,004 B.C.E.		The Ur dynasty fell to the Elamites from the east.

CANAANITE RELIGION

Date originated: 2,500 B.C.E.
Region founded: Levant region
Evolved from: Mesopotamian religion, Egyptian religion
Branched into: Judaism, Edomite religion
Deity: El Elyon (in addition to 100's of gods and goddesses)
Current followers: extinct
Rituals: circumcision

Mesopotamian and Egyptian influence shows up in the Canaanite religion in the form of shared iconography and rituals.

Year	Support	Opposition
1,800 B.C.E.	The Canaanites invade and conquer the eastern Delta of Egypt.	
1,674 B.C.E.	The Canaanites conquer lower Egypt.	
1,595 B.C.E.		The Hittites eject the Amorites from Babylonia.
1,550 B.C.E.		Pharaoh Ahmose drives the Canaanites out of Egypt.
1,307 – 1,077 B.C.E.		Much of Syria and the Mediterranean coastal regions fall to the Assyrian Empire.
934 - 841 B.C.E.		The Neo-Assyrian Empire conquers the entirety of the Canaanite region.
605 B.C.E.		Civil war between the Assyrians weakens control allowing the Babylonians to conquer the western portion.
539 B.C.E.		The Babylonian Empire collapses and Canaan falls to the Persians.
332 B.C.E. - 637 C.E.		Power changes hands from Alexander the Great of Greece, to the Romans, then to Byzantium (Constantinople), and lastly to the Muslims.

EDOMITE RELIGION

Date originated: 1,000 B.C.E.
Region founded: Israel
Evolved from: Mesopotamian religion, Canaanite religion
Deity: Qaus, El (in addition to several gods and goddesses)
Current followers: extinct
Rituals: circumcision

Many of the Edomite deities were influenced by Canaanite mythology.

Year	Support	Opposition
163 B.C.E.		The Edomites were conquered by Judah Maccabee of Jerusalem and forcibly converted to Judaism.

JUDAISM (PHARISEES)

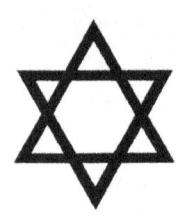

Date originated: 950 - 450 B.C.E.
Region founded: Israel
Evolved from: Canaanite religion
Branched into: Sadducees, Zealotry, Essenes, Elcesaites, Christianity
Deity: Yahweh
Prophet / Teacher: Abraham, Moses, Jacob, Isaac, Isaiah, Amos, Hosea (in addition to approximately 50 others)
Current followers: 13.4 million
Denominations: 8 denominations
Prayer rituals: thrice daily
Other rituals: Shabbat, circumcision
Food restrictions: Cannot eat meat and dairy products together, no pork or shellfish, cannot eat 'non-kosher' food, fasting (Yom Kippur)
Alcohol restrictions: in moderation
Clothing restrictions: head covered during worship (Kippah)
Misc: accept purgatory, animal sacrifice (no longer practiced)

The war god Yahweh enters the faith in 950 B.C.E. and replaces El Elyon of the Canaanite religion. Judaism was championed by the Hebrew prophets Isaiah, Amos, and Hosea in 750 B.C.E., whose legacy was adopted by King Josiah a century later.

Year	Support	Opposition
722 B.C.E.		The Assyrians conquer Israel and the Israelites are displaced to the south.
701 B.C.E.	Hezekiah, King of Judah, removed worship of foreign deities and restored the worship of Yahweh.	
622 B.C.E.	King Josiah of Israel discovers the book of Deuteronomy and declares sole worship to Yahweh.	
586 B.C.E.		The Babylonians under King Nebuchadnezzar conquer Jerusalem.
300 B.C.E.	Primitive Judaism spreads to Egypt.	
163 B.C.E.	The Edomites were conquered by Judah Maccabee of Jerusalem and forcibly converted to Judaism.	
63 B.C.E.		Pompey the Great of the Roman Republic assists Hyrcanus II in his siege of Jerusalem.
73 C.E.		Hadrian of Rome conquers the Judea Province and bans circumcision.
136 C.E.		The Romans under Hadrian bans the study of the Torah.
150 C.E. (approx)	Jews were granted Roman citizenship and Judaism was a recognized religion.	
380 C.E.		Judaism was rejected by the Roman government in favor of Christianity.
523 C.E.	Yūsuf Dhū Nuwās conquers Yemen and persecutes the Christians in favor of Judaism.	
1,099 C.E.		The Catholic crusades results in the massacre of the Jewish inhabitants of Jerusalem.

1,244 C.E.		The Khwarezmids destroys the city of Jerusalem.
1,945 C.E.		Nazi Germany exterminates nearly 6 million Jews during the Holocaust.

SADDUCEES

Date originated: circa 200 B.C.E.
Region founded: Israel
Evolved from: Judaism
Deity: Yahweh
Prophet / Teacher: Tzadok, Boethus (disputed)
Current followers: extinct
Prayer rituals: thrice daily
Other rituals: Shabbat, circumcision
Misc: reject the concept of an afterlife

Sadducees was considered an elite form of traditional Judaism intended for more prosperous members of Judean society.

Year	Support	Opposition
70 C.E.		Roman troops under Titus destroy Herod's Temple during the Siege of Jerusalem.

ESSENES

Date originated: circa 200 B.C.E.
Region founded: Palestine, Syria
Evolved from: Judaism
Deity: Yahweh
Prophet / Teacher: unknown
Current followers: extinct
Prayer rituals: thrice daily
Other rituals: Shabbat, circumcision
Misc: asceticism (celibacy)

The communally stringent Essenes are said to have taken credit for the discovery of the religious documents known as the Dead Sea Scrolls.

Year	Support	Opposition
70 C.E.		Roman troops under Titus destroy Herod's Temple during the Siege of Jerusalem.

ZEALOTRY

Date originated: 6 C.E.
Region founded: Israel
Evolved from: Judaism
Deity: Yahweh
Prophet / Teacher: Judas of Galilee
Current followers: extinct
Rituals: Shabbat, circumcision

The Zealots comprised a political movement that was characterized as 'murderous' towards Roman opposition, as well as other Jews who were against their cause.

Year	Support	Opposition
66 C.E.	The Jewish Revolt succeeded if reclaiming Jerusalem from Rome.	
70 C.E.		Roman troops under Titus destroy Herod's Temple during the Siege of Jerusalem.

ELCESAITES

Date originated: 220 C.E.
Region founded: Sassanid (Persia)
Evolved from: Judaism
Branched into: Mandaeanism, Manichaeism
Deity: Yahweh
Prophet / Teacher: Elchasai, Alcibiades of Apamea
Current followers: extinct
Other rituals: baptism, circumcision

A story from Alcibiades circulated that a giant angel 96 miles tall (the Son of God) accompanied by his sister of similar proportions (the Holy Ghost) presented a book to Elchasai which described a new remission of sins through a contemporary form of baptism.

MANDAEANISM / SABIAN

Date originated: 904 C.E.
Region founded: Yemen
Evolved from: Elcesaites
Deity: a formless representation of two opposites (dualism)
Prophet / Teacher: John the Baptist (also Adam, Abel, Seth, Enosh, Noah, Shem, Aram)
Current followers: endangered (70,000 at its peak)
Prayer rituals: daily
Other rituals: baptism
Food restrictions: no red meat
Alcohol restrictions: not allowed
Clothing restrictions: primarily white

Manchaeans were thought to be a sect of the Elcesaites, as well as exhibiting influences from several other small religious sects of the Mesopotamian region.

Year	Support	Opposition
2,007 C.E.		The Iraq war displaced and eliminated many Mandaean followers.

THELEMA

Date originated: 1,904 C.E.
Region founded: England
Evolved from: Egyptian religion, Buddhism, Astrology
Branched into: Wiccan
Deity: Nuit, Hadit, Ra-Hoor-Khuit, Harpocrates, Babalon, and Therion (Egyptian deities)
Prophet / Teacher: Aleister Crowley
Current followers: 5,000
Denominations: Astrum Argentium, Ordo Templi Orientis
Food restrictions: none
Alcohol restrictions: none
Clothing restrictions: none
Misc: yoga, magic

François Rabelais, a former Catholic monk, was said to have coined the phrase "do what thou wilt" in the 16th century. Sir Francis Dashwood, an English politician, took this theme and established the *Hellfire Club* in 1749. Aleister Crowley, an English occultist, claimed to receive the *Book of Law* from a divine voice named Aiwass during his honeymoon in Egypt.

WICCAN

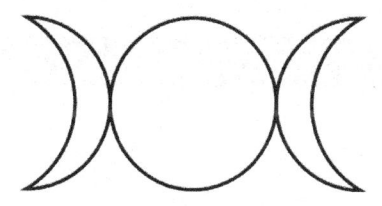

Date originated: 1,954 C.E.
Region founded: England
Evolved from: Thelema
Deity: Triple Goddess and Horned God

Prophet / Teacher: Gerald Gardner
Current followers: 800,000
Denominations: 2 sects
Rituals: meditation, Esbat (coven meeting during full moon)
Food restrictions: none
Alcohol restrictions: none
Clothing restrictions: none
Misc: reincarnation, witchcraft

English author and self proclaimed witch Gerald Gardner was once a high ranking member of the Thelema order until he incorporated the element of witchcraft, ultimately shaping his own belief system.

Near East religions (Christianity branch): Tree of evolution

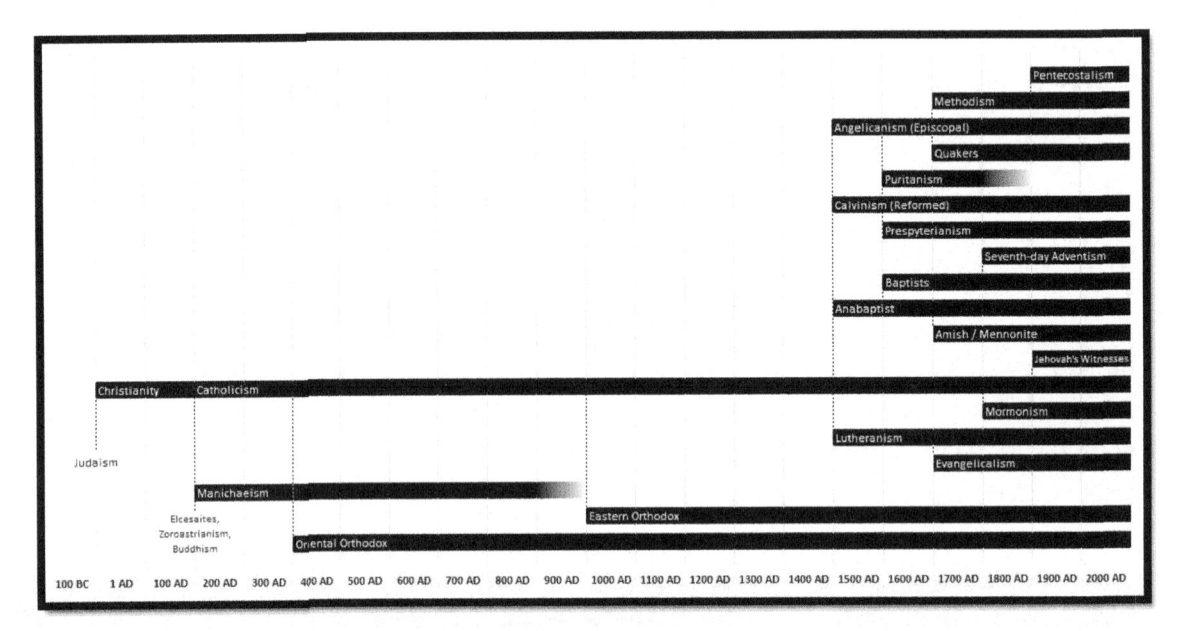

CHRISTIANITY

Date originated: 30 C.E.

Region founded: Levant region
Evolved from: Judaism
Branched into: Catholicism, Protestantism, Mormonism, Jehovah's Witnesses, Manichaeism
Deity: Yahweh
Prophet / Teacher: Jesus of Nazareth
Current followers: 2.2 billion
Denominations: approximately 41,000 denominations
Prayer rituals: daily
Other rituals: baptism
Food restrictions: none
Alcohol restrictions: in moderation
Clothing restrictions: none

Jesus' birth and life was prophesized some 300 times in the Old Testament.

Year	Support	Opposition
30 - 313 C.E.		The Roman Empire begins persecuting Christians resulting in some 50,000 executions.
43 - 430 C.E.	Several African bishops and scholars contribute to the rise of Christianity in northern Africa.	
313 C.E.	Emperor Constantine legalizes Christianity in the Roman Empire.	

CATHOLICISM

Date originated: 200 C.E.
Region founded: Rome
Evolved from: Christianity
Branched into: Orthodoxy

Deity: Yahweh
Prophet / Teacher: Jesus of Nazareth (St Peter)
Current followers: 1.2 billion
Denominations: 9 rites (Benedictine, Cistercian, Carthusian, Carmalite, Dominican, Premonstratensian, Franciscan, Friars Minor Capuchin, Servite)
Prayer rituals: daily
Other rituals: baptism
Food restrictions: fasting (Lent)
Alcohol restrictions: in moderation
Clothing restrictions: none
Misc: ecclesiastical leadership (Pope is highest ranking bishop), penance (confession), accept purgatory

St Peter found the first Catholic Church in Rome and served as its bishop after Jesus' death (i.e. *Matthew 16:18-19*), however the central bishop didn't have authority over the clergy in his city till around 200 C.E.

Year	Support	Opposition
328 C.E.	King Ezana conquers Aksum (Ethiopia) and installed Christianity as the state religion.	
331 C.E.	Alexander the Great of Rome conquers Alexandria in Egypt and installs Christianity several decades later.	
380 C.E.	Christianity becomes the state religion of the Roman Empire under Theodosius I.	
523 C.E.		Yūsuf Dhū Nuwās conquers Yemen and persecutes the Christians in favor of Judaism.
782 C.E.	1000's of Pagan's are massacred in Germany.	
1,184 – 1,860 C.E.	Inquisitions are established throughout Europe utilizing torture and death to suppress heresy and secure religious unity.	
1,204 C.E.		The Crusades fail to stifle Islamic aggression and result in the sacking of Constantinople.
1,453 C.E.		Islam overtakes Christian

		congregations in Africa.
1,567 C.E.	Spanish settlers establish ongoing reforms to forcibly convert Native Americans to Catholicism.	
1,593 C.E.		Calvinism and Catholicism are officially banned in Sweden.
1,685 C.E.	Louis XIV of France revokes the Edict of Nantes, forcing nearly 1 million Protestants to flee France or convert to Catholicism.	
1,864 C.E.	The Taiping Rebellion in southern China resulted in the replacement of Confucianism, Buddhism, and Chinese Folk religion with Christianity.	

MANICHAEISM

Date originated: 228 C.E.
Region founded: Persia (Babylon / Iraq)
Evolved from: Elcesaites, Christianity, Zoroastrianism, Buddhism
Deity: Zurvan (from Zoroastrian mythology) in addition to some 20 deities
Prophet / Teacher: Mani
Current followers: extinct
Prayer rituals: daily
Other rituals: Bema fest
Food restrictions: fasting
Misc: confession

Mani received revelations at the age of 12 and 24. He claimed to be the reincarnation of Buddha, Krishna, Zoroaster, and Jesus, but felt these religious beliefs were incomplete.

Year	Support	Opposition
291 - 296 C.E.		The growth of Manichaeism threatens surrounding religions resulting in their murder and persecution in Persia and Egypt.
382 C.E.		Theodosius of Rome issues a decree for the death of Manichaean monks.

762 C.E.	Khagan Boku Tekin, the king of Uighur (western China), made Manichaeism the state religion (overthrown in 840).	
780 C.E.		Muhammad ibn Mansur al-Mahdi established an inquisition in Persia against Manichaeism.

ORIENTAL ORTHODOXY

Date originated: 451 C.E.
Region founded: Egypt
Evolved from: Catholicism
Deity: Yahweh
Prophet / Teacher: Jesus of Nazareth (Pope Dioscrous)
Current followers: 82 million
Denominations: Coptic, Ethiopian, Eritrean, Syriac, Malankara (Indian), Armenian Apostolic
Prayer rituals: daily
Other rituals: baptism, confession
Food restrictions: fasting
Alcohol restrictions: in moderation
Clothing restrictions: none
Misc: ecclesiastical leadership (4 bishops responsible for 4 separate territories), accept purgatory

The Orthodoxy broke with the Catholic Church after the Council of Chalcedon in 451 C.E. based primarily on disputes over specifics about the 'trinity'. The nomenclature 'oriental' refers to eastern Africa and the Middle East, rather than Asia.

EASTERN ORTHODOXY

Date originated: 1,054 C.E.
Region founded: Rome
Evolved from: Catholicism
Deity: Yahweh
Prophet / Teacher: Jesus of Nazareth (St Paul)
Current followers: 230 million
Denominations: Patriarchate, Nationalist, Traditionalist
Prayer rituals: daily (mostly sung)
Other rituals: baptism, confession
Food restrictions: fasting
Alcohol restrictions: in moderation
Clothing restrictions: none
Misc: ecclesiastical leadership (all bishops are seen as equal), penance (confession), accept purgatory

Disputes with the Catholic Church over specifics about the trinity, original sin, free will, purgatory, hell, but most importantly the hierarchy of bishops resulted in the 'Great Schism' and split with Rome.

LUTHERANISM

Date originated: 1,521 C.E.
Region founded: Germany
Evolved from: Catholicism
Branched into: Evangelicalism

Deity: Yahweh
Prophet / Teacher: Jesus of Nazareth (Martin Luther)
Current followers: 75 million
Prayer rituals: daily
Other rituals: baptism
Food restrictions: none
Alcohol restrictions: in moderation
Clothing restrictions: none
Misc: strict adherence to the Bible

In 1,510 C.E. Catholic priest Martin Luther began questioning the church's interpretation of 'justification', whereby a priest can grant salvation to a sinner. Martin taught that only through God and one's faith in Christ can salvation be granted (i.e. *Psalm 103:19,* et al). This proclaimed heresy led to the Edict of Worms in 1521, where Martin Luther and his followers were excommunicated from the Catholic Church.

Year	Support	Opposition
1,532 C.E.	Two monarchs in Scandinavia adopt Lutheranism resulting in many conversions.	
1,593 C.E.	Calvinism and Catholicism are officially banned in Sweden.	
1,685 C.E.		Louis XIV of France revokes the Edict of Nantes, forcing nearly 1 million Protestants to flee France or convert to Catholicism.

ANABAPTIST

Date originated: 1,525 C.E.
Region founded: Switzerland
Evolved from: Catholicism
Branched into: Baptist, Amish
Deity: Yahweh

Prophet / Teacher: Jesus of Nazareth (Petr Chelcicky)
Current followers: 5 million
Denominations: 6 sects
Prayer rituals: daily
Other rituals: baptism (believers only)
Food restrictions: none
Alcohol restrictions: in moderation
Clothing restrictions: none
Misc: non-violence, cannot take oaths, believers cannot hold government office, excommunication for the unfaithful

In 1,420 C.E. Petr Chelcicky began teaching his beliefs that God is the only power of authority for the believer, who therefore should not hold government office (i.e. *Acts 5:29*). Nearly a century later corruption in the clergy and excessive taxation led to the German Peasants' War. This battle against government and religious oppression, as well as Chelcicky's teachings, inspired the origins of the Anabaptist faith.

Year	Support	Opposition
1,527 C.E.		Roman Catholic leaders and several Protestant monarchs throughout Europe order the persecution of Anabaptists.
1,685 C.E.		Louis XIV of France revokes the Edict of Nantes, forcing nearly 1 million Protestants to flee France or convert to Catholicism.

CALVINISM (REFORMED)

Date originated: 1,536 C.E.
Region founded: Switzerland
Evolved from: Catholicism
Branched into: Anglicanism, Puritanism, Presbyterianism
Deity: Yahweh

Prophet / Teacher: Jesus of Nazareth (John Calvin)
Current followers: 75 million
Denominations: Amyraldism, Hyper-Calvinism, Neo-Calvinism, Christian Reconstructionism, New Calvinism
Prayer rituals: daily
Other rituals: baptism
Food restrictions: none
Alcohol restrictions: in moderation
Clothing restrictions: none
Misc: the 5 points (TULIP): 1. total depravity – man is, by nature, a slave to sin; 2. unconditional election – God has predetermined who will be saved; 3. limited atonement – Jesus' atonement was intended only for the chosen; 4. irresistible grace – God's chosen cannot resist the desire to be saved; 5. perseverance of the saints – the chosen will remain faithful.

Originally a humanist lawyer, John Calvin experienced a religious conversion during his law studies. Soon after the reform break in the Catholic Church, Calvin wrote a book outlining his new found religious beliefs about predestination (i.e. *Romans 8:29*, et al). William Farel, a French reformist, convinced a reluctant Calvin to assist him in his ministry whereby Calvin became immersed in religious duties. Eventually preaching his beliefs in France and Switzerland, he faced constant opposition from other ministers and political figures. But Calvin's teachings continued to spread after his death, and eventually left an impression on the religious leader Frederick III.

Year	Support	Opposition
1,561 C.E.	Frederick III makes Calvinism the official religion of the Rhine (Germany).	
1,593 C.E.		Calvinism and Catholicism are officially banned in Sweden.
1,685 C.E.		Louis XIV of France revokes the Edict of Nantes, forcing nearly 1 million Protestants to flee France or convert to Catholicism.

ANGLICANISM (EPISCOPAL)

Date originated: 1,549 C.E.
Region founded: England
Evolved from: Catholicism, Calvinism
Branched into: Puritanism, Baptists, Quakers, Methodism
Deity: Yahweh
Prophet / Teacher: Jesus of Nazareth (Thomas Cranmer)
Current followers: 85 million
Prayer rituals: 4 times daily
Other rituals: baptism, confession (i.e. *1 John 1:19*)
Food restrictions: none
Alcohol restrictions: in moderation
Clothing restrictions: none

In 1,527 C.E. Henry VIII sought an annulment from his marriage to his second wife Catherine of Aragon based on the grounds that she could not bear him a son to inherit his kingdom. Henry engaged the services of Thomas Cranmer, the recently appointed Archbishop of Canterbury, to lead the proceedings. Cranmer's proclamation that Henry's marriage to Catherine was 'against the law of God' resulted in their preliminary excommunication. This influenced a group effort to establish reformed beliefs based on the newly written tenets of the *Book of Common Prayer*. They authorized that this book be used during mass in their churches, which ultimately led to several arrests and executions, including Cranmer's.

Year	Support	Opposition
1,685 C.E.		Louis XIV of France revokes the Edict of Nantes, forcing nearly 1 million Protestants to flee France or convert to Catholicism.

PURITANISM

Date originated: 1,558 C.E.
Region founded: England
Evolved from: Calvinism, Anglicanism
Deity: Yahweh
Prophet / Teacher: Jesus of Nazareth (the Marian exiles)
Current followers: extinct
Prayer rituals: daily
Other rituals: baptism, strict Sabbatarianism
Food restrictions: none
Alcohol restrictions: in moderation
Clothing restrictions: conservative attire
Misc: exorcisms, no musical instruments in religion services, no dancing

A group of some 800 exiles from England fled to parts of Europe to escape the confines of the Catholic Church. They either assimilated themselves into various positions of political power, or migrated to America.

Year	Support	Opposition
1,685 C.E.		Louis XIV of France revokes the Edict of Nantes, forcing nearly 1 million Protestants to flee France or convert to Catholicism.

PRESBYTERIANISM

Date originated: 1,592 C.E. (1,707)
Region founded: England, Scotland
Evolved from: Calvinism
Deity: Yahweh
Prophet / Teacher: Jesus of Nazareth (John Calvin, Thomas Cartwright)
Current followers: 40 million
Prayer rituals: daily
Other rituals: baptism, strict Sabbatarianism
Food restrictions: none
Alcohol restrictions: in moderation
Clothing restrictions: none
Misc: cannot marry a non-Christian (i.e. *2 Corinthians 6:14*)

In 1,592 C.E. Thomas Cartwright secretly preached Presbyterian views on church leadership in England, and some of these teachings gradually made their way to Scotland. In 1707 the *Acts of Union* was passed to merge the kingdoms of England and Scotland, hence merging the tenets of Calvinism with a revised leadership authority whereby a court of Elders replaced the need for bishops.

BAPTISTS

Date originated: 1,609 C.E.
Region founded: Amsterdam
Evolved from: Anglicanism, Anabaptist
Branched into: Seventh-day Adventism
Deity: Yahweh
Prophet / Teacher: Jesus of Nazareth (John Smyth)
Current followers: 100 million
Prayer rituals: daily
Other rituals: baptism (believers only)
Food restrictions: none
Alcohol restrictions: not allowed (in most sects)
Clothing restrictions: none
Misc: discourage gambling and dancing

John Smyth was an ordained Anglican priest who believed true worship came from the heart, which led to his rejection of infant baptism (i.e. *Acts 2:38-39*). He also believed in a two-fold church leadership of Pastor and Deacon, rather than the typical three-fold leadership of Catholicism and reformed Protestants.

Year	Support	Opposition
1,685 C.E.		Louis XIV of France revokes the Edict of Nantes, forcing nearly 1 million Protestants to flee France or convert to Catholicism.

QUAKERS

Date originated: 1,647 C.E.
Region founded: England
Evolved from: Anglicanism
Deity: Yahweh
Prophet / Teacher: Jesus of Nazareth (George Fox)
Current followers: 400,000
Denominations: 4 sects
Prayer rituals: daily
Other rituals: baptism
Food restrictions: everything in moderation
Alcohol restrictions: not allowed
Clothing restrictions: traditional dress (not enforced)
Misc: non-violence, not allowed to swear oaths, do not observe Christian holidays

George Fox's religious views gradually took shape throughout his childhood and early adult years, focusing on a pure and humble approach to Christianity. Fox's refusal to bear arms (i.e. *Matthew 26:52*) or take oaths (i.e. *James 5:12*) branded him an enemy of the state, turning him into a martyr for persecution by the English government.

Year	Support	Opposition
1,660 C.E.		Puritans ban Quakers from Massachusetts.
1,664 C.E.		Legislation is passed in England officially persecuting Quakers, resulting in their ban across a majority of New England.

EVANGELICALISM (PIETISM)

Date originated: 1,675 C.E.
Region founded: Germany
Evolved from: Lutheranism
Deity: Yahweh
Prophet / Teacher: Jesus of Nazareth (Philip Jacob Spencer, August Hermann Francke)
Current followers: 80 million
Denominations: Conservative, Open, Post
Prayer rituals: daily
Other rituals: baptism
Food restrictions: none
Alcohol restrictions: in moderation
Clothing restrictions: none
Misc: conversionism (i.e. *Mark 16:15-16*), activism (social preaching), sympathy towards the unbeliever

Philip Jacob Spencer studied theology in Strausbourg, and later held meetings in his house based on the movement of 'pietism'. Devout follower August Hermann Francke took over for Spencer upon his death.

AMISH / MENNONITE

Date originated: 1,693 C.E.
Region founded: Switzerland
Evolved from: Anabaptist
Deity: Yahweh
Prophet / Teacher: Jesus of Nazareth (Jacob Ammann, Menno Simons)
Current followers: 250,000
Denominations: 8 sects
Prayer rituals: daily
Other rituals: baptism (after age 18)
Food restrictions: none
Alcohol restrictions: not allowed
Clothing restrictions: traditional dress
Misc: non-violence, do not use insurance or social security, limited or no use of modern technology, members who don't conform are excommunicated

In 1,693 C.E. Jacob Ammann organized a schism amongst the Swiss Brethren seeking unity on several issues, but primarily on the rules surrounding 'shunning' (i.e. *Romans 16:17*, et al). Lack of cooperation and hesitation led to Jacob and his followers excommunicating themselves from the congregation. Those who migrated to Pennsylvania with Ammann were knows as Amish. Those who remained in Europe were knows as Mennonites (after Menno Simons).

METHODISM

Date originated: 1,729 C.E.

Region founded: England
Evolved from: Anglicanism
Branched into: Pentecostalism
Deity: Yahweh
Prophet / Teacher: Jesus of Nazareth (John Wesley)
Current followers: 75 million
Prayer rituals: daily
Other rituals: baptism
Food restrictions: none
Alcohol restrictions: discouraged
Clothing restrictions: none
Misc: missionary work, promote 'logic and reason' in matters of faith

John Wesley was an ordained Anglican priest who believed he was commissioned by God to bring about a revival in the church.

MORMONISM

Date originated: 1,830 C.E.
Region founded: New York, USA
Evolved from: Christianity
Deity: Yahweh
Prophet / Teacher: Jesus of Nazareth (Joseph Smith Jr.)
Current followers: 14.1 million
Denominations: 3 sects
Prayer rituals: several times daily
Other rituals: baptism
Food restrictions: no chocolate
Alcohol restrictions: no alcohol, caffeine, tobacco, or recreational drugs
Clothing restrictions: garments under clothes
Misc: ecclesiastical leadership, polygamy (no longer practiced), missionary work, reject original sin (modern interpretation)

158 | The Evolution of Religion

Joseph Smith was inspired by visions on several occasions, but the most impactful was a visit by the angel Moroni who revealed the location of a buried book of golden plates. After many attempts to find them he successfully recovered them 4 years later. It took 2 years to translate the golden plates from 'reformed Egyptian' into the *Book of Mormon*. Less than a year later Smith formed the Church of Christ of Latter Day Saints.

Year	Support	Opposition
1,838 C.E.		The governor of Missouri bans Mormons from his state.
1,844 C.E.		Joseph Smith was murdered by a violent mob in Illinois, and Mormons fled to Utah.
1,890 C.E.		Plural marriage was banned by Congress resulting in a schism within the faith.

SEVENTH-DAY ADVENTISM

Date originated: 1,840 C.E.
Region founded: New York, USA
Evolved from: Baptists
Deity: Yahweh
Prophet / Teacher: Jesus of Nazareth (William Miller)
Current followers: 17 million
Denominations: 10 sects (5 are extinct)
Prayer rituals: daily
Other rituals: Saturday is the Sabbath (i.e. *Mark 15:42-47*)
Food restrictions: Kosher meat, no pork or shellfish, recommends vegetarianism
Alcohol restrictions: no alcohol or tobacco, avoid caffeine (i.e. *Galatians 5:19-21*)
Clothing restrictions: no body piercings or tattoos (i.e. *Leviticus 19:28*)
Misc: discourage dancing and listening to rock music

William Miller battled with views of Deism and Baptist, until he was inspired when asked to read the day's sermon to his church. He devoted strict attention to the tenets of the Bible (old and new testament), and placed major emphasis on the prophecy of Jesus' second coming.

Year	Support	Opposition
1,844 C.E.		Jesus failed to return as prophesized by William Miller, resulting in lost membership and the formation of new sects.

JEHOVAH'S WITNESSES

Date originated: 1,870 C.E.
Region founded: Pennsylvania, USA
Evolved from: Christianity
Deity: Yahweh
Prophet / Teacher: Jesus of Nazareth (Charles Taze Russell)
Current followers: 7.5 million
Prayer rituals: daily
Other rituals: baptism (believers only)
Food restrictions: none
Alcohol restrictions: in moderation, no tobacco
Clothing restrictions: none
Misc: conversionism (i.e. *Mark 16:15-16*), no gambling (i.e. *Proverbs 13:11*), no blood transfusions, not allowed to marry a non-believer (i.e. *2 Corinthians 6:14*), cannot serve in military (i.e. *Matthew 26:52*), do not observe Christian holidays, no religious symbols, do not believe in Hell

Charles Russell began questioning his Presbyterian faith, as well as all major worldly faiths, at the age of 16. Russell was inspired to reinterpret the Christian Bible in order to remedy the contradictions and improvisations. An unfulfilled prophecy led to a split between Russell and his business partner Nelson Barbour. Russell formed a new partnership with William Henry Conley and formed the *Watch Tower Society* in 1881.

Year	Support	Opposition
1,939 C.E.		Witnesses' refusal to serve in the military during World War II led to their global imprisonment and persecution.

PENTECOSTALISM

Date originated: 1,900 C.E.
Region founded: Kansas, USA
Evolved from: Methodism
Deity: Yahweh
Prophet / Teacher: Jesus of Nazareth (Charles Parham)
Current followers: 279 million
Denominations: 740 sects
Prayer rituals: daily (glossolalia: speaking in tongues)
Other rituals: baptism (believers only)
Food restrictions: none
Alcohol restrictions: in moderation
Clothing restrictions: none
Misc: conversionism, faith healing

Charles Parham left the Methodist ministry because he believed its preachers "were not left to preach by direct inspiration". Parham went on a sabbatical to learn more about modern Christian movements, and heard about an individual who 'spoke in tongues' (i.e. *1 Corinthians 14*). Parham based a new form of ministry on this phenomenon, which both attracted and repelled potential believers.

Near East religions (Islamic branch): Tree of evolution

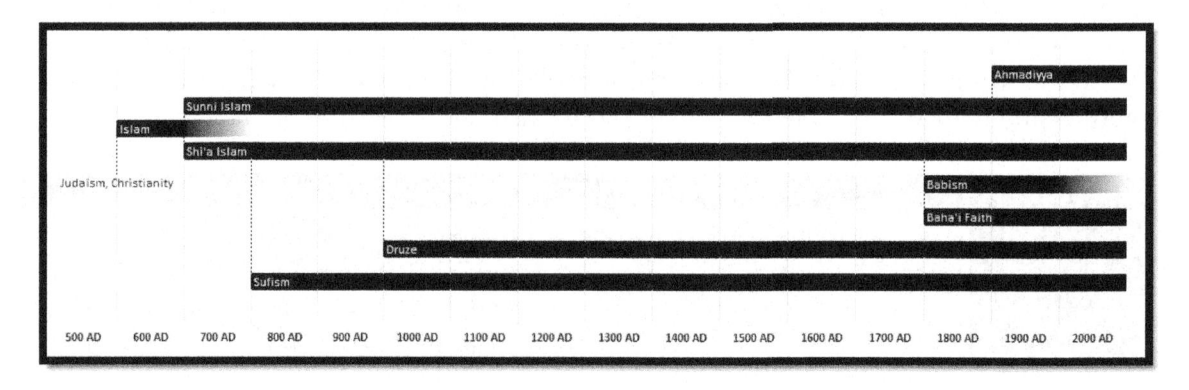

ISLAM

Date originated: 610 C.E.
Region founded: Mecca
Evolved from: Judaism, Christianity
Branched into: Sunni Islam, Shi'a Islam
Deity: Allah (Yahweh)
Prophet / Teacher: Muhammad
Current followers: 1.3 billion
Denominations: 9 sects
Prayer rituals: 5 times daily
Other rituals: circumcision
Food restrictions: fasting (Ramadan), no pork, meat slaughtered by means of 'dhabihah'
Alcohol restrictions: not allowed
Clothing restrictions: strict women's dress code in public
Misc: polygamy (permitted but rarely practiced), no separation of Church and State

Muhammad, a descendant of Ishmael (Abraham's other son Isaac was considered by the Jews to be the symbol of liberty, whereas Ishmael symbolized slavery) had a revelation of the true nature of God and monotheism, which contrasted the existing polytheistic views in 7th century Mecca.

Year	Support	Opposition
629 C.E.	The Muslims conquer Mecca, and their opposition Abu Sufyan adopts Islam.	
634 – 1,453 C.E.	Muslims lead a series of conquests throughout the Middle East, Byzantine, and Ottoman regions.	
1,313 C.E.	Oz Beg Kahn converts to Islam and spreads the faith across the Golden Horde in Turkey.	
1,492 C.E.		King Ferdinand II of Argon

		completes the Reconquista of Granada (Spain), and ends Muslim rule in Iberia.
1,529 C.E.	Suleiman leads the Ottoman Empire's conquest of the Balkans where many convert to Islam.	
1,857 C.E.		The British Empire ends the last Mughal dynasty in India.
1,924 C.E.		The Ottoman Empire was completely dissolved after World War I, and the institution of the Caliphate was abolished.

SUNNI ISLAM

Date originated: 661 C.E.
Region founded: Mecca
Evolved from: Islam
Branched into: Ahmadiyya
Deity: Allah (Yahweh)
Prophet / Teacher: Muhammad
Current followers: 1.1 billion
Denominations: 4 sects
Prayer rituals: 5 times daily
Other rituals: circumcision
Food restrictions: fasting (Ramadan), no pork, meat slaughtered by means of 'dhabihah'
Alcohol restrictions: not allowed
Clothing restrictions: strict women's dress code in public
Misc: polygamy (permitted but rarely practiced)

The Sunni believed Muhammad's successor should be the elected caliph, in this case Muhammad's father-in-law Abu Bakr.

Year	Support	Opposition
1,514 C.E.		Ismael I enforced a mandatory conversion of the Persian Sunnis to Shi'a in an effort to battle the Sunni Ottomans.
1,722 C.E.	Defeat at the hands of the Hotaki Dynasty ends the forceful Shi'a conversion.	

SHI'A ISLAM

Date originated: 661 C.E.
Region founded: Mecca
Evolved from: Islam
Branched into: Sufism, Druze, Babism
Deity: Allah (Yahweh)
Prophet / Teacher: Muhammad
Current followers: 200 million
Denominations: 7 sects
Prayer rituals: 5 times daily
Other rituals: circumcision
Food restrictions: fasting (Ramadan), no pork, meat slaughtered by means of 'dhabihah'
Alcohol restrictions: not allowed
Clothing restrictions: strict women's dress code in public
Misc: polygamy (permitted but rarely practiced), Nikah mut'ah (temporary marriage)

The Shi'a believe Muhammad delivered a sermon at the pond of Khumm a few months before his death where he appointed Ali ibn Abi Talib as his successor.

Year	Support	Opposition
1,514 C.E.	Ismael I enforced a mandatory conversion of the Persian Sunnis to Shi'a in an effort to battle the	

	Sunni Ottomans.	
1,722 C.E.		Defeat at the hands of the Hotaki Dynasty ends the forceful Shi'a conversion.

SUFISM

Date originated: circa 850 C.E.
Region founded: Mecca
Evolved from: Shi'a Islam
Deity: Allah (Yahweh)
Prophet / Teacher: Muhammad (Bayazid Bastami, Junayd Baghdadi, Mansur al-Hallaj)
Current followers: 7.5 million
Denominations: 11 sects
Prayer rituals: 5 times daily
Other rituals: pilgrimage
Food restrictions: fasting (Ramadan), no pork, meat slaughtered by means of 'dhabihah'
Alcohol restrictions: not allowed
Misc: magic, non-violence

Sufism was proclaimed as a way for the 'elite' to reach God, as opposed to the common man.

Year	Support	Opposition
13th – 16th centuries C.E.	Sufism rode the coattails of the growing conquests of Islamic leaders.	
1,925 C.E.		Mustafa Kemal Ataturk of Turkey banned Sufism and closed their temples.

DRUZE

Date originated: 1,017 C.E.
Region founded: Egypt
Evolved from: Shi'a Islam
Deity: Allah (Yahweh)
Prophet / Teacher: Muhammad (Hamza ibn ʿAlī ibn Ahmad)
Current followers: 1 million
Denominations: 2 sects
Prayer rituals: daily
Food restrictions: fasting, no pork
Alcohol restrictions: no alcohol or tobacco
Clothing restrictions: men: mustaches, shirwal (traditional wear), white turban; women: al-mandīl (veil), black shirt, long skirt
Misc: reincarnation

Hamza was allowed to teach his 'reformed' version of Shi'a Islam in Cairo with the permission of the Fatimid Caliph Tāriqu al-Ḥākim. His reformed version spoke out against several distinct Islamic principles such as corruption, polygamy, and remarriage of divorcees.

Year	Support	Opposition
1,017 C.E.	Fatimid Caliph al-Hakim in Persia became a central figure in the Druze faith.	
1,021 C.E.		Sitt al-Mulk takes measures to destroy the movement.
1,305 C.E.		Al-Malik al-Nasir of Egypt defeated the Druze at Keserwan (Lebanon).
1,516 C.E.	Sultan Selim's conquest of Syria allowed Druze villages to prosper in southern Lebanon.	
1,711 C.E.		Arabian Qaysis attack and defeat Yemini Druze diminishing and displacing their power in Lebanon.

1,860 C.E.	Civil War in Lebanon resulted in the defeat of Maronite Christians by the Druze.	
1,909 C.E.		The Hauran rebellion results in the defeat of the Druze at the hands of Ottoman authority.

BABISM

Date originated: 1,844 C.E.
Region founded: Persia
Evolved from: Shi'a Islam
Branched into: Baha'i Faith
Deity: Allah (Yahweh)
Prophet / Teacher: Siyyid `Alí Muhammad Shirazi (Bab)
Current followers: endangered, or converted to Baha'i (100,000 at its peak)
Prayer rituals: daily
Other rituals: pilgrimage
Food restrictions: fasting
Alcohol restrictions: not allowed
Misc: can only marry another believer

Bab acquired 18 disciples while in Persia to assist in the spread of Babism. Their newly founded religious laws ranged from peaceful acceptance to harsh rejection.

Year	Support	Opposition
1,844 C.E.		Uprisings in Iran after the death of Mohammad Shah Qajar resulted in some 20,000 Babi deaths.
1,850 C.E.	The Badasht conference resulted in 100,000 converts to Babism.	
1,852 C.E.		In response to Bab's assassination two years prior, an assassination attempt against Nasser-al-Din Shah resulted

in the killing and imprisonment of several 1,000's Babis.

BAHA'I FAITH

Date originated: 1,863 C.E.
Region founded: Persia
Evolved from: Babism
Deity: Allah (Yahweh)
Prophet / Teacher: Baha'u'llah
Current followers: 6 million
Denominations: 11 sects
Prayer rituals: daily
Other rituals: pilgrimage
Food restrictions: fasting
Alcohol restrictions: not allowed
Misc: no gambling, parental consent for marriage partner

After Bab's execution in 1850, Babism suffered from a lack of solid leadership, to which Baha'u'llah, a respected Babi disciple, attempted to reconcile himself. Mirza Yahya, the flimsy Babi leader, resisted replacement, leading to Baha'u'llah's retreat from Bagdad. The Babi's continued to dissolve and Baha'u'llah was convinced to return where he revived some of his fellowship, revealing to them, in the nearby Garden of Ridvan, the revelation he had during his imprisonment years prior, that he was a Messenger of God. From that point forward their version of Babism morphed into the Baha'i Faith.

Year	Support	Opposition
1,960 C.E.		Gamal Abdel Nasser passes a law in Egypt banning Baha'i institutions and activities.
1,998 C.E.		Some 200 Baha'is are executed over the last 20 years in Iran.

AHMADIYYA

Date originated: 1,889 C.E.
Region founded: British India
Evolved from: Sunni Islam
Deity: Allah (Yahweh)
Prophet / Teacher: Mirza Ghulam Ahmad
Current followers: 10 million
Denominations: 2 sects
Prayer rituals: 5 times daily
Food restrictions: fasting, no pork
Alcohol restrictions: not allowed
Misc: non-violence

Contradictory to Muslim beliefs, Mirza Ghulam Ahmad claimed that Jesus did not die on the cross, but survived the crucifixion and died of old age. He also rejected the idea of armed Jihad.

INDO EUROPEAN RELIGIONS

Indo European religions have supplied the western world with a plethora of epic mythology, the likes of which has fueled fictional entertainment for over a millennium. This is one of the few categories of religion for which this is the case, as every branch has encountered extinction over the ages. As a function of evolution the Gods and stories, which once served as law for entire empires, are demoted to theatrical and literary melodrama upon the rejection of their validity.

The religions categorized in this family are as follows:

Religion	Date originated	Current followers
Minoan Religion	2,200 B.C.E.	*extinct*
Mycenaean Religion	1,600 B.C.E.	*extinct*
Greek Mythology	1,500 B.C.E.	*extinct*
Germanic Mythology	1,000 B.C.E.	*extinct*

Slavic Mythology	750 B.C.E.	*extinct*
Celtic Mythology	500 B.C.E.	*extinct*
Orphism	500 B.C.E.	*extinct*
Hellenistic Religion	313 B.C.E.	*extinct*

Indo European religions: Tree of evolution

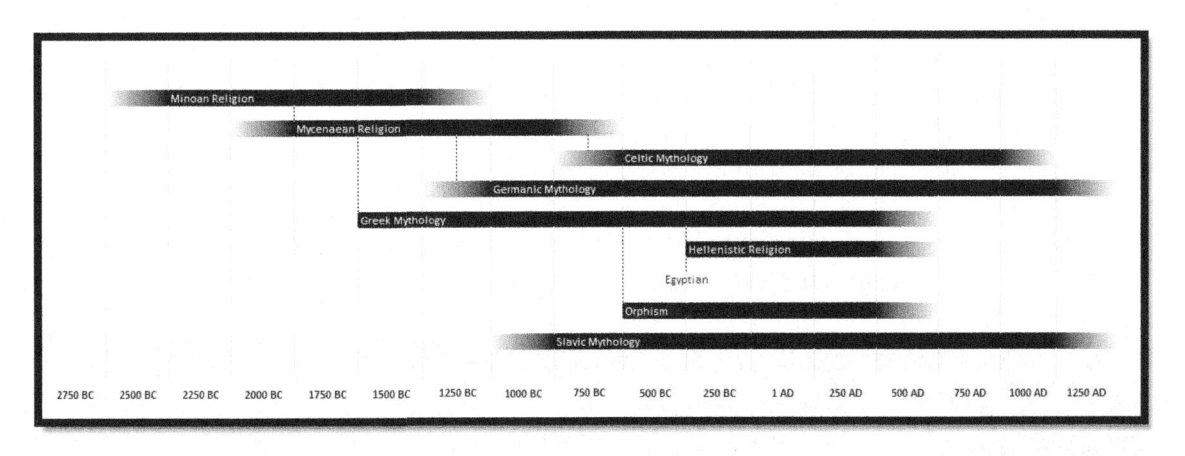

MINOAN RELIGION

Date originated: circa 2,200 B.C.E.
Region founded: Crete
Branched into: Mycenaean Religion
Deity: Mother Goddess (fertility), Mistress of Animals (primarily goddesses, some animal characteristics)
Current followers: extinct
Rituals: Bull dance
Misc: human sacrifice, burial rather than cremation

The Minoan Religion is believed to be to most Matriarchal belief system in recorded history, which was described by Swiss anthropologist Johann Jakob Bachofen as the second of four stages in religious development. Stage one (Hetaerism) being a hunter/gatherer communal society, stage two (Neolithic) represented an agricultural phase, stage three (Dionysian) was a stage of emerging patriarchy, and stage four (Apollonian) represented classical patriarchy.

Year	Support	Opposition
1,400 B.C.E.		The Minoan civilization is defeated by the Mycenaeans.

MYCENAEAN RELIGION

Date originated: circa 1,600 B.C.E.
Region founded: Crete
Evolved from: Minoan Religion
Branched into: Greek Mythology, Celtic Mythology, Germanic Mythology
Deity: primarily goddesses (some animal characteristics), some Roman gods (the twelve-god pantheon)
Current followers: extinct
Rituals: Bull dance
Misc: human sacrifice, burial rather than cremation

The Mycenaean religion represented an almost pure fusion of budding Greek Mythology and the existing Minoan religion.

Year	Support	Opposition
1,400 B.C.E.	The Mycenaeans conquer Crete, the center of the Minoan civilization.	
1,215 – 1,150 B.C.E.		The Hittite Empire and the Egyptian Kingdom gradually fall to the Aegeans and the Dorians.

GREEK MYTHOLOGY

Date originated: circa 1,500 B.C.E.
Region founded: Greece, Rome
Evolved from: Mycenaean Religion
Branched into: Orphism, Hellenistic Religion
Deity: Zeus (in addition to 100's of gods and goddesses)
Current followers: extinct
Prayer rituals: public assembly
Other rituals: votive altar offerings
Misc: animal sacrifice, occasional human sacrifice

Greek Mythology is closely associated with Roman mythology. Military conquests absorbed and adopted new deities for which worship was sometimes permitted, but confined, to that specific territory. Names evolved over time, for example the god Jupiter (in Rome) came first then Zeus (Greek), then eventually fused into a single entity.

Year	Support	Opposition
380 C.E.		Christianity becomes the state religion of the Roman Empire under Theodosius I.

GERMANIC MYTHOLOGY

Date originated: circa 1,000 B.C.E.
Region founded: northern Europe
Evolved from: Mycenaean Religion
Deity: Odin, Thor, Mars, Mercury (in addition to 100's of gods and goddesses)
Current followers: extinct
Prayer rituals: outdoor worship
Misc: animal and human sacrifice

Around 950 C.E. Haakon the Good, King of Norway, converted to Christianity much to the disappointment of his own people. He was forced to rescind his conversion, and upon his death was honored as being received by the Norse gods into Valhalla.

Year	Support	Opposition
1,000 – 1,400 C.E.		Christianity spreads throughout Europe resulting in forcible leadership conversions.

SLAVIC MYTHOLOGY

Date originated: circa 750 B.C.E.
Region founded: Slavia (Russia, eastern Europe)
Deity: Rod, Svarog, Perun (in addition to 100's of god and goddesses)
Current followers: extinct
Rituals: Summer and Winter solstice festivals
Misc: rituals performed in nature (no temples), human sacrifice

Even as Christianity was adopted by Slavic nobility, it was viewed as a 'religion of the elite'. Peasants were baptized, attended mass, and celebrated Christian holidays, yet continued to worship pagan deities to ensure plentiful harvests. Christianity was essentially fused with Slavic mythology providing farmers with both the salvation of the afterlife and the divine protection of their former pantheon. Even Christian saints were used as replacements for pagan gods (e.g. Perun, the god of thunder and lightning, was associated with St Elijah because of his mythical power over weather).

Year	Support	Opposition
600 – 1,100 C.E.		Christianity gradually took over, and pagan practices were outlawed.

CELTIC MYTHOLOGY

Date originated: circa 500 B.C.E.
Region founded: central and western Europe
Evolved from: Mycenaean Religion
Deity: Mercury (in addition to 100's of god and goddesses)
Current followers: extinct
Misc: animal and nature worship (trees, weather, water), human sacrifice, head hunting

Celtic Mythology encompassed a great many pantheons of the region including Irish, Scottish Welsh, British, Breton (France), and Gaulish (Netherlands and Switzerland), all of whom were influenced by the Mycenaean 12 (Mercury, Mars, Jupiter, etc).

Year	Support	Opposition
54 C.E.		Druid rituals are banned (focused primarily on the removal of human sacrifice) by the Roman Emperor Augustus.
600 - 900 C.E.		Christianity gradually took over, and Celtic (pagan) practices were outlawed.

ORPHISM

Date originated: circa 500 B.C.E.
Region founded: Greece
Evolved from: Greek Mythology
Deity: Zeus (in addition to 100's of gods and goddesses)
Current followers: extinct
Food restrictions: vegetarianism
Misc: reincarnation

Orphism differed from Greek Mythology in the following ways, which bore some striking similarities to Christianity and Hinduism: belief in a 'grievous circle' of immortality (reincarnation), the practicing of secret initiation rites to achieve release from the 'grievous circle' (sacraments), the cautioning of afterlife punishment (Hell), and they were founded upon sacred writings depicting their cosmology (Bible, Rigveda).

Year	Support	Opposition
380 C.E.		Christianity becomes the state religion of the Roman Empire under Theodosius I.

HELLENISTIC RELIGION

Date originated: 313 B.C.E.
Region founded: Crete
Evolved from: Greek Mythology, Egyptian Religion
Deity: primarily Greek and Egyptian gods and goddesses
Current followers: extinct
Misc: astrology, magic, animal sacrifices

After the conquests of Alexander the Great, Greek culture gained influence from Egyptian mythology as well as Judaism, which both diluted and expanded belief systems in Greece. This has been regarded as a decline in religious belief for the time, where even atheistic skepticism became prevalent.

Year	Support	Opposition
204 B.C.E.	The Roman Senate permits the worship of Atargatis (Aphrodite Derceto).	
362 C.E.	Emperor Julian promulgates freedom of religion in an attempt to restore Hellenistic beliefs.	
380 C.E.		Christianity becomes the state religion of the Roman Empire under Theodosius I.

/ The Evolution of Religion

INDIGENOUS RELIGIONS

Indigenous religions tend to be isolated – and generally non-branching – belief systems of various rural cultures. As their evolutionary relations are only quasi-tangential at best, they are subdivided by their region of origin: African, Pacific, and American.

The religions categorized in this family are as follows:

African

Religion	Date originated	Current followers
Serer Religion	10,000 B.C.E.	*endangered*
Yoruba Religion	5,000 B.C.E.	20 million
Vodou	1,791 C.E.	5 million

Pacific

Religion	Date originated	Current followers
Aboriginal Religion	8,000 B.C.E.	*endangered*
Indonesian Religion	2,000 B.C.E.	*endangered*
Polynesian Religion	1,000 B.C.E.	*endangered*
Hawaiian Religion	500 C.E.	*endangered*

American

Religion	Date originated	Current followers
Olmec Religion	1,500 B.C.E.	*extinct*
Aztec religion	1,200 B.C.E.	*extinct*
Native American Religion	500 B.C.E.	*endangered*
Mayan Religion	200 B.C.E.	*endangered*
Incan Religion	1,200 C.E.	*extinct*

Comparison: The Stats | 175

Indigenous religions: Tree of evolution

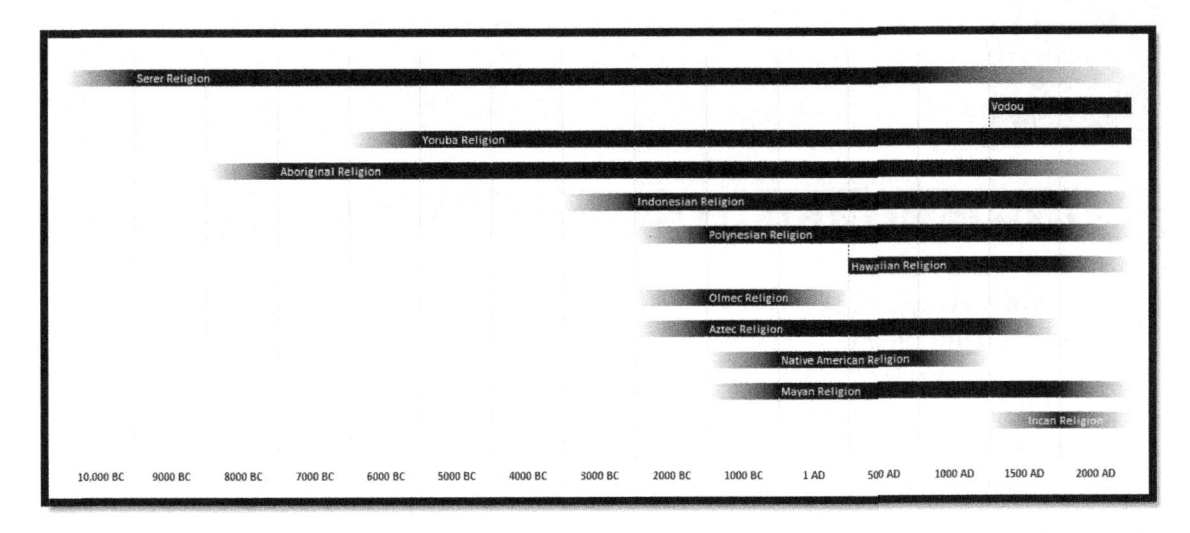

AFRICAN

SERER RELIGION

Date originated: circa 10,000 B.C.E.
Region founded: western Africa
Deity: Roog (in addition to many gods and goddesses)
Current followers: endangered
Rituals: Monday is the day of rest
Clothing restrictions: displaying of juju (ancestral belongings used for witchcraft)
Misc: reincarnation, witchcraft

The Serer 'pentagram' symbol represents the star *Yoonir*, also known as the Star of Sirius. The ancient Serer farmers relied on Yoonir's placement in the sky to know when to plant their seeds. It is believed that the ancient Egyptians derived several of their gods (e.g. Ra, Sopdet, Ma'at) from the Serer pantheon.

Year	Support	Opposition
1,875 C.E. (approx)		The Muslims conquered the Serers, and those who survived either converted to Islam, or committed martyrdom.

YORUBA RELIGION

Date originated: circa 5,000 B.C.E.
Region founded: Nigeria
Branched into: Vodou
Deity: Olódùmarè (in addition to approximately 20 gods and goddesses: Orishas)
Current followers: 20 million
Denominations: Santeria, Lukumi, Umbanda, Candomblé, Qadiriyya, Tijaniyya, Cherubim, Seraphim, Aladura
Prayer rituals: morning worship
Other rituals: outdoor offerings
Misc: reincarnation, animal sacrifice, magic, human sacrifice (no longer practiced)

The Yoruba religion has become somewhat diluted through African slavery. To keep their belief system relevant, Yoruban worshippers would pay homage to the Orishas through Catholic ceremonies as if they were Christian saints.

VODOU

Date originated: 1,791 C.E.
Region founded: Haiti
Evolved from: Yoruba religion
Deity: Bondyè
Current followers: 5 million
Denominations: Orthodox, Makaya, Kongo
Prayer rituals: prayers offered to Loa (spirit messengers of Bondyè)
Other rituals: Loa ceremony
Misc: magic, voodoo dolls

In 1685, after western and central Africans were sold into slavery in Saint-Domingue (Haiti), King Louis XIV of France prohibited the practice of traditional African religions. While practicing their religion underground, their polytheistic pantheon merged with Catholicism to create a monotheistic worship, as well as filling in the gaps of lost traditions. In 1804 the Haitian Revolution freed the Haitians from French

Colonial rule and religious freedom was restored. The ceremonial sacrifice of a black pig that preceded the revolution was considered by Christian commentators to be a "pact with the devil", which has tainted Christian perspectives of Vodou as a Satanic based religion.

PACIFIC

ABORIGINAL RELIGION

Date originated: circa 8,000 B.C.E.
Region founded: Australia
Deity: Rainbow Serpent, Baiame, Dirawong, Bunjil (belief varied)
Current followers: endangered (less than 10,000)
Rituals: spiritual dances
Misc: magic

The Aboriginal creation story and spiritual overview known as 'The Dreaming' (or Dreamtime) is a common thread in an otherwise diverse world of Australian culture.

INDONESIAN RELIGION

Date originated: circa 2,000 B.C.E.
Region founded: Indonesia
Deity: Barong (in addition to approximately a dozen gods and goddesses)
Current followers: endangered
Denominations: Dayak, Baduy, Batak, Toraja, Asmat, Sunda, Java, Minangkabau, Malay
Prayer rituals: some sects confine prayer to the shaman
Alcohol restrictions: some sects prohibit alcohol
Other rituals: season feasts
Misc: karma, reincarnation, animal sacrifice

The diverse culture of the Indonesians and integration of Islam, Christianity, and Hinduism has significantly clouded their religious heritage.

Year	Support	Opposition
100 C.E.		Influences from mainland Hindus and Buddhists were adopted, diluting the original Indonesian mythology.

800 C.E. (approx)		Islamic influences further dilute Indonesian beliefs.

POLYNESIAN RELIGION

Date originated: circa 1,000 B.C.E.
Region founded: Tonga, Samoa, Tahiti, New Zealand
Branched into: Hawaiian religion
Deity: Rangi (in addition to 15 gods and goddesses)
Current followers: endangered
Rituals: drinking of kava
Misc: magic, human sacrifice

Relying heavily on sea travel the Polynesians, worshipping both the sea and sky, developed an early understanding of star navigation as well as an impressive comprehension of seasonal cycles.

Year	Support	Opposition
1,700 C.E. (approx)		The influx of Christianity greatly diluted the Polynesian belief system.

HAWAIIAN RELIGION

Date originated: circa 500 C.E.
Region founded: Hawaii
Evolved from: Polynesian religion
Deity: Kāne (in addition to 100's of gods and goddesses)
Current followers: endangered
Prayer rituals: several times daily
Other rituals: drinking of 'awa (kava)
Misc: hula, various sacrifices

11 years after Ka'ahumanu, Hawaii's 19th century leader, was converted to Christianity, all aspects of the Hawaiian religion, including the hula, were outlawed. But traditional worship continued to be practiced in secrecy.

Year	Support	Opposition
1,820 C.E.		Missionaries arrive and convert most of the Hawaiians to Christianity.

AMERICAN

OLMEC RELIGION

Date originated: circa 1,500 B.C.E.
Region founded: southern Mexico
Deity: 8 genderless Supernaturals
Current followers: extinct
Rituals: bloodletting
Misc: disputed evidence of infant sacrifice

The Olmec civilization was mysteriously wiped out around 350 B.C.E., most likely due to a depletion of their natural resources or disease, leaving behind almost no direct accounts of their religious heritage.

AZTEC RELIGION

Date originated: circa 1,200 B.C.E.
Region founded: central Mexico
Deity: Huitzilopochtli (in addition to approximately 36 gods and goddesses)
Current followers: extinct
Rituals: 19 Aztec calendar rituals, New Fire ceremony every 52 years
Misc: human sacrifice, animal sacrifice, some auto-sacrifice

A smallpox outbreak in 1520 led to the decisive downfall of the Aztec civilization, resulting in an estimated 50% reduction in their population.

Year	Support	Opposition
1,521 C.E.		The Aztecs were conquered by Spain under Cortez who was aided by many citizens of Tlaxcala.

NATIVE AMERICAN RELIGION

Date originated: circa 500 B.C.E.
Region founded: North America
Deity: various polytheistic pantheons
Current followers: endangered
Denominations: Algonquian, Plains, Muskogean, Iroquois, Alaskan, Uto-Aztecan
Rituals: weather dances, consumption of peyote
Misc: human and animal sacrifice

Similar to the Hindu sanctity of cows, the rare white buffalo was considered sacred to many Native American religions. In general, Native American beliefs were very diverse in regards to deities, burial ceremonies, healing, sorcery, and piousness.

Year	Support	Opposition
1,567 C.E.		Spanish settlers establish ongoing reforms to forcibly convert Native Americans to Catholicism.

MAYAN RELIGION

Date originated: circa 200 B.C.E.
Region founded: Central America
Deity: Itzamna (in addition to approximately 100 gods and goddesses)
Current followers: endangered (2 million at its peak)
Prayer rituals: daily
Other rituals: confession, bloodletting
Food restrictions: fasting
Misc: animal sacrifice, pilgrimage, astrology

The Mayan civilization mysteriously went into decline around 800 C.E.

INCAN RELIGION

Date originated: circa 1,200 C.E.
Region founded: Peru
Deity: Viracocha, Pachamama (in addition to several dozen gods and goddesses)
Current followers: extinct

Prayer rituals: divination (occultic fortune-telling)
Other rituals: monthly festivals
Misc: human sacrifice (usually a child or slave), ancestor worship

The Incas established one of the most powerful and short lived empires in western South America. All that exists of Inca mythology today is a wavering belief in the goddess Pachamama combined with Christian rituals.

Year	Support	Opposition
1,532 C.E.		The Battle of Cajamarca launches a 40 year campaign resulting in the conquering of Peru by the Spanish.

CHAPTER 9

CONCLUSIONS:

Where Are We Headed?

"An Inuit hunter asked the local missionary priest: 'If I did not know about God and sin, would I go to hell?' 'No,' said the priest, 'not if you did not know.' 'Then why,' asked the Inuit earnestly, 'did you tell me?'"
- Annie Dillard

Questions Answered
The Theological Pyramid
What Would Society Be Like Without Religion?
The Damage

Why did certain religions flourish while others faded away?

We've explored nearly 100 religions in relative detail, some still being practiced, some extinct. Together with their tangentially referenced sects and denominations compile a six-digit total. But it's important to note that there are literally thousands of religions still in practice that were not acknowledged, and many more thousands that are extinct. Common to many indigenous beliefs, the evolutionary path of these 'neglected' faiths tend to be a straight line as they were less influential members of the theological family tree. Religions born from a region outside the economic super-powers (i.e. Roman Empire, Persian Empire, India, and China) had the survival odds immediately stacked against them. A thriving economy is needed to effectively build a military, and militaries defend and expand cultures.

A religion's shelf-life depended greatly on everything *but* the religion itself (i.e. which government supported it, which governments were against it, did they proselytize, did they persecute, did they evolve in accordance with economic change). Every one of our ancient ancestors started off as a polytheist. Warfare inspired monotheism, which became the calling card of the Roman and Persian Empires, which replaced and wiped out hundreds of polytheistic faiths, by force. But India and the Far East stayed basically true to their religious origins, primarily because their geography prevented them from assimilating with the cultures of the west. The majority of the Far East's failed religious endeavors were due to a surplus of philosophical schools of thought (i.e. too much supply, not enough demand). India enjoyed a relatively stable economy, which influenced religious stability. But during an economic collapse when social change was inevitable, or if leadership stability was uncertain, a budding religion with strong potential could be given the opportunity of a lifetime.

Can we predict which modern religions will excel or decline?

A good indicator of a religion's peak (i.e. when society was the least skeptical of its origin and claims) was when a faith's tenets were the most structured, the followers were the most unified, and their government exhibited the most control over its citizens. Much of this came about due to cultural advancement (e.g. written language, improved methods of law enforcement), which segued into industrial advancement where superfluous gods were ironically recognized as obsolete. The notion that a single God could replace a pantheon of deities, one for each aspect of nature, indicated that technology was more reliable than prayer. This point in history was incited between 1,500 – 500 B.C.E.

The question really becomes "which religions hinder survival rather than enable it?" The amount of Gods has little bearing on the rules that religion imposes, and these rules can be pivotal. Modern survival has been redefined as 'who can keep up?' Africa has basically been stripped of its indigenous religious beliefs and is now essentially comprised of an Islamic northern half and a Christian southern half. Africa has become the spiritual step-child of both the Near East and the West. Instead of developing their own system on their own terms, their politics, government, and religion has been forced upon them by two economic and cultural opposites, which has turned a slow, but functioning system, into a slow, non-functioning system. Political neglect on the part of the Near East and the West, rather than religion, shoulders the majority of the blame. If the notion that exposure to Christianity and Islam was the first and only step toward economic salvation, then perhaps the 'diamond market' was their divine reward. Unfortunately religious intervention stopped there, doing little to suppress the increasing warlord insurgence financed by blood diamonds (it's easy to see why suppressed societies were attracted to a 'war god' such as Yahweh).

The anti-progressive nature of Islam, on the other hand, has painted itself into a corner. One of three scenarios is most likely to unfold in the not too distant future. One:

the terrorism stops, Islam remains static, and Islamic economies fall further behind. Two: the terrorism stops, Islam evolves, and Islamic economies gradually improve. Three: the terrorism persists, and Islam is forced to evolve through western intervention (i.e. warfare). History has revealed two factors whose influence can be more powerful than religion: money and death. One or both of these factors will result in the decline of religious beliefs that deny their authority, and Islam is apt to put this to the test.

The Theological Pyramid

Three questions posed in the first chapter remain unaddressed:

- What factors that once affected religious evolution are no longer valid today?
- Can we predict how modern society will affect religion in the future?
- Will religion ever go away?

All three questions can be dealt with through the concept of the *theological pyramid*. Religious belief can be divided into five elements, each evolving separately, in order, and ultimately decreasing in their significance to human nature.

Belief in the *afterlife* arose first, and is potentially present in any being who mourns the dead (e.g. chimpanzees). Afterlife in this phase is strictly limited to the undying mind and transference to a spiritual plane of existence entirely beyond the physical world. Belief in *spirits* incorporates the interaction between the physical and spiritual world. This includes communication, emotional stimulation, and physical manipulation through the dead. The spirits are omnipresent, possibly omnificent, but not yet omnipotent. Belief in *gods* introduces omnipotence, as well as man's prerogative to request assistance through prayer. Each god controlled a specific aspect, or several aspects, of nature, and our potential to connect with them via divine ritual could harness their omnipotence. But prayer eventually came with a cost. The price for divine intervention required believers to live life by a divine code, or *rules*. These rules generally involved sacrificing valuable possessions, as well as conducting oneself in an ethical manner that benefitted society as a whole. Lastly, belief in *salvation* was God's reward in the spiritual world for following his or her rules during our physical existence.

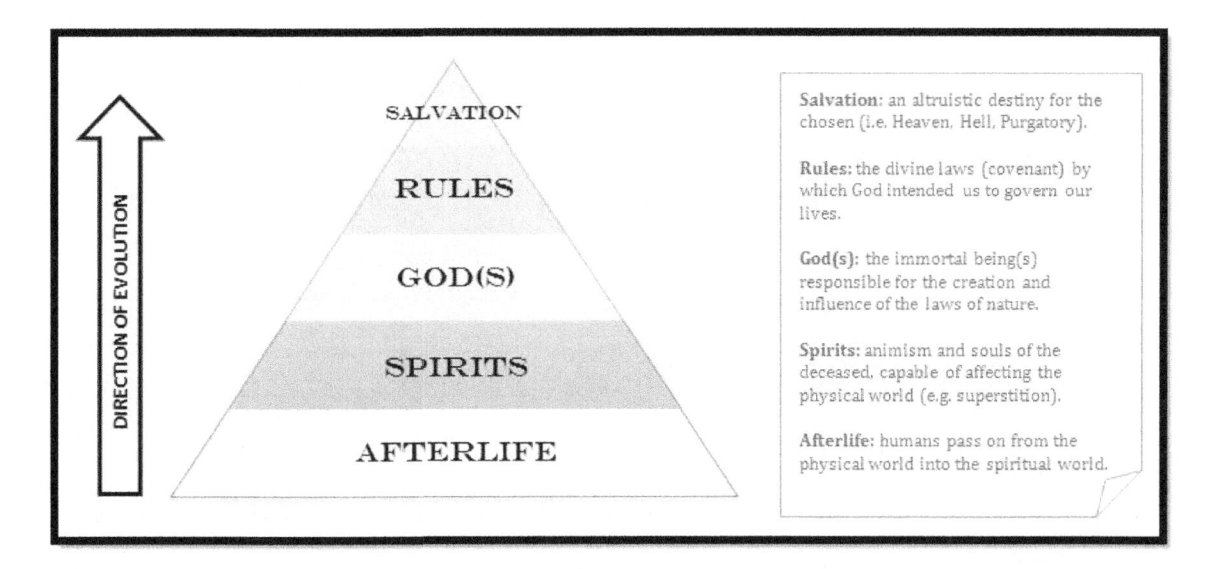

Anthropological pyramid (bottom to top): AFTERLIFE, SPIRITS, GOD(S), RULES, SALVATION. Arrow indicates DIRECTION OF EVOLUTION.

Salvation: an altruistic destiny for the chosen (i.e. Heaven, Hell, Purgatory).

Rules: the divine laws (covenant) by which God intended us to govern our lives.

God(s): the immortal being(s) responsible for the creation and influence of the laws of nature.

Spirits: animism and souls of the deceased, capable of affecting the physical world (e.g. superstition).

Afterlife: humans pass on from the physical world into the spiritual world.

As commonplace as these beliefs are, they took nearly 200,000 years to fully evolve. What's also commonplace are certain requirements modern humans must have to form a cohesive society capable of long term stability. These are structured in an *anthropological pyramid*. Mankind has learned over time that even though these are requirements for optimum survival, he will inevitably fall short of accomplishing them. Our lack of *immortality* does not actually have to be learned as we are naturally pre-wired to comprehend this, but only the more highly evolved species are prone to ponder this. *Understanding* is man's primal method for claiming power over the elements that both aid and hinder his survival. This can be done by understanding the origins of nature. For example, now that we understand the origins of vegetables, we can provide seeds with the proper nourishment to ensure a harvest, as well as cross-breed and engineer seeds that generate superior crops. *Technology* utilizes our current level of understanding to enhance survival. *Culture* expands the survival process beyond the self and incorporates societal behavior. Similar to our desire to understand the origins of nature, we strive to understand the origins of human nature and values. The origin of any organic entity is imagined to be pure, and our need to connect with our 'pure self' is thought to be accomplished through the appreciation of culture (i.e. nostalgia). Once cultural values are established, those who do not abide must be corrected through a system of *justice*.

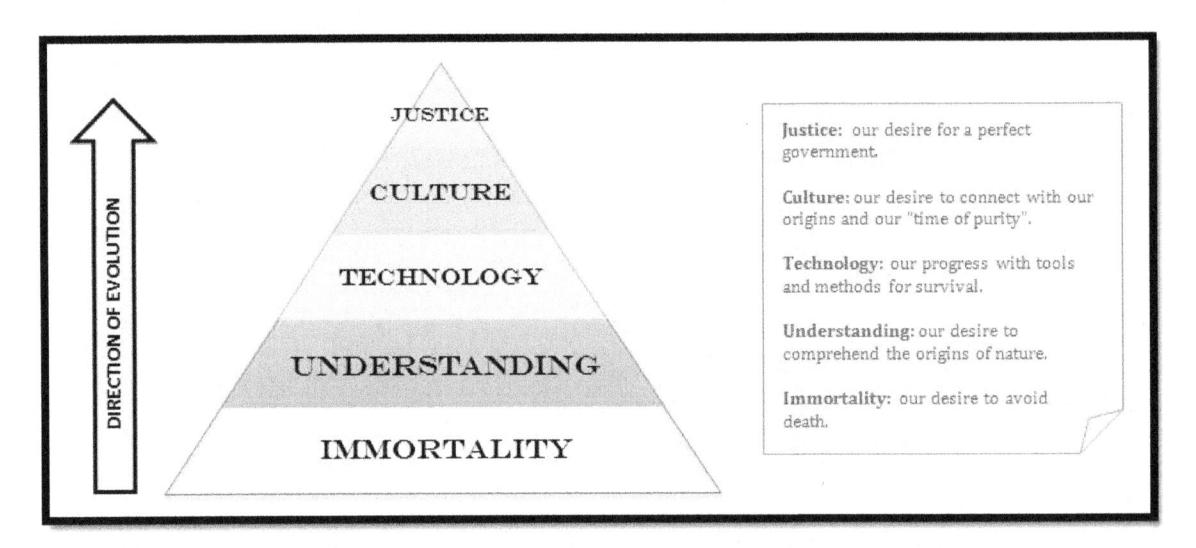

186 | The Evolution of Religion

[Pyramid diagram: from bottom to top — IMMORTALITY, UNDERSTANDING, TECHNOLOGY, CULTURE, JUSTICE; arrow on left indicates DIRECTION OF EVOLUTION]

Justice: our desire for a perfect government.

Culture: our desire to connect with our origins and our "time of purity".

Technology: our progress with tools and methods for survival.

Understanding: our desire to comprehend the origins of nature.

Immortality: our desire to avoid death.

The establishment of the theological pyramid relies on our inevitable failure to accomplish the needs of the anthropological pyramid (e.g. our inability to achieve or perfect *justice* results in *no reliable system of punishment and reward*, therefore we have *salvation*).

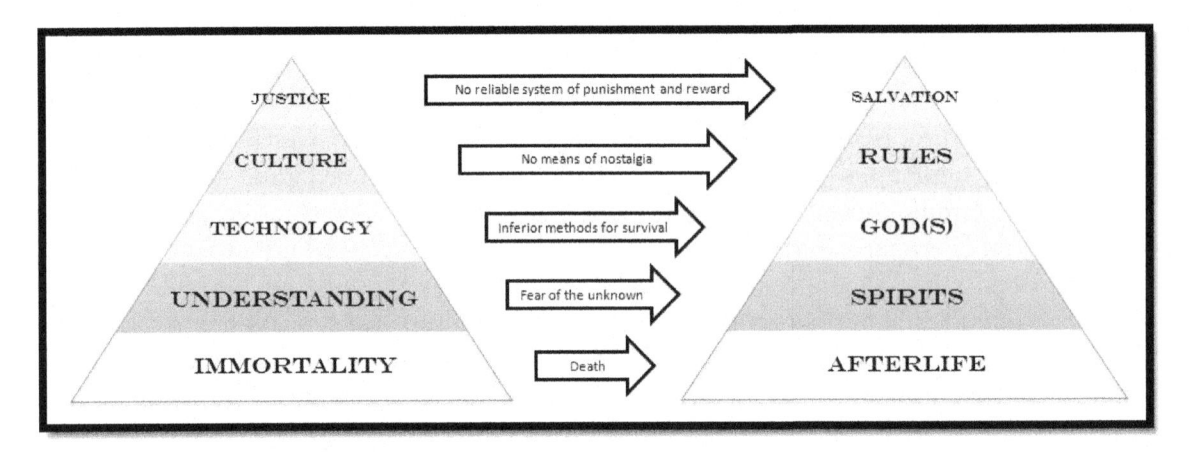

*[Two pyramids side by side with arrows between them:
Left pyramid (bottom to top): IMMORTALITY, UNDERSTANDING, TECHNOLOGY, CULTURE, JUSTICE
Right pyramid (bottom to top): AFTERLIFE, SPIRITS, GOD(S), RULES, SALVATION
Arrows: JUSTICE → "No reliable system of punishment and reward" → SALVATION; CULTURE → "No means of nostalgia" → RULES; TECHNOLOGY → "Inferior methods for survival" → GOD(S); UNDERSTANDING → "Fear of the unknown" → SPIRITS; IMMORTALITY → "Death" → AFTERLIFE]*

Our inability to meet the demands of the anthropological pyramid has inspired the five elements of religion. The problem is, and continues to be, that religion fills an emotional need rather than a practical need. The elements of the anthropological pyramid are not solved by religion, they are simply addressed. Whether man is conscious of this or not, the believer continues his attempts to rectify these issues unaware that religion is an unnecessary component. The ambiguity that surrounds these elements arises from a range of potential solutions whose aspects are universally appealing to some degree. Yet every government has managed to settle on a distinct value system, values that incidentally run the gamut. This ambiguity catalyzed our need to reach beyond politics and turn to religion: an authority beyond man established to resolve ambiguity.

Justice / Salvation

The 2002 sci-fi film *Minority Report* may very well have demonstrated the only method by which a crime free society could actually be established[29]. Short of that, the government would have to turn its citizens into emotionless robots via some other 'sci-fi themed' method. Actual technological advances are aiding in bringing criminals to justice (e.g. surveillance, satellite tracking, communication tracing, forensic evidence), but motivations for deterrence remain a dilemma. Religion's attempt to establish a reward/punishment system (i.e. Heaven and Hell), based on the results, has fallen short as well.

One of the key problems of global conformity is evident in our current means of punishment. The nations of the world are very much at odds when it comes to the definition of a crime, or, more specifically, the degree of punishment. Many Islamic nations still practice harsh methods of persecution for practicing non-Islamic religions, and especially target sex, sodomy, and the use of alcohol and narcotics.

Malaysia (Islam): 5 years imprisonment for possession of a single marijuana seed
Indonesia (Islam): death penalty for drug trafficking
Singapore (Buddhist, Christian, Islam): caning for vandalism, jail for littering and possession of pornography
China (Taoist, Buddhist, Folk): death penalty for tax evasion, life for owning a pornographic website
Sudan (Islam): death penalty for prostitution
Nigeria (Christian, Islam): death penalty for homosexual acts and adultery

Enforcing our laws has been handled more efficiently over time, but our desire for justice is counter balanced by awareness. Before crime in the media could be instantly communicated from literally anywhere in the world to a device that fits in your pocket, ignorance was bliss. Our paranoia is no longer afforded the luxury of ignorance, and knowing what is possible heightens our desire for reliable justice. Perhaps the other end of the judicial spectrum (i.e. reward), if it were economically feasible, could yield results. In other words, if the government cut you a quarterly check for *not* committing crimes, would you obey the laws?

Abstract: Our collective uncertainty surrounding degrees of applicable justice results in a desire for divine salvation.

---

[29] The premise of the sci-fi thriller *Minority Report* involves a technique utilized by Washington DC to predict homicides before they happen, thereby arresting the would-be murderer for the crime they were 'planning' to commit.

Culture / Rules

Establishing a set of universal human rights is the modern day cultural equivalent of cracking the *da Vinci Code*. On the heels of World War II, the 30 articles of the *Universal Declaration of Human Rights* did little more than outlaw slavery. Even moral agreement on something as palpable as murder poses problems. Apologists argue that unity under one religion is the solution to establishing human rights. For this to be true, compliance is not merely limited to judicial laws, but would apply to several facets of everyday cultural existence: marriage, economy, diet, and health care.

Marriage

Monogamy and the institute of marriage pre-dates recorded history (prior to 3,000 B.C.E), which also means it predates all documented modern religions. Religion has attempted to monopolize this establishment, which has led to several conflicting issues. Polygamy, which is mentioned no less than 16 times in the Old Testament, is generally considered unacceptable by Christian standards, though this grey area has allowed for multiple interpretations (i.e. Mormonism, Islam), not to mention the 65 countries that legally recognize plural marriage. Underage marriage for females (i.e. under the age of 18) is mentioned once in the Qur'an, but is fully permitted under Sharia Law[30]. Homosexuality on the other hand, even as it is mentioned only twice in *Leviticus* (18:22, 20:13), is almost entirely forbidden by Christianity, Islam, and certain denominations of Judaism. A consistency issue arises when we derive our values from antiquated scriptures.

> *"This was established by decree of Almighty God... it is sanctioned in the Bible, in both Testaments, from Genesis to Revelation... it has existed in all ages, has been found among the people of the highest civilization, and in nations of the highest proficiency in the arts."*
> —Jefferson Davis (President, Confederate States of America)

> *"Every hope of the existence of church and state, and of civilization itself, hangs upon our arduous effort to defeat the doctrine of [their] suffrage."*
> —Rev. Robert Dabney (19th century Presbyterian pastor)

> *"... the right of [persecuting them] is clearly established in the Holy Scriptures, both by precept and example."*
> —Richard Furman (President, South Carolina Baptist Convention)

---

[30] Islamic beliefs aside, underage marriage is fairly common in Africa and much of Latin America.

The portion in brackets intentionally conceals the nature of these quotes, which actually address 'slavery' in America before the Civil War. Regardless of how we view slavery today, these three men, as well as many others of their time, were completely accurate in their biblical justification. Even though slavery persists on a relatively limited basis, slavery is outlawed in all countries. Society evolved, and religious interpretations were forced to evolve with it. Yet modern biblical justification against homosexuality is rife amongst apologists and some politicians.

"Homosexuality is clearly condemned in the Bible. It undermines the basis of God's created order where God made Adam, a man, and Eve, a woman – not two men, not two women – to carry out his command to fill and subdue the earth. Homosexuality cannot carry out that command. It also undermines the basic family unit of husband and wife, the God-ordained means of procreation. It is also dangerous to society."
—Matt Slick (Christian apologist)

"If the Supreme Court says that you have the right to consensual sex within your home, then you have the right to bigamy, you have the right to polygamy, you have the right to incest, you have the right to adultery. You have the right to anything. Does that undermine the fabric of our society? I would argue yes, it does."
—Rick Santorum (Republican Party politician)

It seems like only a matter of time before societal views on homosexuality takes a similar route as slavery, only without military intervention. According to *PollingReport.com* America's attitude toward same-sex marriage, based on eight national polls, shows that cultural values are evolving regardless of religious influence.

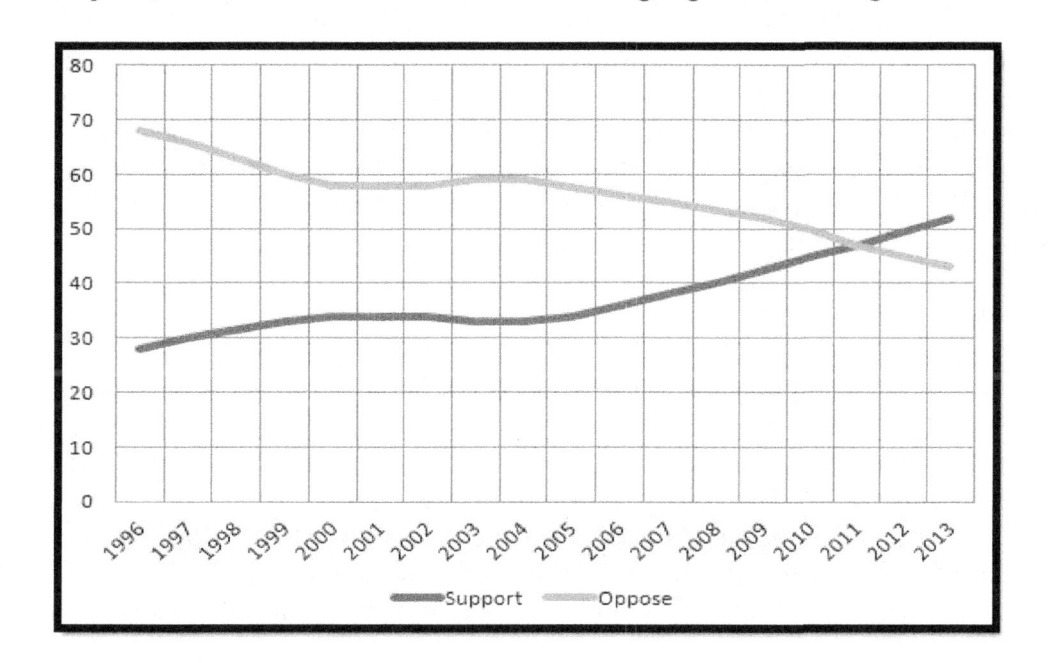

Economy

Universal agreement on an economic system may be the biggest pipe dream of the bunch. Not only are we at odds with capitalism versus socialism, and all variations in between, but our relatively recent biases against environmental harm, and unethical work environments creates additional obstacles. There are numerous environmental hazards that are, unfortunately, extremely profitable. Offshore oil drilling and power plant emissions are at least limited by government regulations, but the same can't be said for Brazil. The deforestation of the Amazon rainforest generates 8.6% of Brazilian trade revenue, which amounts to $22 billion annually and 6.5 mil jobs. Halting this industry equates to America losing the majority of her entire agricultural trade revenue. A globalized economy would be a necessity in order to eliminate ethical quandaries, like 'sweat-shop' wages. And then there are economic hindrances, as with Islamic inheritance and usury regulations. Economic systems, even prosperous ones, generally involve a highly convoluted balancing act just to remain stable, and the last thing they need are reforms from an archaic prophet with no financial background.

Diet

What we eat has recently afforded us the luxury of 'being picky'. In countries like Zambia, Haiti, and Ethiopia (just to name a few) the notion that someone would pay more money for a lower calorie food option is entirely outside of their perspective. This isn't to say that international vegetarianism isn't worth pursuing, but until technology can turn deserts into gardens, economic and trade reforms are just a starting point.

As diet is directly linked to our survival, our dietary culture can serve as a barometer for morality. What we eat says a lot about our values, and technology plays a significant role. Let's imagine we are able to 'grow' meat substitutes whose taste and texture are virtually indistinguishable from any meat, as well as being healthier and more economical. How would our views on animal slaughter be affected by this? On that note, was it necessary to keep slaves after the industrial revolution when machines could surpass human labor? Our morality is highly dependent on our ease of survival, and ease of survival is dependent on technology.

Heath Care

Even the richest country in the world is not immune to ethical difficulties when to comes to health care. But what are our options: higher quality health care with shorter lines at a higher cost – abundant heath care with waiting lists and higher taxes – or something in-between? The downside of a primarily capitalist economic system is that some 'essential' products can inherit the characteristics of a 'luxury'. Religion may offer individual health guidance in the way of alcohol consumption, diet, sexual practices, meditation rituals, excessiveness, and overall balance in one's lifestyle, but none of them offer a value system by which social health care should be structured. When medical treatment came in the form of 'miracle cures' for healing the blind and the crippled, or holistic recipes composed of bone fragments and snake venom, health care was apparently less of an issue.

Specifics aside, sometimes the values dictated by culture are harder to quantify, like the elusive yet eternal question, 'what's my purpose in life?' The one thing our general motivations have in common (e.g. family, art, politics, philanthropy) is that they seek to enhance the survival of our species. Even something as seemingly selfish as 'earning money' can only be accomplished by providing a service or product to another consumer. But even as these endeavors only partially fill our void, an answer like 'serving God' (which can be translated into 'serving yourself') only carries value when an actual person gains benefit from it, which, in this particular case, ties into our social camaraderie with other worshippers in pursuit of the same goal (i.e. salvation in Heaven would be more like Hell if you were 'alone' for eternity).
Abstract: The ambiguity surrounding opposing views on marriage, economy, diet, health care, and purpose (among other issues) inspired divine laws.

Technology / God(s)

Our survival instinct is a lot like the engine of a high performance sports car – even if you drive slowly you get horrible gas mileage. In other words, our instincts don't idle well. There is a correlation between our ease of survival and our level of misdirected anxiety. When we're not busy surviving (i.e. hunting, avoiding predators, earning a paycheck) we're often worrying about it. Technology is a very positive side affect of that worry. And where technology fell short, prayer took over[31]. Survival based prayers came in the form of language, which guided the evolution of the recipient of these prayers into sympathetic, language oriented beings (although the concept of spiritual cause and effect, as with *karma*, promotes positive deeds over verbal gratitude). It wasn't until technology evolved that prayers found an additional purpose: personal motivation. Man realized he possessed the potential to control his survival, but the worry was still there. Unsure about the origins of inspiration and mental clarity, he sought guidance to unleash this potential. As long as there is anxiety associated with our future, and the key to unlocking our brain's full potential remains a mystery, there is the potential for prayer, and therefore God.

Abstract: Our lack of a technological solution for our survival and cognitive shortcomings led to the creation of God(s).

---

[31] No longer limited to underdeveloped societies, even in modern times the more pious amongst us (generally priests and clerics) find it necessary to boost their importance by inserting a caveat to science and technology and sighting the causes of phenomenon like earthquakes, tsunamis, and other natural disasters to the sins of mankind.

Understanding / Spirits

The main difference between this level of the pyramid and the previous is that the supernatural aspect of this level does not seek a following. In other words, ghosts are either powerless to help or they don't have egos. The spiritual world may have arisen due to a lack of scientific understanding, but it persists primarily due to a lack of perspective. There is the potential for overlap between the two levels through the acceptance of Deism (i.e. belief in a super-natural creator who does not intervene), or simply the idea that God takes action of his own accord independent of our religious beliefs or prayers. Valid or not, horoscopes and astrology continue to ring true with over a billion people worldwide. In fact, if Astrology were a religion, it would rank third in popularity, essentially tied with Hinduism. Whether it's a belief in pre-destiny, spiritual guidance, or fortune-telling, they accomplish two things that appeal to our human nature: they reduce accountability and increase self importance. In other words, the very nature of something, or someone, guiding our choices counter-acts our fear of the unknown and feeds our ego.

The *Forer effect* is a classic example of the biases we attribute to favorable data (e.g. horoscopes). In 1949 psychologist Bertram Forer passed out the following 'unique' personality evaluation to his students:

> *You have a great need for other people to like and admire you. You have a tendency to be critical of yourself. You have a great deal of unused capacity which you have not turned to your advantage. While you have some personality weaknesses, you are generally able to compensate for them. Your sexual adjustment has presented problems for you. Disciplined and self-controlled outside, you tend to be worrisome and insecure inside. At times you have serious doubts as to whether you have made the right decision or done the right thing. You prefer a certain amount of change and variety and become dissatisfied when hemmed in by restrictions and limitations. You pride yourself as an independent thinker and do not accept others' statements without satisfactory proof. You have found it unwise to be too frank in revealing yourself to others. At times you are extroverted, affable, sociable, while at other times you are introverted, wary, reserved. Some of your aspirations tend to be pretty unrealistic. Security is one of your major goals in life.*

The students were unaware that they were all given the exact same evaluation, and when told to rate its accuracy on a scale of zero to five (five being the highest) the ratings averaged 4.26.

There are many fields of knowledge for which we have accumulated a great deal of understanding based on confirmed evidence (e.g. evolution, carbon dating, vaccinations, climatology) yet inevitably fail to monopolize when up against 'denialism'. Perhaps the main reason this attitude persists is because accepting this knowledge as 'true' does not immediately affect our survival. There are only a handful of essentials we require to maintain our health: food, water, hygiene, and, in most cases, clothing; even shelter is negotiable if you reside in a temperate region. Social backlash aside, in general, your day-to-day would not be the slightest bit disrupted if you believed the earth was flat, the rain was God's tears, or sickness was caused by demons. However, others in this world (e.g. astronomers, meteorologists, farmers, engineers, physicists, biologists, doctors) are not afforded the luxury of ignoring science. Thankfully the efforts and knowledge of a few can, and do, benefit the many.

If you were given the choice of camping for a night in the African Serengeti (host to over 70 species of large mammals) or a cemetery in Iowa, it might not be an easy decision. Even as there are no proven cases of anyone being physically harmed by a ghost or spirit, there are several instances, since the advent of clinical psychology, where demonic possession was believed to have occurred.

1906 – Clara Germana Cele (South Africa)
1949 – Robbie Mannheim – aka Roland Doe (United States)
1974 – Michael Taylor (England)
1975 – Anneliese Michel (Germany)

The symptoms described in all of these cases largely resemble those of dissociative identity disorder, schizophrenia, Tourette's syndrome, epilepsy, bipolar disorder, or sleep paralysis, but that's not to say the explanation is this simple. The evidence for demonic possession is about as strong, and actually less prevalent, as alien abductions. And if you subscribe to the idea that the exorcisms performed by Catholic priests are effective, these particular examples, from a theological standpoint, are mutually exclusive[32].

The *God(s)* level of the pyramid relies on several factors to remain structurally sound: the myths must endure to preserve the rituals (what do I believe?), worshippers must overlook the paradox of multiple 'supreme' Gods attached to multiple world religions (who do I worship?), and a justification for bad things happening to good people (why does God allow evil?[33]). Spirituality, on the other hand, is often not bound by rituals, exclusivity, or divine morality. It capitalized on our lack of understanding for why things happen, be it circumstantial, psychological, or in instances of presumed supernatural activity, scientific. Compared to organized religion, there is far less social pressure to adhere to specific spiritual beliefs, which allows for a freedom of credence that appeals to many. But perhaps most essential to our 'pattern seeking' instincts,

---

[32] The Christian stance on extraterrestrials is ambiguous as they are not specifically addressed in the Bible, but to keep consistent with traditional beliefs the only acceptable position is that God created life on this planet only, therefore alien life forms do not exist.
[33] The Christian concept of 'the fall of man' offers the explanation that all of humanity is held accountable for the wrongful actions of the first humans, which contradicts human nature (i.e. an unjust rule from a 'moral' God).

spiritual guidance seeks to remedy the randomness of events. We gain a survival advantage when we can predict negative outcomes, thus allowing us time to plan accordingly. Whether we are successful at this or not, belief in some form of spiritual guidance eliminates the daunting conclusion that negative events may very well have no explanation or justification.

Abstract: Our inability to fully understand science or cope with the emotional dissonance linked to negative events influences our belief in spiritual guidance.

Immortality / Afterlife

Do human beings have a soul? Our fear of death incorporates the lives of loved ones as well as our own, but upon reaching the bottom of the theological pyramid the philosophical waters grow murkier. Our primitive instincts presume that our mind lives on, but, unlike spirits, are unable to affect or interact with the physical world. The ongoing argument on this subject is between *substance dualism* (the mind and brain are separate) and *monism* (the mind is a product of the brain). It wasn't until around 1,700 B.C.E. that the Egyptians acquired knowledge of brain damage, but it was still generally accepted worldwide that the heart – not the brain – housed the soul as well as intellect. In 1637 René Descartes made philosophical history with the statement, "I think, therefore I am," which opened the door for theories on consciousness and dualism.

One of the arguments on the subject is the monist argument from *brain damage*. This links thoughts and consciousness to the brain due to the fact that brain damage, be it degenerative (e.g. Alzheimer's disease) or injury related, directly, and often permanently, impairs our ability to think. This is also evident with TMS (trans-cranial magnetic stimulation), which can produce, enhance, or slow down motor activity and receptors. The dualist counter argument is that the brain is merely a gateway between the spiritual world and the physical. The mind produces 'pure' thoughts that, when filtered through a damaged brain, are processed imperfectly. When the brain deteriorates after death the mind detaches and is released into the spiritual world. However, our understanding of the nature of thought is now in question with a recent discovery of neurologist V.S. Ramachandran at Cal Tech University in 2006. A split brain patient (i.e. the corpus callosum was severed essentially creating two distinct personalities) was asked a series of questions directed at both the right and left hemispheres of his brain. When asked if he believed in God, the right half answered "yes", while the left half answered "no". Ramachandran posed the facetious, yet relevant, question: when this man dies, does only the right half of his soul go to Heaven?

Another argument from the dualist perspective is the argument from *irreducibility*, which insists that the properties of the 'whole' must be evident in the 'parts'. The brain is made up of molecules, which themselves are not capable of consciousness, therefore billions of unconscious molecules cannot create a conscious brain (i.e. consciousness is supplied by a separate component: the soul). The monist counter to this argument is to demonstrate that a species without a soul (e.g. a chimpanzee) can display consciousness.

In 2011 Takaaki Kaneko and Masaki Tomonaga conducted research with chimpanzees to determine if they could display characteristics of self awareness. Three female chimps were utilized in the experiment. The chimps witnessed two blinking cursors on a computer screen. One of the cursors could be controlled by a mouse, for which the chimp could access and manipulate. The catch was that both cursors would move – one via the mouse, the other was a previously recorded movement intended to distract. The chimps were then given a reward if they could correctly identify which cursor movement was theirs during a playback of the event. Even as the actions of the 'distracter cursor' were nearly identical to the chimps', the three subjects achieved 90% accuracy in identifying their own cursor.

A deeper understanding of the origins of thought is required to settle these arguments; nevertheless there will always remain a desire to escape the finality and mystery of 'not thinking'. To alleviate some of the mystery, it can be argued that the familiarity of death is something we've all experienced during a night of dreamless sleep.

Abstract: Our inability to fully understand the nature of thought, both in life and in death, influences our belief in the soul.

An additional factor that spans the entirety of our existence is the *social amity* surrounding religion stemming from our desire to seek out like-minded individuals. The communal dividends associated with each level of the pyramid can be accomplished through secular social groups.

- Social means designed to improve our imperfect justice system: pursuing a criminal justice degree, pursuing a career in politics, or joining the N.R.A.

- Social means designed to embrace nostalgia and culture: joining the N.C.L.R.C. (National Capital Language Resource Center), joining the American Historical Association, or joining a local culture group found in most major cities.

- Social means designed to explore modern technology: joining the A.I.T.P (Association of Information Technology Professionals), or joining a local computer club.

- Social means designed to further our understanding of science and nature: joining Mensa International (if your I.Q. is at least 132), joining the Night Sky Network (astronomy based), or joining a local science club found in most major cities.

- Social means designed to compensate for our mortality: joining a local bereavement support group.

There is an undeniable 'tongue in cheek' aspect to these pursuits, but the social advantages of religion are clear: joining one church satisfies all five categories.

Where religion falls short is that it offers no evidence of providing justice, it replaces actual culture with myths, prayer does not replace technology, and there is no evidence to back up any of its explanations for the origins of nature or spiritual guidance. And religion may have conceived the afterlife, but it does not own it. In other words, if the mind can survive death, you don't have to commit to a belief system to reap the benefits. Of course accepting the principle of an afterlife inevitably leads to conceiving the other layers of the theological pyramid. Until we are able to experience the spiritual world, and quantifiably communicate our findings with the living, the afterlife will undoubtedly conform to the buoyancy of our imaginations.

What's the next tier to come once our desire to resolve the current pyramid apex has tapered? Where can we redirect our worries in the future? It's not always easy to conceive 'potential' problems that society can agree upon. It could be animal rights, or some developing environmental issue, or perhaps it will loop back around to immortality coat tailing on our quest to cure diseases. But what we're inevitably doomed to take for granted is how far we've actually progressed. To abandon a pursuit like 'resolving social injustice' should only come about because both parties (i.e. believers and non-believers) are actually satisfied with the results. In other words, the believers are truly at ease knowing the sinners will repent in hell, and the non-believers are content with the product of our justice system. I venture to say that neither side has collectively come to this conclusion. Imagining a physical world where no evil deed goes unpunished seems utterly unachievable. But if this ever became a reality, we would undoubtedly celebrate by redirecting our fears toward whatever issue happens to be next in line. Perhaps the real problem lies not in the issue itself, but in the dismissal placed upon it after crafting an unsubstantiated resolution.

What would society be like without religion?

A question that wasn't posed in the first chapter seems relevant to address: what would society be like without religion? If we disregard knee-jerk apologist responses like, "there would be no morality, monogamy, or reason to remain civil," we are left with several secular examples from which we can draw conclusions. In regards to counter acting xenophobia, society already has a variety of positive secular lifestyle choices to bond over. In the same way that religion can restrict diet, provide rituals, and manage appearance, the west coast is notorious for their affinity for healthy eating, exercise, and concern for fashion – although they collectively serve the same goal.

If we want a broader example of a secular society, we can look to Europe. Once governed by the church, it can be argued that Europe displays a largely anti-religious attitude because of its past. The laws of the United States were established based on religious freedom, but most of Europe didn't adopt a separation of church and state until the 20th century, and some countries are only partially separated (e.g. Germany). It's possible that European atheism is a form of rebellion against their government or a cathartic display of their religious freedom, whereas America's religious demographics have remained relatively unchanged since its origins in 1776 (i.e. the way Europe used to be).

Let's compare social statistics of the seven most atheistic countries in Europe (Czech Republic, Denmark, Estonia, France, Netherlands, Norway, and Sweden) to Romania (a highly Christian European country), Turkey (a highly Islamic European country), and the United States. The statistics being analyzed are tangential to issues religion often addresses, like food restrictions, caring for the ill (health care), philanthropy (economy versus poverty rate), family values (same-sex marriage status, polygamy status, divorce rate, abortion rate), and crime (homicide rate, prison population, capital punishment status).

COUNTRY	BELIEF	MEDICAL	DIETARY	ECONOMIC		MARRIAGE & FAMILY				CRIME & JUSTICE		
	Believe in God / Believe in Spirits	Health Care Ranking (WHO stats from 2000)	Vegetarian	Economy Ranking	Poverty Rate	Same-sex Marriage Status	Polygamy Status	Divorce Rate	Abortion Rate (per 100,000 pregnancies)	Homicide Rate (per 100,000 population)	Prisoners (per 100,000 population)	Capital Punishment (amount executed in 2011)
Czech Republic	19% / 50%	48	1.5%	51	9%	Recognized (cannot adopt)	Not legal	66%	21	1.7	178	Abolished
Denmark	31% / 49%	34	1.5%	34	13.4%	Recognized	Not legal	46%	16	0.9	72	Abolished
Estonia	16% / 54%	77	Almost none	101	17.5%	Not recognized	Not legal	58%	54	5.2	339	Abolished
France	34% / 27%	1	2%	5	6.2%	Recognized	Not legal	55%	12	1.1	102	Abolished
Netherlands	34% / 37%	17	4.5%	18	10.5%	Recognized	Cohabitation Agreement (2 partners)	43%	7	1.1	112	Abolished
Norway	32% / 47%	11	2%	23	4.3%	Recognized	Not legal	44%	17	0.6	73	Abolished
Sweden	23% / 53%	23	Almost none	22	6.6%	Recognized	Not legal	47%	19	1.0	75	Abolished
Romania	90%	99	Almost none	56	21.1%	Not recognized	Not legal	28%	78	2.0	193	Abolished
Turkey	90%	71	Almost none	17	16.9%	Not recognized	Not legal	20%	25	3.3	92	Abolished
United States	90%	38	5%	1	15.1%	Recognized in 11 states	Not legal	53%	23	4.8	716	43

If religion isn't the catalyst for these beliefs and behaviors, what is? Some might call it 'bold' to claim that our intrinsic sense of morality could yield results like what we might observe in France or Norway. The other end of the spectrum would entail state authorized atheism, like Marxism in Stalinist Russia (1929 – 1939), or the influence of the Communist climate in China, post revolution (after 1949). This attitude, government sanctioned or not, actually ties in to our subconscious desire for 'fairness'.

Alberto Alesina (Harvard University) and George-Marios Angeletos (MIT) conducted an economic study in 2002 to explain the difference in cultural attitudes between the United States and Europe. 71% of Americans display a 'capitalist' mindset in that they believe people are ultimately in control of their financial destiny. However, only 40% of Europeans agree and instead believe that 'bad luck' plays just as strong a role as personal effort. Americans also exhibit a general belief that market conditions (i.e. business growth, supply, demand) play out fairly, whereas Europeans believe these conditions are often unfair. These somewhat polarized mindsets have yielded two significant outcomes. Firstly, American tax rates are lower (10% average), while European tax rates are nearly double (average of the atheistic nations is nearly 18%). Secondly, there is a greater division between the rich and the poor in America, while in Europe, partially due to larger tax revenue, their poor are better protected.

An arguable conclusion can be drawn from these statistics: we *desire* to have faith in an overall governing body. In America this faith is in God, therefore we can comfortably limit government interference. In Europe they compensate for their lack of godly belief by entrusting more regulatory power in their government. American culture tends to discriminate in that those who are lazy, and therefore poor, are ungodly – a classic example of religious xenophobia. Yet the European attitude, which accepts 'bad luck' as a pretext, doesn't attribute motive to this undesirable situation. Conservative Americans offer advice (e.g. God helps those who help themselves) while Europeans offer money.

The diversity of world religions and governments creates a paradox when determining if mankind has a common social nature. Are we best adapted to cohabitate in a caste system (a sanctioned division of classes), a capitalist society (a natural division of classes), some form of egalitarianism (equality), or some combination of the three? Retroactive analysis may be required to determine this, nonetheless, our nature seems to require, at the very least, 'fairness' in the form of religion counter to the degree of state involvement. Unfortunately, the balancing act is nullified when both religion and government are one in the same.

The Damage

A humble kingdom was under constant attack by a neighboring rival. On his death bed, the King entrusted his twin sons with an epic project: build a wall around the city for protection. He stated that whichever son laid the most bricks would inherit his throne. After the King died his sons began crafting each brick and laying them by hand. Many years later, and after many hard fought enemy battles, they could see the other end of the wall which would complete the circle, but they realized the old bricks were crumbling and would have to be replaced. One son designed a machine that would craft bricks twice as fast, which would ultimately complete the wall, but it would have to be renovated regularly. The other son decided instead of clay bricks he would use stone. The first son stated, "To inherit the throne we have to use clay bricks," to which the other son replied, "Not only is dad not alive to clarify his wishes, I thought the goal was to protect the city."

The 'brick wall' analogy illustrates the mindset religion aims to instill on society. It establishes rules, applies those rules towards the 'greater good', and then, regardless of the outcome, justifies the results to reinforce the religion itself. Religion tends to establish divine rules with the best of intentions, but like many flawed regulations, the damage will eventually become magnified. For example, 30 years ago Mexico City had what was widely considered to be the highest levels of air pollution on the planet. In 1989 they created a law to reduce vehicle emissions known as *Hoy No Circula* (a.k.a. one day without a car). The rule was that all non-commercial vehicles must stay off the road at least one day a week on a rotating basis (stickers were issued based on the last digit of the license plate number). The idea was that 20% less cars on the road per day would improve the air quality over time. Did it work? Naturally people didn't like not being able to drive for a day, so families who could afford a second car bought one and kept their old car. This resulted in the same amount of cars on the road as before the regulation, with most people using their older car for commuting and their new car one day a week. Mexico City's air pollution got worse, and the policy was eventually dropped in favor of mandatory emissions testing.

In addition to promoting 'ethical' business practices, Islamic dogma drastically stifled their business growth. And now the United States, and its trepidation towards stem-cell research, faces a similar situation regarding health. Federal funding for this medical research (e.g. treatment for cancer, Parkinson's, spinal cord injuries, and multiple sclerosis) has been restricted due to religious influence based on 'the sanctity of a soul', or, to tie back into the analogy, the wall is weaker because stronger materials are forbidden[34]. This is also evident with the rise of HIV in southern Africa. Safe-sex campaigns and condoms (which yielded a 10% decrease in AIDS in Uganda between 1991 and 2000) have been banned due to the influence of Christian and Islamic religious leaders. Their goal of promoting abstinence and monogamy has led to a gradual increase rather than a decline in the spread. It's easy to justify this outcome as 'God's way of punishing the sinners'. And it will likely follow a similar path if the epidemic crosses continental borders into Europe and the Middle East as 'God's way of punishing those who allow the sins to continue'.

Religion actually magnifies instincts in humans that are not evident in nature, not necessarily because we are more highly evolved, but because we are too prolific at what we do best: survive. Humans and animals alike are genetically and emotionally wired to preserve their own species, but this begins with their own kin, extending to parents, siblings, cousins, second cousins, and so on[35]. In the hunter-gatherer era, bands were essentially an oligarchy comprised of fifty members of your extended family, give or take. Communal preservation wasn't just a social instinct, it was a family instinct. When human populations grew beyond family based communities, our mentality changed. We realized that values are subjective based on culture. But rather than explore these

---

[34] Coupled with federal funding restrictions, 14 states are in the process of completely banning the use of human embryos for stem cell research.

[35] Bottlenose dolphins have been observed biting through nets to save a captured companion, and supporting ill companions close to the ocean's surface to prevent them from drowning. Adult meerkats will climb to a vantage point to spot predators on behalf of the group, but this behavior is particularly evident when young pups are present.

differences we were inclined to fear them. Perhaps our zeal for religious branching is nature's way of thinning out the herd. Our cultural isolation embraces belief systems that reduce sympathy for those who think differently. The larger our population the more obvious this partition becomes, thus the more inclined we are towards apathy, neglect, and ultimately war. At first glance these attributes strike us as negative, but perhaps religion and religious branching is just another survival instinct: a method to reduce over-population. Religion comes in the guise of humanity, but ultimately, and ironically, results in dehumanization. And if this disconnect does not result in warfare or poverty, religion's fear of science (i.e. the stifling of technological advances) may hinder our survival. But like many fear based instincts we manage to suppress a majority of these urges in favor of civil brotherhood, only to leave us with a dubious question: should we listen to our instincts?

Is religious branching trying to tell us something? Are there too many of us? An important attribute our instincts tend to lack is 'perspective'. Unmoved by data or reason, instincts and emotion function on a timeline of immediate gratification. They come from a primal fear that food, water, shelter, and mating privileges are limited resources that must be competed for. Religion reacts to this by attempting to unite mankind in a common goal of poise and benevolence. But unlike government, religion was not designed to evolve. And despite efforts to prevent evolution, religion does so for one main reason: change over time is inevitable. Nothing in nature stays the same for very long. Religion can be viewed as a paradox: the desire of an evolving species to cling to its un-evolved origins. But to keep religion free from the clutches of xenophobia, faithful followers must remain wary of the ambition of their leaders. Uniting the planet in a common belief is a noble pursuit, but if God designed us with this in mind, he created the ultimate test of human perseverance: bonding foreigners with a belief system that arouses our xenophobia.

Auditing the path laid out by the Abrahamic religions yields a timeline that hardly resembles a divine plan.

- Polytheism in the Near East creates a pantheon of thousands of gods
- The Canaanites establish divine supremacy amongst a handful of these gods
- *Judaism* establishes monotheism through Yahweh, but believes the Jewish race was segregated for his divine protection
- *Christianity* adapts Judaism to encompass all races through Yahweh's arrival on earth in human form
- *Islam* reinterprets Judaism and Christianity through a divine revelation via the prophet Muhammad
- Islamic leadership reinterprets its legacy resulting in a schism that divides the Shi'a from the Sunni
- Christian leadership is reinterpreted resulting in a schism that divides the Catholics from Protestants
- Protestants reinterpret Christianity creating numerous divisions

- The reinterpretations continue for all three branches...

If an observer from another planet sought to integrate with our society, they would be confronted with the choice of which religion to choose. A belief system communicated to us through divine means would still be in practice today. Based on this, the decision can be broken down into four categories: cumulative, singular, open, and synthetic.

Cumulative assumes that all, or at least more than one religion, are divinely inspired regardless of their contradictions (e.g. Judaism, Christianity, and Islam are all correct). This carries some philosophical baggage due to the contradiction of omnificence when applied to monotheism. In other words, an all-knowing and autonomous god is either deceitful or is not omnificent if in fact there are other gods (and/or paths to salvation). *Singular* implies that there is in fact only one true religion. Unfortunately we are left to our own devices to determine which. The differences are not only subtle but often arbitrary and self-serving[36]. And if one religion did stand out as being truly inspired, what's to be said of the religions it evolved from? How much should we invest in divine insight that's been repeatedly misinterpreted, and at what point in the timeline was it properly conveyed? *Open* assumes there is a God, or at least a creative force, but this supernatural entity is either incapable of desire, or simply has no desire to be worshipped (e.g. Deism). Lastly *synthetic* implies that the tenets of all religions – past, present, and future – are manmade and carry no divine value.

There is a caveat to the *singular* category that allows it to flourish, but, in addition to being the most mystifying of the four options, it hemorrhages severely from Occam's razor. There is a creator and his religion endures in modern times. But this creator chose to remain anonymous amongst the various theologies by observing mankind's inherent propensity for religion and patterns for spirituality, and then inspired a prophet accordingly. This prophet led a life like the others, spread his gospel like the others, and communicated a flawed set of beliefs and values like the others. The only difference between this prophet and the others is that the voice inside his head was actually God, and this God knowingly fed him misinformation in order to camouflage the one true religion. This God knew that a religion which can be confirmed through physical evidence would not inspire a nutritious following – it would inspire fascism. The laws of this religion are not divine, for they perfectly mimic manmade concepts. Its theories of origin and myths mirror those of the other faiths, which reduce its rituals to manmade constructs as well. Its followers will reap the benefits of salvation, but for no other reason than sheer, blind luck. Unfortunately, we do not know which religion this is or which prophet this God chose to inspire, and we never will.

Contradictions and inaccuracies aside, as long as we have the catalysts of four key psychological ingredients, religion will continue to flourish is some capacity.

---

[36] To use Christianity as an example, its dogmatic differences from Judaism revolve around its holy days (e.g. Sabbath and Passover) and its stance on accepting the resurrection of a prophet as an unsupported miracle. Your position on these key issues determines whether or not you are saved or tortured for eternity.

Ingredient number one: exposure to a **mortality salience** (e.g. economic decline, insufficient technology). Ingredient two: **fear of change** (e.g. overpopulation, negative media coverage). Ingredient three: **cultural camaraderie** (i.e. a locally reinforced religious assembly). And ingredient four: **foreign oppression** (e.g. the threat of insurgence from a foreign entity).

Unfortunately we are hard-wired to detect a *mortality salience* even if one doesn't exist, but improved technology has gradually diluted its severity. Our exposure to *change* has become, ironically enough, a rapidly evolving phenomenon. As technology improves our longevity and communication, it exposes us to greater vehicles for change, thus cancelling out any ground gained in that realm. *Cultural camaraderie* has been a constant throughout history, but the difference here is in government and whether or not we are bound by law to participate in religious rituals or not. Improved survival methods created a more humanistic society, which has led to more humanistic politics. Lastly, *foreign oppression* too is coupled with technology via democracy, improved communication (i.e. a means to create world-wide alliances like NATO), and, ironically, better weapons (i.e. our capacity to cause our own extinction has created a welcome trepidation towards extreme military campaigns). We are less likely to fall victim to xeno-dichotomy now than we were as recently as half a century ago.

In the epic battle of 'science versus religion' the tide is starting to shift in the direction of science. In other words, the value of technology is beginning to detract from the value of spirituality. But this may come at a price. Reserving a portion of our psyche for 'spiritual protection' may be the catalyst for exploiting our passions. If all of life's problems could be addressed via technology, the burden of accountability may take a toll. Too much control can be equally unhealthy, so perhaps 'fear in small doses' is the ideal prescription. But human nature will undoubtedly stride to keep worry at bay, and this bodes poorly for the future of organized religion. Does the innovation of industry mean religion as a whole will someday be demoted to mythology? If God goes away, the ambiguous forces of superstition are next on the chopping block, followed by mourning rituals – it's hard to imagine the death of a loved as a potentially hollow and immediately resolvable event. We may never fully realize the benefits, or potential hazards, of a Godless human culture. It's within our nature to rebel almost as much as it is to conform, so the pendulum may eventually swing back in the other direction. But unsubstantiated beliefs take a backseat to the policies we employ to keep society in line. It's becoming harder to ignore the results.

EPILOGUE:

The Burden of Proof

Religion exists in two verifiable places: in the minds of humans, and in media (e.g. books, video, etc). If the media is destroyed (e.g. the Zoroastrian Avesta around 500 B.C.E.) and the human worshippers destroyed along with it (e.g. the Olmec civilization around 350 B.C.E.) their god would have to re-inspire a human prophet, or civilization, in order to revive its theology. Thelema, which reinterpreted the Egyptian religion, and a few Pagans – who are essentially rebelling against Christianity – are among the few modern examples of this phenomenon, neither of which approaches mainstream status. So if religions have documentable starting points, as well as ending points, what happens to their gods before and after their reign? The esoteric question *if a tree falls in the forest and there's no one there to hear it, does it make a sound* comes to mind. Unlike gods, sound possesses physical qualities that can be measured. If there's no one there to hear the tree fall, the sound is still a tangible entity regardless of human verification. Gods, on the other hand, have been defined as immaterial, immeasurable, and therefore must live vicariously through human acknowledgment to retain value. Can the Babylonian god Marduk be considered a god after 500 C.E.? Can Yahweh be considered a god before 950 B.C.E.? Perhaps we need to redefine what a god is.

The characteristics and desires of a god are established by the religious leaders who interpret their wishes. In other words, if you want to know what Waheguru expects of his worshippers, you should consult a Sikhi priest, or read the *Gurū Granth Sāhib*, compiled by a Sikh guru. Based on this there are three absolutes we can apply in our pursuit to define God:

1. His/her existence is dependent on documentation and worshippers
2. His/her teachings are subject to human interpretation
3. His/her teachings are limited by our capacity to circulate them

These absolutes can be reworded without necessarily altering their meaning:

1. God is not omnipotent
2. God is not omnificent
3. God in not omnipresent

As creative beings we can apply any characteristics to an entity that is transcendent, like "perfect, timeless, mysterious", etc. Only a delusional political leader would dare use these terms to describe their government or economic system, yet these systems are the accepted basis of society. It is, however, understood that laws and governments are capable of evolution, but when a religion evolves, you've created a new religion. But how far has religion really evolved? Since the birth of religious rituals, as archaic as many of them are (e.g. bloodletting, body mutilation, idolatry) perhaps the only truly extinct practice is human sacrifice. Unfortunately technology has enabled its bleak replacement: suicide bombings. This is not a ritual per se, but it is religiously motivated.

On the surface, religion appears to have evolved. Belief systems in existence now (e.g. theism, prayer, salvation) did not exist when religion originated. In this regard religion, like biology, grew more complex with evolution. However, the mindset of the worshipper has not. This is the primary difference between biological evolution and theological evolution. Even as there are alpha personalities in nature, the genetics across a species are essentially identical. There is an evolutionary divide in religion that makes it unique. Three tiers have been established: the divine, the human vessel, and the worshipper. The *worshippers* follow what the human vessel (i.e. the prophet) instructs. This tier has remained evolutionarily unchanged throughout history. The *human vessel* does what the *divine* (i.e. God) instructs. It is on this tier where the evolution has taken place, but here too is where a disconnect arises. When is a prophet truly a prophet, and when are they defiant worshippers with vivid imaginations?

If we tally the worshippers who would claim that God has directly spoken to them, which would include, by definition, almost every Evangelical and Pentecostal

Christian (approx 350 million), not to mention the worshippers of countless other gods, and most certainly would include the majority of priests of all faiths (approx 2 million), the final number would easily reach half a billion. If 1 out of every 5,000 of these 'chosen' are ambitious enough to break from the flock and convince others to follow, you'd have the global array of religious denominations we have today (to put things in perspective, 1 in out of 50 Americans have the ambition to start a small business with employees).

If you concede that prophets and religious leaders are a true representation of God's wishes, you have to ask yourself, "why would our creator care about our politics?" Are we not capable of war, genocide, and segregation without God's guidance? Religion is how mankind countered fear, with God as our immortal bodyguard. But over the millennia religion was substituted for culture, and it catered to our instincts. The ironic balance of 'too little technology, too much fear' versus 'too much technology, too little compassion' tightened the union between religion and politics.

"The only way to reduce the number of nuclear weapons is to use them."
—Rush Limbaugh

"As soon as Jesus sits on his throne he's gonna rule the world with a rod of iron. That means he's gonna make the ACLU do what he wants them to. That means you're not gonna have to ask if you can pray in public school. We will live by the law of God and no other law."
—Rev. John Hagee

"Let's teach them about the big bang theory, let's teach them about evolution – I've got no problem if a school board, a local school board, says we want to teach our kids about creationism, that people, some people, have these beliefs as well, let's teach them about intelligent design. Bottom line, at the end of the day, we want our kids to be exposed to the best facts."
—Bobby Jindal (Governor of Louisiana)

"A thorough knowledge of the Bible is worth more than a college education."
—Theodore Roosevelt

A reoccurring issue in theological debates is "who carries the burden of proof?" Do theists need to prove there is a God, or do atheists need to prove there is no God? American theoretical physicist Richard Feynman was famously asked if he could, "prove that flying saucers are impossible?" This was a rebuttal to a statement Feynman made about the improbability of UFOs actually existing. His assumption was based on what little evidence Feynman did have, which was the propensity for human irrationality, versus the 'unknown' efforts of extraterrestrial beings. Feynman conceded that he can't prove UFOs are impossible, they're just unlikely.

Is there a reason to believe UFOs do exist? If we are to trust personal accounts then there is a reason to believe. Based on personal accounts alone would you vote for a federal tax increase to devote a division of the military toward defense against potential UFO attacks? How about sacrificing your time to attend weekly meetings or raise public UFO awareness? What if a proclaimed victim of alien abduction asserted that his captors utilized fermentation to poison their enemies, so as a gesture of solidarity we should prohibit alcoholic beverages? The more sacrifices we make the less appealing a commitment to UFO belief sounds, but it doesn't have to end there. What if another victim of abduction claimed his technologically superior captors possessed an age reversal machine, and they were willing to share it with anyone who volunteers to be 'examined'? The more complex UFO worship becomes (i.e. the eventual addition of a reward: age reversal) the more its evolution begins to mirror theological evolution (i.e. the eventual addition of salvation).

Why do we require certain criteria to confirm some claims but dismiss it for others? We are ultimately we're left asking "are there instances where we should dismiss physical evidence and trust our instincts?" If going to church, saying prayers, and talking to dead relatives makes you happy, what's the harm? Philosopher and neuroscientist Sam Harris wrote an article entitled *The Fireplace Delusion* which illustrates the byproduct of religion in a telling analogy.

> *On a cold night, most people consider a well-tended fire to be one of the more wholesome pleasures that humanity has produced. A fire, burning safely within the confines of a fireplace or a woodstove, is a visible and tangible source of comfort to us. Here is what we know from a scientific point of view: There is no amount of wood smoke that is good to breathe. It is at least as bad for you as cigarette smoke, and probably much worse. The unhappy truth about burning wood has been scientifically established to a moral certainty: That nice, cozy fire in your fireplace is bad for you. Burning wood is also completely unnecessary, because in the developed world we invariably have better and cleaner alternatives for heating our homes. In fact, wood smoke often contributes more harmful particulates to urban air than any other source.*

The side-effects of religion are not confined to analogy, nor are they limited to third world cultures. Prioritizing emotion and instinct over reliable evidence indicates a regression toward primitive behavior – it's a dubious state of mind, and one we should collectively discourage and rise above. Allowing fear to dictate important decisions is, for example, detrimental to our justice system: over 30 deaths during the Salem witch trials in 1692, over 50 falsely executed murderers in the last 50 years[37], and literally

---

[37] This statistic is based on official government documentation, which does not take into account cases the justice departments were not willing to conceded, as well as those who were not fortunate enough to have

1000's of falsely accused rapists since the advent of DNA testing in 1985. Regardless of a judge's instructions to base a decision on evidence, a skilled attorney, or a heinous enough crime, can influence a jury member to 'go with their gut'.

Granted, there are situations where emotion can be a more practical guide than evidence. When we first meet someone for whom we plan to invest our time and/or money, we often rely on emotion to gage how trustworthy this person is. Unfortunately first impressions based on emotion can often blind us to contrary follow-ups, not to mention the fact that masking one's malicious intentions is a skill most politicians and businessmen have perfected. Self awareness of our 'emotional radar' should be exercised as often as possible. We can start by asking ourselves 'what's at stake when we rely on our emotions?' Are we being asked to donate our life savings because the rapture is imminent? Are we trusting the word of the Bible over the word of scientific data when it comes to global warming? Are we voting 'guilty' to condemn three teenage boys to death row because the victims were allegedly killed as part of a satanic ritual?[38]

Obviously not every situation involving emotion is as grave as these examples, but to put things into perspective we should be aware of where the burden of proof truly resides. When Christian apologists attempt to shift the burden of proof for the existence of God by claiming that, "there's no evidence that God does *not* exist", I'd like to make my point by comparing and contrasting Christianity (the largest religion in the world) with Mormonism (an offshoot and unfortunate 'punch-line' of Christianity). The problem with assigning the 'existence of God' as the default position is that it makes two dubious assumptions: 1) what we don't understand can only be explained by the existence of a God (e.g. as a society we will not now, nor in the future, advance our current understanding of science and nature); and 2) humans are the only creatures capable of understanding what God expects of us.

Both of these assumptions are essentially one in the same as they lead us down the same path: how can we quantify what's not there? In other words, if someone makes a claim for which there is no evidence, how do we know if it's true? Before the proponents of theism take the position that 'one set of rules must apply to all' (i.e. there is only one true religion), they must first come to agreement on what the rules are. As difficult as it may be for scientists to uncover the origins of our universe by studying physical evidence, it is exponentially more difficult to uncover the origins for something that presents no physical evidence whatsoever, which includes both the existence of a God, as well as its dogma.

Let's begin our comparison of Christianity to its bastardized offshoot by indentifying significant ambiguities that surround Mormonism.

---

undergone a post-mortem analysis.

[38] In 1994 the 'West Memphis Three' were convicted of capital murder by a jury in Arkansas, but ultimately released in 2010 upon entering an Alford plea after newly produced DNA evidence was introduced.

Ambiguity 1: The 'golden plates', from which the *Book of Mormon* was interpreted, were supposedly written in 'reformed Egyptian'. In 1829 Columbia College professor Charles Anthon was presented a transcribed sample of this language to authenticate its source. According to Joseph Smith, Anthon certified the text, only to rescind after hearing that the source was an angel. According to Anthon, he suspected fraud from the beginning. Also, no non-Mormon scholar acknowledges the existence of a 'reformed Egyptian' language.

Ambiguity 2: Other than Joseph Smith, there were eleven actual eye witnesses of the golden plates (and for some, the angel Morini as well), all of which were former members of the Latter Day Saints church:
- Oliver Crowley: also experienced divine visions similar to Joseph Smith's.
- Martin Harris: changed his religion five times before he became a Mormon, and was said to have walked and talked with Jesus (who was in the guise of a deer) for several miles.
- David Whitmer: also claims to have seen ancient relics possessed by the various characters in the Book of Mormon.
- The remaining eight witnesses were all members of David Whitmer or Joseph Smith's family.

Ambiguity 3: In 1830 the golden plates were returned to the angel Morini and have yet to be produced or examined since.

Ambiguity 4: Smith had a dubious track record for acquiring buried treasure, receiving visions, and financial debt.
- 1811 – 1819: Prior to the golden plate visions, Smith receives seven separate visions of various spiritual natures.
- 1820: Using his divinely acquired 'seer stone', Smith sends the owner of a stolen roll of cloth on a three mile trip to retrieve it. It was never found.
- 1820 – 1826: Smith and his family embark on a series of no less than seven treasure digging expeditions in and around the New York town of Palmyra, one of which involved Smith exhuming his older brother Alvin to prove to his family that he didn't exhume him prior.
- 1822: After sacrificing a black sheep to break a spell, Smith organized a group to dig for a chest of money, but the mission failed because a party member 'broke the silence' during the excavation.
- 1824 – 1825: The Smith family is delinquent on their home mortgage on three separate occasions.
- 1826: Smith goes on trial in a South Bainbridge court for 'disturbing the peace' due to being a 'glass looker', which at the time was a familiar con in New York farm country.

- 1828: Smith uses his seer stone (the same technique he used to find treasure) to translate the 'reformed Egyptian' from the golden plates into the Book of Mormon.

Ambiguity 5: Many of the historical accounts offered in the Book of Mormon (supposedly originating around 600 B.C.E. and buried in New York around 400 C.E.) contradict the archeological evidence we have today.
- *Book of Mormon*: up until 400 C.E. the Lamanites spoke Hebrew (or a modified Semitic language) and were the principle ancestors of the American Indians. *Evidence*: no Semitic languages provided influence or were spoken natively in America.
- *Book of Mormon*: horses, elephants, cattle, sheep, and goats are mentioned (placing their American inhabitance between 2,500 B.C.E. – 400 C.E.). *Evidence*: these animals were either extinct or did not exist in the Western Hemisphere till the Spaniards brought them over in the 15th century.
- *Book of Mormon*: barley, wheat, iron, and steel are mentioned. *Evidence*: barley and wheat were brought by the Spaniards, and metallurgy wasn't present in America until 400 years after the golden plates were supposedly written.
- *Book of Mormon*: the population of the Jaredites (a literate society with writing skills) numbered at least 2 million. *Evidence*: no archeological remains have been found of the Jaredite civilization, which were, by size and sophistication, comparable to the Ancient Egyptians or Romans, who left behind numerous artifacts and structures.

Rather than express my personal opinion on the validity of the Mormon faith, I will allow others the privilege.

> "I could not believe that heaven was organized as the Mormons asserted. Rather, I asked myself, where on earth did Joseph Smith acquire these ceremonies?"
> —Martin Wishnatsky (author and former LDS member)

> "Make no mistake about this. Mormonism is a cult. I know the Holy Bible is a decoy to the Mormon faith. If the Holy Bible contradicts the Mormon scriptures, the Holy Bible is wrong!"
> —Todd K. Olson (former Mormon elder)

> "You can take it to the bank, that if Romney [a Mormon] were President, the church leaders would have another 'vision,' that a church takeover must happen."
> —James Martin (former LDS member)

To draw a parallel with Mormonism we can compare several ambiguities of Christianity.

Ambiguity 1: The Old Testament was originally written in Aramaic and Hebrew (which contained no vowels). It was represented as being written by Moses, but the consensus amongst scholars is that it was written and edited by numerous anonymous sources, and that the fifth book, Deuteronomy, was a forgery. The New Testament was originally written in Koine Greek, whose original manuscripts have not survived. The surviving translations spanned three different traditional Greek text-types. Several of the gospel's authors are unknown, and none were eye witnesses to the supernatural accounts they described.

Ambiguity 2: According to biblical scholars, the accounts of Jesus' birth date is between 6 – 4 B.C.E., and the date of his crucifixion and resurrection somewhere between 30 – 36 C.E. The day of the week of the crucifixion was a Wednesday, Thursday, or Friday. The gospel of Mark places the time of the crucifixion at 9am, and his death at 3pm. However, the gospel of John places Jesus in Pilate's presence at noon.

Ambiguity 3: Jesus' ascension into heaven after his resurrection is described in Mark, Luke, and Acts as being "received *up* into heaven". Archaic cosmology understood heaven to be physically located above our atmosphere, whereas space travel and radio telescopes reveal otherwise.

Ambiguity 4: The track record of many Christian leaders paints an unflattering portrait of the morality required to preach their gospel.
- In 1968 self-proclaimed Christian prophet and faith healer Peter Popoff declared bankruptcy as a result of losing his ministry. Noted skeptic James Randi exposed his scam that the 'messages' he was receiving from God about audience members was actually via an in-ear receiver fed verbally by his wife backstage.
- Pentecostal pastor Tony Alamo was convicted of tax evasion in 1969 and 1994, and ten counts of sexual child abuse in 2009.
- Baptist reverend Henry J. Lyons was convicted of racketeering and grand theft in 1999.
- Pentecostal minister Jim Bakker was involved in a rape scandal in 1987, and convicted on 24 counts of accounting fraud in 1989.
- Anglican minister Graham Capill was convicted on multiple charges of sexual child abuse in 2005.
- Over the last 70 years 1,670 Catholic bishops were accused, sued, or convicted of child molestation.

Ambiguity 5: Many of the historical accounts offered in the Bible contradict the archeological and anthropological evidence we have today.
- *Bible*: according to the Creation myth, the earth and first life originated approximately 6,000 years ago. *Evidence*: multiple scientific disciplines place the

earth's age around 4.5 billion years, and the origins of life around 2.5 billion years ago.
- *Bible*: Seth, Enos, Cainan, Mahalaleel, Jared, Enoch, Methuselah, and Lameh all lived to be anywhere from 777 – 969 years old. *Evidence*: the oldest documented human was Jeanne Calment, 1875 – 1997 (122 years old).
- *Bible*: Noah fit two (or seven) of every species of walking, creeping, and flying animal onto a 450 foot ark in one day. *Evidence*: there are over 6.5 million species of land animals spread across seven continents.
- *Bible*: the Tower of Babel myth asserts that there was only one universal language spoken around 2,400 B.C.E. *Evidence*: early forms of written language reveal a difference in the Sumerian, Egyptian, Akkadian, and Indus languages dating back to 3,000 B.C.E.
- *Bible*: mentions actual giants, unicorns, and dragons. *Evidence*: there is no confirmed archeological evidence for the existence of giants, unicorns, or dragons.

The primary gripe of Christians about Mormonism is that they are essentially a contradictory cult riding the coattails of acceptance that Christianity has established. This is a legitimate concern, but it ignores the big picture. The primary gripe of atheists about religion is that religious beliefs and rituals contradict scientific evidence and social and economic evolution, and aspires to ride on the coattails of government. Because of this, religious influence must remain separate from education (i.e. it contradicts scientific evidence), government or politics (i.e. it contradicts social and economic evolution).

There is a side effect that accompanies the intelligence we have acquired: we are compelled to ask 'why'. If we know why we get sick, why food grows, why the sun rises, etc. we increase our chances for survival. But nature and society is constantly changing, which inevitably leads to different strategies and beliefs for how to navigate through life. If religion held up to all manners of reasoning and scrutiny, there would be a case for elevating it to a platform above traditional government. But religion not only fails at establishing consistency within itself, much less within the world surrounding it, it reverses our survival instincts. Survival of religion itself takes priority over the survival of its believers – an understandable side effect when your followers believe they possess an immortal soul. When the wellbeing of society as a whole is not our primary objective, what's the point?

Unfortunately we are ill-equipped to analyze the world through a different set of eyes and establish a broader perspective. The theist might say religion is to mankind as a parachute is to a skydiver. Whereas the atheist might say religion is to mankind as a parachute is to bird. 'Do we need religion' is still a hot topic for debate, but perhaps a few clues from nature can help put things in perspective. Such godless species like jellyfish and sponges have managed to endure the hardships of this world for nearly 500 million years. Homo sapiens have been around a mere 200,000. It would be like comparing their time on this plant to a day, and ours to a little over 90 seconds. Why do *we* need God to survive, but they don't? Those of us with the luxury of technology might scoff at the idea of comparing ourselves to primates, much less jellyfish. But the reality is all roads lead to survival. To a naive observer, a middle-class family in America focused on career and lifestyle would not appear to need religion. By comparison, a tribe of Bushmen in Central Africa who rarely live beyond age fifty seem to be in dire need of celestial guidance. Yet people from either culture can be equally pious, equally thirsty for knowledge, yet pale in comparison to the survival track record of the jellyfish.

Once you acknowledge the possibility that God is an unnecessary addition to the universe, you begin to realize how we as humans 'tick'. The more we know and understand, the less necessary God becomes. It's only a matter of time before the last drop of theology is squeezed dry from the realm of the unknown. Losing God does not mean losing hope, reason, or purpose – it means losing a major catalyst for discrimination and alienation. Only after we can remove the walls built by unsubstantiated belief systems can we even begin to establish a global culture. Perhaps someday the concept of borders will reside only in our history books.

REFERENCES

FOREWORD: IS RELIGION THE ANSWER?

- Jackson, Wayne. Christian Courier. "The Use of "Hell" in the New Testament." https://www.christiancourier.com/articles/406-use-of-hell-in-the-new-testament-the (2013).
- 43alley. YouTube. "Realizing Hell Does Not Exist." http://www.youtube.com/watch?v=Wgj65-EfmoA (Apr 9, 2013).
- ProgressIllinois. YouTube. "Rep. John Shimkus: God decides when the earth will end." http://www.youtube.com/watch?v=_7h08RDYA5E (Mar 27, 2009).
- CurrentNewsPolitics. YouTube. "Republican Congressman Cites Biblical Great Flood To Say Climate Change Isn't Man-Made." http://www.youtube.com/watch?v=3EAfVVf-Efc (Apr 10, 2013).

1
INTRODUCTION: YOU CAN'T COMPARE RELIGION TO EVOLUTION!

- Wikipedia. "Catholic sex abuse cases." http://en.wikipedia.org/wiki/Catholic_sex_abuse_cases (Apr 2013).
- Smith, Mark. Contra Craig. "Comments on Craig's Book: Reasonable Faith." http://www.jcnot4me.com/Items/contra_craig/contra_craig.htm (Mar 2013).
- The Daily Beast. "18 Outrageous Conservative Quotes." http://www.thedailybeast.com/articles/2009/09/10/18-outrageous-christian-right-quotes.html (Mar 2013).
- Wikipedia. "Catholic Church and evolution." http://en.wikipedia.org/wiki/Catholic_Church_and_evolution (Apr 2013).
- Wikipedia. "Evolution." http://en.wikipedia.org/wiki/Evolution (Mar 2013).
- Wikipedia. "Documentary hypothesis." http://en.wikipedia.org/wiki/Documentary_hypothesis (Apr 2013).
- Truth in Science. "The Peppered Moth." http://www.truthinscience.org.uk/tis2/index.php/component/content/article/127.html (Mar 2013).
- Understanding Evolution. "Toxic river means rapid evolution for one fish species." http://evolution.berkeley.edu/evolibrary/news/110301_pcbresistantcod. (Mar 2011).
- Wikipedia. "Culture." http://en.wikipedia.org/wiki/Culture (Apr 2013).
- Wikipedia. "List of languages by first written accounts." http://en.wikipedia.org/wiki/List_of_languages_by_first_written_accounts (Mar 2013).
- Wikipedia. "Indo-European languages". http://en.wikipedia.org/wiki/Indo-European_languages (Mar 2013).
- Science Daily. "New Evidence of Culture in Wild Chimpanzees'" http://www.sciencedaily.com/releases/2009/10/091022122321.htm (Jan 4, 2010).
- Wikipedia. "Kalam cosmological argument." http://en.wikipedia.org/wiki/Kal%C4%81m_cosmological_argument (Apr 2013).
- Wikipedia. "Chicago Statement on Biblical Inerrancy." http://en.wikipedia.org/wiki/Chicago_Statement_on_Biblical_Inerrancy (Apr 2013).
- Dallas Theological Seminaries Archives. "International Council on Biblical Inerrancy." http://library.dts.edu/Pages/TL/Special/ICBI_1.pdf (1978).
- Wikipedia. "List of ancient legal codes." http://en.wikipedia.org/wiki/List_of_ancient_legal_codes (Apr 2013).
- Crabtree, Vexen. Academic Studies of Religion. "Legislation and Faith: Religious Rights and Religions Wrongs." http://www.humanreligions.info/religious_rights.html (Jan 16, 2013).

2
RELIGION'S STORY: IN THE BEGINNING...

- Wikipedia. "Johann Jakob Bachofen." http://en.wikipedia.org/wiki/Johann_Jakob_Bachofen (May 2013).
- Wikipedia. "Civilization." http://en.wikipedia.org/wiki/Civilization (Feb 2013).
- Wikipedia. "Evolutionary origins of religion." http://en.wikipedia.org/wiki/Evolutionary_origin_of_religions (Jan 2013).
- Wikipedia. "Timeline of religion." http://en.wikipedia.org/wiki/Timeline_of_religion (Jan 2013).
- Timelines. "Anthropology." http://timelinesdb.com/listevents.php?subjid=765&title=Anthropology (Mar 2013).
- Wikipedia. "Human evolution." http://en.wikipedia.org/wiki/Human_evolution (Jan 2013).
- Pinker, Steven. "The Evolutionary Psychology of Religion." http://pinker.wjh.harvard.edu/articles/media/2004_10_29_religion.htm (Oct 29, 2004).
- Wikipedia. "Timeline of human evolution." http://en.wikipedia.org/wiki/Timeline_of_human_evolution (Jan 2013).
- Wikipedia. "Timeline of human prehistory." http://en.wikipedia.org/wiki/Timeline_of_human_prehistory (Jan 2013).
- Wikipedia. "Timeline of historic inventions." http://en.wikipedia.org/wiki/Timeline_of_historic_inventions (Jan 2013).
- Hopkin, Michael. Nature. "Jaw-dropping theory of human evolution." http://www.nature.com/news/2004/040322/full/news040322-9.html (Mar 25, 2004).
- Wade, Nicholas. New York Times. "Scientist Finds the Beginnings of Morality in Primate Behavior." http://www.nytimes.com/2007/03/20/science/20moral.html?pagewanted=all&_r=0 (Mar 20, 2007).
- Boyle, Alan. NBC News: Science. "How monkeys handle moral outrage." http://www.nbcnews.com/science/how-monkeys-handle-moral-outrage-6C10402459?franchiseSlug=sciencemain (Feb 20, 2012).
- Bekoff, Marc. Daily Good/Yes Magazine. "Emotional Lives of Animals." http://www.dailygood.org/view.php?sid=28 (May 17, 2011).
- SlideShare. "Civilization: An Introduction to the Origins of Society, Government, and Culture – Lecture Notes for Part 2: Politics – From bands to states."

- Godfrey, Neil. Vridar. How Polytheism morphed into Monotheism: first steps. http://vridar.org/2008/04/27/how-polytheism-morphed-into-monotheism-a-first-step/ (Apr 27, 2008).
- Saldana, Stephanie. Daily Star. "Temple reveals secrets of the one God." http://cogweb.ucla.edu/Culture/Monotheism.html (Mar 5, 2002).
- Evid3nc3. YouTube. "3.3.3 Atheism: A History of God (Part 1)." http://www.youtube.com/watch?v=MlnnWbkMlbg (Jan 7, 2011).
- Wikipedia. "Canaanite Religion." http://en.wikipedia.org/wiki/Canaanite_religion (Apr 2013).
- Wikipedia. "Mircea Eliade." http://en.wikipedia.org/wiki/Mircea_Eliade (May 2013).
- Wikipedia. "Joseph Campbell." http://en.wikipedia.org/wiki/Joseph_Campbell (May 2013).
- Carey, Benedict. New York Times. "I'm Not Lying, I'm Telling a Future Truth. Really." http://www.nytimes.com/2008/05/06/health/06mind.html?_r=0 (May 6, 2008).
- McHenry, Larry. "Star Myths." http://home.comcast.net/~lsmch/starmyths.htm (Apr 2013).
- Brian Hare, Josep Call, Michael Tomasello. "Chimpanzees deceive a human competitor by hiding." http://email.eva.mpg.de/~tomas/pdf/Chimpanzees%20deceive%20a%20human%20competitor_06.pdf (Jan 19, 2004).

3
COGNATIVE ANALYSIS: IT'S ALL IN YOUR MIND

- Wikipedia. "God gene." http://en.wikipedia.org/wiki/God_gene (Mar 2013).
- Barrett, Justin L. Test of Faith. "Why Would Anyone Believe in God." http://www.testoffaith.com/resources/resource.aspx?id=557 (2004).
- Wikipedia. "Harry Harlow." http://en.wikipedia.org/wiki/Harry_Harlow (May 2013).
- Wikipedia. "Blaise Pascal." http://en.wikipedia.org/wiki/Blaise_Pascal (Apr 2013).
- Skeptic Magazine. YouTube. "Michael Shermer Out of Body Experiment." http://www.youtube.com/watch?v=nCVzz96zKA0 (Jun 19, 2007).
- village1diot. YouTube. "Religion Explained – The Atheist Experience #341." http://www.youtube.com/watch?v=roceluRvhHM (May 7, 2010).
- Wikipedia. "Prayer." http://en.wikipedia.org/wiki/Prayer (Mar 2013).
- Wikipedia. "B. F. Skinner." http://en.wikipedia.org/wiki/B._F._Skinner (Apr 2013).

- Asser, Seth M. and Rita Swan. American Academy of Pediatrics. "Child Fatalities From Religion-motivated Medical Neglect". http://pediatrics.aappublications.org/content/101/4/625.abstract (Jan 13, 1997).
- Leath, Colin. "The experience of meaning in life from a psychological perspective." http://e-a.freehostia.com/cleath/docs/meaning.htm (Jan 10, 1999).
- Wikipedia. "Colbie Caillat." http://en.wikipedia.org/wiki/Colbie_Caillat (May 2013).
- Wikipedia. "Max Weber." http://en.wikipedia.org/wiki/Max_Weber (Mar 2013).
- Funch, Flemming. "Symbol Test." http://www.worldtrans.org/essay/symboltest.html (Jan 22, 1995).
- Wikipedia. "Religious Symbols." http://en.wikipedia.org/wiki/Religious_symbols (May 2013).
- Wikipedia. "Christianity and anti-Semitism." http://en.wikipedia.org/wiki/Christianity_and_antisemitism (Apr 2013).
- Wikipedia. "Dabru Emet." http://en.wikipedia.org/wiki/Dabru_Emet (May 2013).
- Wikipedia. "Phineas Gage." http://en.wikipedia.org/wiki/Phineas_Gage (Apr 2013).
- Gedrose, Alexandra. Cracked. "5 Psychological Experiments That Prove Humanity is Doomed." http://www.cracked.com/article_16239_5-psychological-experiments-that-prove-humanity-doomed.html (May 6, 2008).
- Gregory S. Berns, Jonathan Chappelow, Caroline F. Zink, Giuseppe Pagnoni, Megan E. Martin-Skurski, Jim Richards. "Neurobiological Correlates of Social Conformity and Independence During Mental Rotation." http://www.ccnl.emory.edu/greg/Berns%20Conformity%20final%20printed.pdf (2005).
- Wikipedia. "Milgram experiment." http://en.wikipedia.org/wiki/Milgram_experiment (Apr 2013).
- Wikipedia. "Religion and happiness." http://en.wikipedia.org/wiki/Religion_and_happiness (Mar 2013).
- The Clergy Project. http://www.clergyproject.org/ (Mar 2013).
- Mayo Clinic. "Red wine and resveratrol: Good for your heart?" http://www.mayoclinic.com/health/red-wine/HB00089 (Mar 2013).
- Newport, Frank. Gallup Politics. "In U.S., 46% Hold Creationist View of Human Origins." http://www.gallup.com/poll/155003/hold-creationist-view-human-origins.aspx (Jun 1, 2012).
- Wikipedia. "Terror management theory." http://en.wikipedia.org/wiki/Terror_management_theory (Apr 2013).
- Wikipedia. "Japanese American interment." http://en.wikipedia.org/wiki/Japanese_American_internment (Apr 2013).

- Danielle Foster, Jamila Reynolds, Amy Oliver. "Terror Management Theory." http://www.trinity.edu/mkearl/death10/TerrorManagement.swf
- Vey, Gary. Viewzone. "What's Behind Beauty?" http://www.viewzone.com/TMT.html (2011).
- Beck, Richard. Experimental Theology. "Death, Art & Christian Aesthetics: Part 2, A Terror Management Perspective." http://experimentaltheology.blogspot.com/2008/11/why-is-christian-art-so-bad-part-2.html (Nov 24, 2008).
- Howardell, Douglas. ACA Group. "Overcoming People's Fear of Change." http://theacagroup.com/overcome.htm (2004).

4
RELIGIOUS BRANCHING: PART 1 – WHY SO MANY?

- Wikipedia. "Council of Chalcedon." http://en.wikipedia.org/wiki/Council_of_Chalcedon (Mar 2013).
- Montero, David. The Christian Science Monitor. "Shiite-Sunni conflict rises in Pakistan." http://www.csmonitor.com/2007/0202/p01s02-wosc.html (Feb 2, 2007).
- Wikipedia. "Efficacy of prayer." http://en.wikipedia.org/wiki/Efficacy_of_prayer (Feb 2013).
- Wikipedia. "Concordat of Worms." http://en.wikipedia.org/wiki/Concordat_of_Worms (Mar 2013).
- Wikipedia. "Catharism." http://en.wikipedia.org/wiki/Catharism (Mar 2013).
- Anon. "Corruption in the Medieval Catholic Church." http://www.vashonsd.org%2Fteacherweb%2Fzecher%2Ffiles%2FCorruption_in_the_Medieval_Catholic_Church.doc (Mar 2013).
- Wikipedia. "A Letter Concerning Toleration." http://en.wikipedia.org/wiki/A_Letter_Concerning_Toleration (Mar 2013).
- Wikipedia. "Origins of Christianity." http://en.wikipedia.org/wiki/Origins_of_Christianity (Apr 2013).
- Wikipedia. "Split of early Christianity and Judaism." http://en.wikipedia.org/wiki/Split_of_early_Christianity_and_Judaism (Apr 20313).
- Wikipedia. "Christianity and Judaism." http://en.wikipedia.org/wiki/Christianity_and_Judaism (Apr 2013).
- 43alley. YouTube. "The Evolution of Jesus in the Bible." http://www.youtube.com/watch?v=XKAHoYCWXF8 (Sept 3, 2010).
- Wikipedia. "Diocletianic Persecution." http://en.wikipedia.org/wiki/Diocletianic_Persecution (Apr 2013).

- Wikipedia. "History of Islam." http://en.wikipedia.org/wiki/History_of_Islam (Apr 2013).
- Wikipedia. "Muhammad." http://en.wikipedia.org/wiki/Muhammad (Apr 2013).
- Wikipedia. "Catholic Church and evolution." http://en.wikipedia.org/wiki/Catholic_Church_and_evolution (Apr 2013).

5 RELIGIOUS BRANCHING: PART 2 – WHAT'S THE DIFFERENCE?

- Wikipedia. "Thelema." http://en.wikipedia.org/wiki/Thelema (Apr 2013).
- Wikipedia. "God Is Not Great." http://en.wikipedia.org/wiki/God_Is_Not_Great (Apr 2013).
- Wikipedia. "Female genital mutilation." http://en.wikipedia.org/wiki/Female_genital_mutilation (Apr 2013).
- Byskov, Else. "Death is an Illusion: Children that remember previous lives." http://www.deathisanillusion.com/page.pl?id=2&cid=3 (2009).
- Wikipedia. "Miraculous births." http://en.wikipedia.org/wiki/Miraculous_births (Mar 2013).
- Wikipedia. "Jesus Christ in comparative mythology." http://en.wikipedia.org/wiki/Jesus_Christ_in_comparative_mythology (Mar 2013).
- Wikipedia. "Nakayama Miki." http://en.wikipedia.org/wiki/Nakayama_Miki (Mar 2013).
- Wikipedia. "Resurrection." http://en.wikipedia.org/wiki/Resurrection (Mar 2013).
- Marigny, Lauretta. Pathlights Press. "Resurrection: Bible Characters Raised from the Dead." http://www.pathlightspress.com/resurrection.html (2011).
- Tomes, Nigel. Church in Toronto. "Belief in Miracles Growing: Surprising Trend Presents Challenges & Opportunities" http://churchintoronto.blogspot.com/2012/11/belief-in-miracles-growing.html#!/2012/11/belief-in-miracles-growing.html (Nov 5, 2012).
- Sivananda, Sri Swami. "Lives of Saints: Zoroaster." http://www.dlshq.org/saints/zoroaster.htm (Oct 17, 2004).
- Wikipedia. "Miracles of Guatama Buddha." http://en.wikipedia.org/wiki/Miracles_of_Gautama_Buddha (May 2013).
- Wikipedia. "Baha'i Faith and Zoroastrianism." http://en.wikipedia.org/wiki/Bah%C3%A1'%C3%AD_Faith_and_Zoroastrianism (May 2013).
- Wikipedia. "Ichadon." http://en.wikipedia.org/wiki/Ichadon (May 2013).
- Wikipedia. "Splitting of the moon." http://en.wikipedia.org/wiki/Splitting_of_the_moon (May 2013).

- Wikipedia. "Jehoshua." http://en.wikipedia.org/wiki/Jehoshua (May 2013).
- Wikipedia. "Atra-Hasis." http://en.wikipedia.org/wiki/Atra-Hasis (Mar 2013).
- Wikipedia. "Epic of Gilgamesh." http://en.wikipedia.org/wiki/Epic_of_Gilgamesh (Mar 2013).
- Wikipedia. "Enuma Elis." http://en.wikipedia.org/wiki/En%C3%BBma_Eli%C5%A1 (Mar 2013).
- Wikipedia. "Rigveda." http://en.wikipedia.org/wiki/Rigveda (Mar 2013).
- Wikipedia. "Avesta." http://en.wikipedia.org/wiki/Avesta (Mar 2013).
- Wikipedia. "Tanakh." http://en.wikipedia.org/wiki/Tanakh (Mar 2013).
- Wikipedia. "Documentary hypothesis." http://en.wikipedia.org/wiki/Documentary_hypothesis (Apr 2013).
- Wikipedia. "The Bible and History." http://en.wikipedia.org/wiki/The_Bible_and_history (Mar 2013).
- Media History Project. "When Were the Books of the Bible Written?" http://www.mediahistory.umn.edu/archive/biblicaldates.html (May 18, 2012).
- Wikipedia. "Q source." http://en.wikipedia.org/wiki/Q_source (Mar 2013).
- Wikipedia. "Quran." http://en.wikipedia.org/wiki/Quran (Mar 2013).
- Wikipedia. "Tao Te Ching." http://en.wikipedia.org/wiki/Tao_Te_Ching (Mar 2013).
- NOVA. "Writers of the Bible." http://www.pbs.org/wgbh/nova/ancient/writers-bible.html (Nov 18, 2008).
- Wikipedia. "Typhon." http://en.wikipedia.org/wiki/Typhon (Mar 2013).
- Wikipedia. "Garden of the gods (Sumerian paradise). http://en.wikipedia.org/wiki/Garden_of_the_gods_(Sumerian_paradise) (Mar 2013).
- Wikipedia. "Flood myth." http://en.wikipedia.org/wiki/Flood_myth (Mar 2013).
- Wikipedia. "Tower of Babel." http://en.wikipedia.org/wiki/Tower_of_Babel (Mar 2013).
- Wikipedia. "End time." http://en.wikipedia.org/wiki/End_time (Mar 2013).
- Evid3nc3. YouTube. "3.3.3 Atheism: A History of God (Part 1)." http://www.youtube.com/watch?v=MlnnWbkMlbg (Jan 7, 2011).
- Jewish Atheist. "Ancient Judaism and Canaanite Religions." http://jewishatheist.blogspot.com/2006/05/ancient-judaism-and-canaanite.html (May 31, 2006).
- Wikipedia. "Feng shui." http://en.wikipedia.org/wiki/Feng_shui (Mar 2013).

6
WAR: WHAT IS IT GOOD FOR?

- Wikipedia. "NATO." http://en.wikipedia.org/wiki/NATO (Feb 2013).

- Wikipedia. "Protests against the Vietnam War." http://en.wikipedia.org/wiki/Protests_against_the_Vietnam_War (May 2013).
- Wikipedia. "Weather Underground." http://en.wikipedia.org/wiki/Weather_Underground (May 2013).
- Wikipedia. "War Before Civilization." http://en.wikipedia.org/wiki/War_Before_Civilization (Apr 2013).
- SlideShare. "Civilization: An Introduction to the Origins of Society, Government, and Culture – Lecture Notes for Part 2: Politics – From bands to states." http://www.slideshare.net/mmcrivera29/socsci-2-four-types-of-societies (Jul 21, 2010).
- Experience Ancient Egypt. "Ancient Egyptian Armies." http://www.experience-ancient-egypt.com/ancient-egyptian-armies.html (2012).
- Wikipedia. "Circumcision." http://en.wikipedia.org/wiki/Circumcision (Mar 2013).
- Wikipedia. "Franz Boas." http://en.wikipedia.org/wiki/Franz_Boas (Mar 2013).
- Signs of the Times. "Soursop Fruit Kills Cancer 100-Fold better Than Chemotherapy." http://www.sott.net/article/242555-Soursop-Fruit-Kills-Cancer-100-Fold-better-Than-Chemotherapy (Feb 21, 2012).
- Wikipedia. "Pledge of Allegiance." http://en.wikipedia.org/wiki/Pledge_of_Allegiance (Oct 2013).
- Wikipedia. "Gullah language." http://en.wikipedia.org/wiki/Gullah_language (Apr 2013).
- Wikipedia. "Jerusalem." http://en.wikipedia.org/wiki/Jerusalem (Feb 2013).
- Wikipedia. "History of ancient Israel and Judah." http://en.wikipedia.org/wiki/History_of_ancient_Israel_and_Judah (Mar 2013).
- Wikipedia. "Lists of wars by date." http://en.wikipedia.org/wiki/Category:Lists_of_wars_by_date (Mar 2013).
- Wikipedia. "History of Russia." http://en.wikipedia.org/wiki/History_of_Russia (Mar 2013).
- Diffen. "Confucianism vs Taoism." http://www.diffen.com/difference/Confucianism_vs_Taoism (Mar 2013).
- Wikipedia. "List of Chinese wars and battles." http://en.wikipedia.org/wiki/List_of_Chinese_wars_and_battles (Feb 2013).
- Wikipedia. "Confucianism." http://en.wikipedia.org/wiki/Confucianism (Mar 2013).
- Wikipedia. "History of Taoism." http://en.wikipedia.org/wiki/History_of_Taoism (Mar 2013).
- RationalWiki. "Evidence for the Exodus." http://rationalwiki.org/wiki/Evidence_for_the_Exodus (Apr 2013).

7
ECONOMICS: EXPENSIVE BIBLES SELL BETTER

- Wikipedia. "Terror management theory." http://en.wikipedia.org/wiki/Terror_management_theory (Apr 2013).
- Gallup. "Presidential Approval Ratings – George W. Bush." http://www.gallup.com/poll/116500/presidential-approval-ratings-george-bush.aspx (Mar 2013).
- Wikipedia. "Roman Republic." http://en.wikipedia.org/wiki/Roman_Republic (Mar 2013).
- Wikipedia. "History of Roman Empire." http://en.wikipedia.org/wiki/History_of_the_Roman_Empire (Mar 2013).
- Wikipedia. "History of the Middle East." http://en.wikipedia.org/wiki/History_of_the_Middle_East (Mar 2013).
- Wikipedia. "Economic history of China." http://en.wikipedia.org/wiki/Economic_history_of_China (Mar 2013).
- Wikipedia. "History of China." http://en.wikipedia.org/wiki/History_of_China (Mar 2013).
- Wikipedia. "History of India." http://en.wikipedia.org/wiki/History_of_India (Mar 2013).
- V, Jayaram. HinduWebsite. "Hinduism and Caste System." http://www.hinduwebsite.com/hinduism/h_caste.asp (Apr 2013).
- Wikipedia. "Caste system in India." http://en.wikipedia.org/wiki/Caste_system_in_India (Apr 2013).
- Wikipedia. "List of countries by GDP (nominal)." http://en.wikipedia.org/wiki/List_of_countries_by_GDP_(nominal) (Apr 2013).
- Kuran, Timur. "Why the Middle East Is Economically Underdeveloped: Historical Mechanisms of Institutional Stagnation." http://www.international.ucla.edu/cms/files/kuran.0130.pdf (Nov 30, 2003).
- Institute of Islamic Banking and Insurance. "Islamic Economics." http://www.islamic-banking.com/islamic-economics.aspx (Mar 2013).
- Postrel, Virginia. The New York Times. "Economic Scene; The decline of the Muslim Middle East, and the roots of resentment, can be traced to Islamic inheritance law." http://www.nytimes.com/2001/11/08/business/economic-scene-decline-muslim-middle-east-roots-resentment-can-be-traced-islamic.html (Nov 8, 2001).
- Abbasi, Zubair. "The Genesis of Business Corporations: A Comparative Historical Analysis." http://www.uc3m.es/portal/page/portal/instituto_figuerola/home/events_news/7summerschool_2012/programme/Gods%20Law%20v%20Corporations-%20A%20Critique%20of%20Islamic%20Law%20Matte.pdf (Mar 2013).

- Wikipedia. "Iranian Revolution." http://en.wikipedia.org/wiki/Iranian_Revolution (Mar 2013).

8
COMPARISION: THE STATS

- Wikipedia. "List of religions and spiritual traditions." http://en.wikipedia.org/wiki/List_of_religions_and_spiritual_traditions (Jan 2013).
- Religion Facts. "The Big Religion Comparison Chart." http://www.religionfacts.com/big_religion_chart.htm (Feb 2013).
- ProCon. "All Religions and Denominations in the US." http://undergod.procon.org/view.resource.php?resourceID=000068 (Oct 24, 2008).
- Wikipedia. "Al-Hakim bi-Amr Allah." http://en.wikipedia.org/wiki/Al-Hakim_bi-Amr_Allah (Mar 2013).
- Wikipedia. "Chinese folk religion." http://en.wikipedia.org/wiki/Chinese_folk_religion (Feb 2013).
- Wikipedia. "Wonderism." http://en.wikipedia.org/wiki/Wonderism (Feb 2013).
- Wikipedia. "Taoism." http://en.wikipedia.org/wiki/Taoism (Feb 2013).
- Wikipedia. "Confucianism." http://en.wikipedia.org/wiki/Confucianism (Feb 2013).
- Wikipedia. "Mohism." http://en.wikipedia.org/wiki/Mohism (Apr 2013).
- Wikipedia. "Shinto." http://en.wikipedia.org/wiki/Shinto (Feb 2013).
- Wikipedia. "Mazu (goddess)." http://en.wikipedia.org/wiki/Mazu_(goddess) (Feb 2013).
- Wikipedia. "Cao Dai." http://en.wikipedia.org/wiki/Cao_%C4%90%C3%A0i (Feb 2013).
- Wikipedia. "Historical Vedic religion." http://en.wikipedia.org/wiki/Historical_Vedic_religion (Feb 2013).
- Wikipedia. "Hinduism." http://en.wikipedia.org/wiki/Hinduism (Feb 2013).
- Wikipedia. "Hindu denominations." http://en.wikipedia.org/wiki/Hindu_denominations (Mar 2013).
- Wikipedia. "Zoroastrianism." http://en.wikipedia.org/wiki/Zoroastrianism (Feb 2013).
- Wikipedia. "Buddhism." http://en.wikipedia.org/wiki/Buddhism (Feb 2013).
- Wikipedia. "Schools of Buddhism". http://en.wikipedia.org/wiki/Schools_of_Buddhism (Feb 2013).
- Wikipedia. "History of Buddhism." http://en.wikipedia.org/wiki/History_of_Buddhism (Feb 2013).
- Wikipedia. "Jainism." http://en.wikipedia.org/wiki/Jainism (Feb 2013).

- Wikipedia. "Mazdak." http://en.wikipedia.org/wiki/Mazdak (Feb 2013).
- Wikipedia. "Mithraic mysteries." http://en.wikipedia.org/wiki/Mithraic_mysteries (Feb 2013).
- Wikipedia. "Sikhism." http://en.wikipedia.org/wiki/Sikhism (Feb 2013).
- Wikipedia. "Tenrikyo." http://en.wikipedia.org/wiki/Tenrikyo (Feb 2013).
- Wikipedia. "Brahma Kumaris beliefs and practices." http://en.wikipedia.org/wiki/Brahma_Kumaris_beliefs_and_practices (Feb 2013).
- Wikipedia. "Scientology." http://en.wikipedia.org/wiki/Scientology (Feb 2013).
- Wikipedia. "Ancient Mesopotamian religion." http://en.wikipedia.org/wiki/Mesopotamian_mythology (Feb 2013).
- Wikipedia. "Ancient Semitic religion." http://en.wikipedia.org/wiki/Ancient_Semitic_religion (Feb 2013).
- Wikipedia. "Ancient Egyptian religion." http://en.wikipedia.org/wiki/Ancient_Egyptian_religion (Feb 2013).
- Wikipedia. "Sumerian religion." http://en.wikipedia.org/wiki/Sumerian_religion (Feb 2013).
- Wikipedia. "Canaanite religion." http://en.wikipedia.org/wiki/Canaanite_religion (Feb 2013).
- Wikipedia. "Edom." http://en.wikipedia.org/wiki/Edom (Feb 2013).
- Wikipedia. "Judaism." http://en.wikipedia.org/wiki/Judaism (Feb 2013).
- Katz, Lisa. About: Judaism. "Branches of Judaism." http://judaism.about.com/od/denominationsofjudaism/p/branches.htm (Mar 2013).
- Wikipedia. "Outline of Judaism." http://en.wikipedia.org/wiki/Outline_of_Judaism (Mar 2013).
- Finkelshteyn, Leah. "Jewish Diversity: The Chart Paths to One God." http://web.clas.ufl.edu/users/kenwald/pos4291/spring_00/jewish_practice.htm (Mar 2013).
- Rich, Tracey R. "Judaism 101: Movements of Judaism." http://www.jewfaq.org/movement.htm (2011).
- Wikipedia. "Sadducees." http://en.wikipedia.org/wiki/Sadducees (Mar 2013).
- Wikipedia. "Essenes." http://en.wikipedia.org/wiki/Essenes (Mar 2013).
- Wikipedia. "Zealotry." http://en.wikipedia.org/wiki/Zealotry (Mar 2013).
- Wikipedia. "Elcesaites." http://en.wikipedia.org/wiki/Elcesaites (Mar 2013).
- Wikipedia. "Mandaeism." http://en.wikipedia.org/wiki/Mandaeism (Feb 2013).
- Wikipedia. "Thelema." http://en.wikipedia.org/wiki/Thelema (Feb 2013).
- Wikipedia. "Francois Rabelais." http://en.wikipedia.org/wiki/Fran%C3%A7ois_Rabelais (Mar 2013).
- Wikipedia. "Wicca." http://en.wikipedia.org/wiki/Wicca (Feb 2013).

- Wikipedia. "Gerald Gardner (Wiccan)." http://en.wikipedia.org/wiki/Gerald_Gardner_(Wiccan) (Mar 2013).
- Wikipedia. "Protestant branches." http://en.wikipedia.org/wiki/File:Protestantbranches.svg (Feb 2013).
- Wikipedia. "List of Christian denominations by number of members. "http://en.wikipedia.org/wiki/List_of_Christian_denominations_by_number_of_members (Feb 2013).
- Fairchild, Mary. About: Christianity. "Comparing Christian Denominations – Beliefs (Part 2)." http://christianity.about.com/od/denominationscomparison/ss/comparebeliefs2.htm (Mar 2013).
- Wikipedia. "Christianity." http://en.wikipedia.org/wiki/Christianity (Feb 2013).
- Wikipedia. "History of Christianity." http://en.wikipedia.org/wiki/History_of_Christianity (Feb 2013).
- Wikipedia. "List of Catholic rites and churches." http://en.wikipedia.org/wiki/List_of_Catholic_rites_and_churches (Apr 2013).
- Wikipedia. "Catholicism." http://en.wikipedia.org/wiki/Catholicism (Feb 2013).
- Wikipedia. "History of the Catholic Church." http://en.wikipedia.org/wiki/History_of_the_Catholic_Church (Feb 2013).
- Wikipedia. "Manichaeism." http://en.wikipedia.org/wiki/Manichaeism (Feb 2013).
- Wikipedia. "Oriental Orthodoxy." http://en.wikipedia.org/wiki/Oriental_Orthodoxy (Feb 2013).
- Wikipedia. "Eastern Orthodox Church." http://en.wikipedia.org/wiki/Eastern_Orthodox_Church (Feb 2013).
- Wikipedia. "Lutheranism." http://en.wikipedia.org/wiki/Lutheranism (Feb 2013).
- Wikipedia. "Martin Luther." http://en.wikipedia.org/wiki/Martin_Luther (Feb 2013).
- Wikipedia. "Anabaptist." http://en.wikipedia.org/wiki/Anabaptist (Feb 2013).
- Wikipedia. "Petr Chelcicky." http://en.wikipedia.org/wiki/Petr_Chel%C4%8Dick%C3%BD (Feb 2013).
- Wikipedia. "Calvinism." http://en.wikipedia.org/wiki/Calvinism (Feb 2013).
- Wikipedia. "John Calvin." http://en.wikipedia.org/wiki/Calvinism
- Wikipedia. "Anglicanism." http://en.wikipedia.org/wiki/Anglicanism (Feb 2013).
- Wikipedia. "Thomas Cranmer." http://en.wikipedia.org/wiki/Thomas_Cranmer (Feb 2013).
- Wikipedia. "Puritan." http://en.wikipedia.org/wiki/Puritan (Feb 2013).
- Wikipedia. "Presbyterianism." http://en.wikipedia.org/wiki/Presbyterianism (Feb 2013).
- Wikipedia. "Baptists." http://en.wikipedia.org/wiki/Presbyterianism (Feb 2013).

- Wikipedia. "John Smyth (Baptist minister)." http://en.wikipedia.org/wiki/John_Smyth_(Baptist_minister) (Feb 2013).
- Wikipedia. "Quakers." http://en.wikipedia.org/wiki/Quakers (Feb 2013).
- Wikipedia. "George Fox." http://en.wikipedia.org/wiki/George_Fox (Feb 2013).
- Wikipedia. "Evangelicalism." http://en.wikipedia.org/wiki/Evangelicalism (Feb 2013).
- Wikipedia. "Amish." http://en.wikipedia.org/wiki/Amish (Feb 2013).
- Wikipedia. "Jakob Ammann." http://en.wikipedia.org/wiki/Jakob_Ammann (Feb 2013).
- Wikipedia. "Methodism." http://en.wikipedia.org/wiki/Methodism (Feb 2013).
- Wikipedia. "Mormonism." http://en.wikipedia.org/wiki/Mormonism (Feb 2013).
- Wikipedia. "Joseph Smith." http://en.wikipedia.org/wiki/Joseph_Smith (Feb 2013).
- Wikipedia. "Seventh-day Adventist Church." http://en.wikipedia.org/wiki/Seventh-day_Adventist_Church (Feb 2013).
- Wikipedia. "William Miller (preacher)." http://en.wikipedia.org/wiki/William_Miller_(preacher) (Feb 2013).
- Wikipedia. "Jehovah's Witnesses." http://en.wikipedia.org/wiki/Jehovah's_Witnesses (Feb 2013).
- Wikipedia. "Charles Taze Russell." http://en.wikipedia.org/wiki/Charles_Taze_Russell (Feb 2013).
- Wikipedia. "Pentecostalism." http://en.wikipedia.org/wiki/Pentecostalism (Feb 2013).
- Wikipedia. "Charles Fox Parham." http://en.wikipedia.org/wiki/Charles_Parham (Feb 2013).
- Wikipedia. "Islamic schools and branches." http://en.wikipedia.org/wiki/Islamic_schools_and_branches (Feb 2013).
- Wikipedia. "Islam." http://en.wikipedia.org/wiki/Islam (Feb 2013).
- Wikipedia. "Muhammad." http://en.wikipedia.org/wiki/Muhammad (Feb 2013).
- Wikipedia. "Sunni Islam." http://en.wikipedia.org/wiki/Sunni (Feb 2013).
- Wikipedia. "Shia Islam." http://en.wikipedia.org/wiki/Shia_Islam (Feb 2013).
- Wikipedia. "Sufism." http://en.wikipedia.org/wiki/Sufism (Feb 2013).
- Wikipedia. "Druze." http://en.wikipedia.org/wiki/Druze (Feb 2013).
- Wikipedia. "Babism." http://en.wikipedia.org/wiki/B%C3%A1bism (Feb 2013).
- Wikipedia. "Bab." http://en.wikipedia.org/wiki/B%C3%A1b (Feb 2013).
- Wikipedia. "Baha'i Faith." http://en.wikipedia.org/wiki/Bah%C3%A1%27%C3%AD_Faith (Feb 2013).
- Wikipedia. "Baha'u'llah." http://en.wikipedia.org/wiki/Bah%C3%A1%27u%27ll%C3%A1h (Feb 2013).
- Wikipedia. "Ahmadiyya." http://en.wikipedia.org/wiki/Ahmadiyya (Feb 2013).

- Wikipedia. "Minoan religion." http://en.wikipedia.org/wiki/Ahmadiyya (Mar 2013).
- Wikipedia. "Johann Jakob Bachofen." http://en.wikipedia.org/wiki/Johann_Jakob_Bachofen (May 2013).
- Wikipedia. "Mycenaean Greece." http://en.wikipedia.org/wiki/Mycenaean_Greece (Feb 2013).
- Wikipedia. "Greek mythology." http://en.wikipedia.org/wiki/Greek_mythology (Mar 2013).
- Wikipedia. "Germanic paganism." http://en.wikipedia.org/wiki/Germanic_paganism (Apr 2013).
- Wikipedia. "Slavic mythology." http://en.wikipedia.org/wiki/Slavic_mythology (Apr 2013).
- Wikipedia. "Celtic mythology." http://en.wikipedia.org/wiki/Celtic_mythology (Apr 2013).
- Wikipedia. "Orphism (religion)." http://en.wikipedia.org/wiki/Orphism_(religion) (Apr 2013).
- Wikipedia. "Hellenistic religion." http://en.wikipedia.org/wiki/Orphism_(religion) (Feb 2013).
- Wikipedia. "Serer religion." http://en.wikipedia.org/wiki/Serer_religion (Mar 2013).
- Eades, J.S. "The Yoruba Today: 6 Belief systems and religion organization." http://lucy.ukc.ac.uk/YorubaT/yt6.html (1980).
- Wikipedia. "Yoruba religion." http://en.wikipedia.org/wiki/Yoruba_religion (Mar 2013).
- Adelowo, E. Dada. "Rituals, Symbolism and Symbols in Yoruba Traditional Religious Thought." http://obafemio.weebly.com/uploads/5/1/4/2/5142021/04-1_162.pdf (Apr 1, 1990).
- Wikipedia. "Haitian Vodou." http://en.wikipedia.org/wiki/Haitian_Vodou (Mar 2013).
- Wikipedia. "Australian Aboriginal mythology." http://en.wikipedia.org/wiki/Australian_Aboriginal_mythology (Apr 2013).
- Wikipedia. "Mythology of Indonesia." http://en.wikipedia.org/wiki/Mythology_of_Indonesia (Apr 2013).
- Studies of Religion. "Religions of Ancient Origin: Celtic & Polynesian." http://studiesofreligion.org.au/members/resource/05_celtic_polynesian/polynesian_summary.html (Apr 2013).
- Myths Encyclopedia. "Polynesian Mythology." http://www.mythencyclopedia.com/Pa-Pr/Polynesian-Mythology.html (Apr 2013).
- Wikipedia. "Polynesian mythology." http://en.wikipedia.org/wiki/Polynesian_mythology (Apr 2013).

- Wikipedia. "Hawaiian mythology." http://en.wikipedia.org/wiki/Hawaiian_mythology (Apr 2013).
- Wikipedia. "Hawaiian religion." http://en.wikipedia.org/wiki/Hawaiian_religion (Apr 2013).
- Wikipedia. "Olmec religion." http://en.wikipedia.org/wiki/Olmec_religion (Apr 2013).
- Wikipedia. "Aztec religion." http://en.wikipedia.org/wiki/Olmec_religion (Apr 2013).
- Wikipedia. "Native American religion." http://en.wikipedia.org/wiki/Native_American_religion (Apr 2013).
- Wikipedia. "Maya religion." http://en.wikipedia.org/wiki/Maya_religion (Apr 2013).
- Wikipedia. "Religion of the Inca Empire." http://en.wikipedia.org/wiki/Religion_in_the_Inca_Empire (Nov 2013).
- Wikipedia. "Inca mythology." http://en.wikipedia.org/wiki/Inca_mythology (Nov 2013).
- Wikipedia. "Pachamama." http://en.wikipedia.org/wiki/Pachamama (Nov 2013).

9
CONCLUSIONS: WHERE ARE WE HEADED?

- Voyer, Marc. "Top 10: Harsh Legal Systems." http://www.askmen.com/top_10/travel/top-10-harsh-legal-systems.html (2013).
- Wikipedia. "Marriage." http://en.wikipedia.org/wiki/Marriage#History_of_marriage (Apr 2013).
- Wikipedia. "Christian views on slavery." http://en.wikipedia.org/wiki/Christian_views_on_slavery (Apr 2013).
- Silver, Nate. The New York Times. "How Opinion on Same-Sex Marriage Is Changing, and What It Means." http://fivethirtyeight.blogs.nytimes.com/2013/03/26/how-opinion-on-same-sex-marriage-is-changing-and-what-it-means/?_r=0 (Mar 26, 2013).
- Wikipedia. "Economy of Brazil." http://en.wikipedia.org/wiki/Economy_of_Brazil (May 2013).
- Wikipedia. "Forer effect." http://en.wikipedia.org/wiki/Forer_effect (Apr 2013).
- Wikipedia. "Exorcism." http://en.wikipedia.org/wiki/Exorcism (May 2013).
- Wikipedia. "Dualism (philosophy of mind)." http://en.wikipedia.org/wiki/Dualism_(philosophy_of_mind) (Apr 2013).
- Wikipedia. "Monism." http://en.wikipedia.org/wiki/Monism (Apr 2013).
- wimsweden. YouTube. "Split brain with one half atheist and one half theist." http://www.youtube.com/watch?v=PFJPtVRlI64 (Jun 3, 2010).

- AFP. Discovery News. "Chimps Are Self Aware." http://news.discovery.com/animals/zoo-animals/chimpanzees-self-awareness-110504.htm (May 4, 2011).
- Cowen, Nick. Civitas Crime. "Comparisons of Crime in OECD Countries." http://www.civitas.org.uk/crime/crime_stats_oecdjan2012.pdf (Apr 2012).
- Wikipedia. "Demographics of atheism." http://en.wikipedia.org/wiki/Demographics_of_atheism (Apr 2013).
- Wikipedia. "World Health Organization ranking of health systems." http://en.wikipedia.org/wiki/World_Health_Organization_ranking_of_health_systems (Apr 2013).
- Wikipedia. "List of countries by GDP (nominal)." http://en.wikipedia.org/wiki/List_of_countries_by_GDP_(nominal) (Apr 2013).
- Wikipedia. "State atheism." http://en.wikipedia.org/wiki/State_atheism (Jun 2013).
- Alesina, Alberto and George-Marios Angeletos. "Fairness and Redistribution: US versus Europe." http://aida.wss.yale.edu/~shiller/behmacro/2003-11/alesina-angeletos.pdf (Oct 2002).
- Wheelan, Charles. Naked Economics. New York: W.W. Norton & Company. 2003.
- Wikipedia. "Religion and HIV/AIDS." http://en.wikipedia.org/wiki/Religion_and_HIV/AIDS (Apr 2013).
- Wikipedia. "Stem cell laws and policy in the United States." http://en.wikipedia.org/wiki/Stem_cell_laws_and_policy_in_the_United_States (Apr 2013).
- Cole, Simone. eHow. "Moral Traits of Animals." http://www.ehow.com/info_8619922_moral-traits-animals.html (Apr 2013).
- Science Daily. "Meerkat Predator-Scanning Behavior is Altruistic." http://www.animalliberationfront.com/Philosophy/Morality/Speciesism/MeerkatsAltruistic.htm (Feb 4, 2013).

EPILOGUE: THE BURDEN OF PROOF

- Wikiquote. "Unidentified flying object." http://en.wikiquote.org/wiki/Unidentified_flying_object (Dec 2013).
- Harris, Sam. "The Fireplace Delusion." http://www.samharris.org/blog/item/the-fireplace-delusion (Feb 2, 2012).
- Linder, Douglas O. "Salem Witch Trials 1692: The Dead." http://law2.umkc.edu/faculty/projects/ftrials/salem/asal_de.htm (Sept 2009).
- Wikipedia. "Wrongful execution." http://en.wikipedia.org/wiki/Wrongful_execution (Nov 2103).
- Wikipedia. "West Memphis Three."

- http://en.wikipedia.org/wiki/West_Memphis_Three (Nov 2013).
- Wikipedia. "Mormonism and history." http://en.wikipedia.org/wiki/Mormonism_and_history (May 2013).
- Wishnatsky, Martin. "Mormonism: A Latter Day Deception." http://www.goodmorals.org/mormons/index.asp?poetlist=ChapterTwo.htm (2002).
- Olson, Todd K. Faith Facts. "Ex-Mormon Testimony." http://www.faithfacts.org/world-religions-and-theology/ex-mormon-testimony (2008).
- Wood, Sarah. Addicting Info. "Former Mormon Explains Why Mitt Romney Should Never Be President." http://www.addictinginfo.org/2012/05/13/former-mormon-explains-why-mitt-romney-should-never-be-president/ (May 13, 2012).
- Wikipedia. "List of religious leaders convicted of crimes." http://en.wikipedia.org/wiki/List_of_religious_leaders_convicted_of_crimes (May 2013).
- BishopAccountability.org. "Database of Publicly Accused Priests in the United States." http://bishop-accountability.org/priestdb/PriestDBbylastName-A.html (May 2013).

Made in the USA
Middletown, DE
11 April 2021